James Russell Lowell

JAMES RUSSELL LOWELL IN 1842

From a crayon drawing by William Page

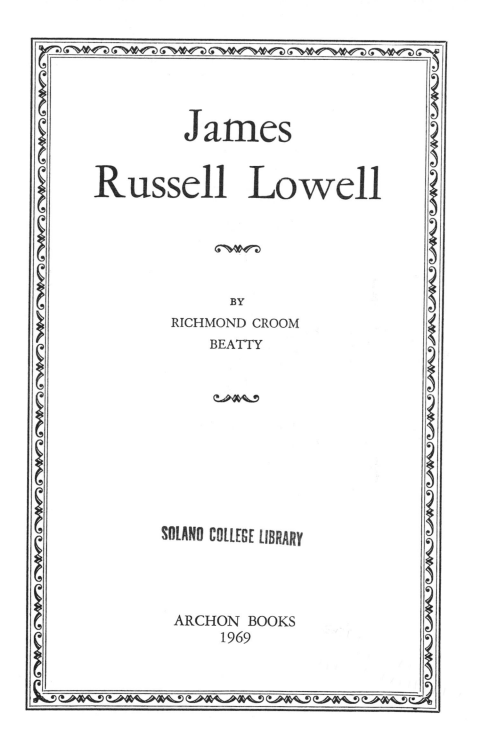

James Russell Lowell

BY

RICHMOND CROOM
BEATTY

ARCHON BOOKS
1969

SBN: 208 00752 0
LIBRARY OF CONGRESS CATALOG CARD NUMBER: 69-13623
PRINTED IN THE UNITED STATES OF AMERICA

--◦⊰{ iv }⊱◦--

To
C. B. B.
AND THE MEMORY OF
W. H. B.

--•◦❖{ v }❖◦•--

PREFACE

I CAN remember the seven of them, done impartially in sepia, framed above the large mahogany bookcase in the back hall—Emerson, Holmes, Hawthorne, Whittier, Bryant, Longfellow, and Lowell. The beards of the last three were remarkably rich, leaving nothing below the nose particularly visible, so that the name of each author had been discreetly printed beneath his face, in a delicate arc. Their works—the Cambridge, the Riverside, or some other properly *collected* edition—were ranged below them on the shelves, rank upon rank, "with strict impunity." Here, I was given to understand, was American Literature, along with pictures of the major American writers. I should dutifully read their books. And I should also strive to be good and great, as they had been as persons. I was considerably advanced in years and indiscretions before I heard of Whitman, or Mark Twain, or Poe; was of voting age before I learned about Melville. But since that time—especially during the past twelve years—I have wondered a great deal about that set of faces and have tried to study, as well as I could, the problem of what peculiar dispensation made them, exclusively, into what Meredith might have termed our "army of unalterable law."

To seek an answer through an investigation of the life of one of these men evokes a dilemma which, it appears to me, no biographer can entirely escape. For almost invariably he is a man of one age, while his subject belongs to another. Where shall the emphasis be placed, then? The strictest scholarship would dictate, of course, that the author immerse himself in his subject's era and see him altogether within its frame of reference. I would not for a moment question this principle insofar as it suggests that the biographer learn as much as he possibly can about the age he is treating. But to stop with that learning would be, I am afraid, to render himself the victim of a serious inadequacy. For the biographer's subject— especially if he be a literary figure—belongs not only to his own age but to the present; and what he means to us, no less than what he was to his contemporaries, must somehow be discovered and set down. Why, for instance, have certain of his writings failed to survive, although others continue to be read? When one begins to deal with this sort of query, he finds himself in the field of criticism —that most confused of all the mediums of literature, certainly a medium in which no absolutes exist. He must therefore simply do the best he knows how, which means, in turn, that he *may* please those who tend to share his critical (or political or economic) pre- suppositions, but that he will certainly irritate those who do not.

This latter group will likely charge the author with being biased, and the charge will be just. My own reply to it would be somewhat as follows: Unless one's interest as biographer is merely in the chronological recording of events (as in the adventure novel or the detective story), a bias is inescapable. For a bias, as I see it, is merely a point of view, and almost everybody appears to have one. In a critic, for example, it may be humanist, Marxian, royalist, neo-Catholic, impressionist, southern liberal, or what not. And this point of view will inevitably reflect itself in any honest and extended piece of critical writing. One can only try to be scrupulously fair in presenting the evidence upon which his conclusions are based.

One method of doing this is through a frequent reliance upon history. The failure of so many literary biographers to take advan- tage of historical scholarship in their efforts to get at the truth behind their subjects' opinions has made for no end of shoddy guesses and errors. Yet in the case of American literature I have never been able to define the point at which this field ends and that of American history begins. Nor is the matter important. For both are facets of American culture, and it is this culture which we are all attempting, variously, to explore.

It might be added, in connection with the present book, that probably some revealing insights into the rich diversity of American opinion would be made available were a number of the leading figures of a given region examined in detail by students of another. There can be such a thing as too much inbreeding in scholarship, no less than in a Jukes family, and perhaps with respect to the writers of New England this is already the case. Of course that student who is not native to the tradition he is exploring will always suffer from certain disadvantages. The countless small truths that fall unconsciously upon the minds of the indigenous he is compelled to acquire laboriously at second hand, if indeed he is able to acquire them at all. But at least, by way of compensation, he will be free from the temptations of idolatry. Moreover—to alter somewhat the modest apology of Darwin—those natives who are better informed are still left with the always delectable privilege of indicating wherein the intruder's judgments are unsound.

R. C. B.

ACKNOWLEDGMENTS

THE manuscript of this volume has been read by several good friends of mine, and their criticisms of it have proved profitable beyond measure. I think especially of the solid comments of Dean John E. Pomfret and of Professors Donald Davidson, Knox Chandler, Edwin Mims, Frank Owsley, E. H. Duncan, and Dan Robison—all of Vanderbilt University. For its point of view, however, these gentlemen are in no way responsible, except insofar as several of them have contributed vicariously to my education. To thank them in detail would be an act of supererogation. But I should certainly be negligent not to confess an indebtedness to the Guggenheim Foundation for making possible the leisure to explore my subject rather extensively.

CONTENTS

Preface vii

Acknowledgments xi

List of Illustrations xvii

I
. . . "My earliest impressions" 1

II
"I continue as juvenile as ever." 9

III
"A University is a place where nothing useful is taught" . . 17

IV
"My pen has not yet traced a line of which I am either proud
or ashamed." 36

V
"I know more of the history of Ancient Rome than I do that
of America." 57

VI
. . . "I am the first poet who has endeavored to express the
American idea." 75

VII
. . . "Nothing more depressing than to look one's old poems in
the face." 91

VIII
"I had never before any adequate idea of the barbarism of
these Western people" 101

IX
"He [Michael Angelo] is the apostle of the exaggerated, the
Victor Hugo of painting and sculpture." 114

X

"I will take care to keep it [*Leaves of Grass*] out of the way of
the students." 124

XI

"She has only one fault . . . she is not rich." 136

XII

. . . "The strongest battalions are always on the side of God." . 150

XIII

"One must swallow the truth, though it makes one's eyes
water." 166

XIV

"They [the English] have as little tact as their *totem* the Bull." 179

XV

We must acknowledge the negro "as our brother . . . ere
Amerca can penetrate the southern states." 188

XVI

"England is the only country where things get a thorough
discussion, and by the best men." 196

XVII

"I . . . am astonished to find how clever I used to be." . . . 209

XVIII

"If I am not an American, who ever was?" 227

XIX

"I wish I could feel, as I did then [50 years ago] that we were
a chosen people." 238

XX

"We are now expecting General Grant with terror." 247

XXI

"One of the worst diseases we have to cure in the Irish . . . is
their belief that the laws are their natural enemies." 256

XXII

"The throng was such as only London could pour forth." . . 265

XXIII
"Come early and come often, as they say to the voters in New
York." 280
XIV
"Death is a private tutor" 294

Notes , ... 298

Bibliographical Note 310

Index 312

LIST OF ILLUSTRATIONS

Lowell in 1842 . . . . Frontispiece

Elmwood (Lowell's birthplace) 11

Maria White Lowell 40

Hosea and the "Creutin Sarjunt" 77

Lowell in 1875 236

Lowell in His Library at Elmwood 281

I

*"I . . . received my earliest impressions in a community
the most virtuous, I believe, that ever existed."*
Lowell to Joel Benton, January 19, 1876
Works, XV, 376

ONE COULD approach the village, as it was called in 1819, by
a ride of a few miles, mostly eastward from Boston, turning
gradually toward a wider and slowly rising terrain. Laid out by
Governor John Winthrop, in 1632, to function as a fortified town,
it was settled now—immemorially, it appeared—beside the broad
and serpentine river, a sleepy community of five thousand souls.

Traveling the New Road, one might pause on the brow of
Symond's Hill to take in the view lying before him. In the fore-
ground stretched the town itself, tufted with elms, lindens, and
horse-chestnuts—trees which had seen Massachusetts a colony.
Over it rose the noisy belfry of the oldest college in America, the
square brown tower of the church, the thin yellow spire of the
parish meetinghouse. To one's left hand, on the Old Road, stood
some half-dozen dignified houses of colonial days, all comfortably
fronting southward. On the right, the Charles glided through
green and purple salt meadows, darkened at intervals with blossoming black grass. Beyond the marshes that surrounded it, low hills
defined a gray horizon.[1]

English this Cambridge of President Monroe's day really was,
in particulars too obvious to escape notice. Quiet, unspeculative,
without enterprise, self-sufficient, it revealed only such differences
from the original type as might be imposed by a system of local
government and by the public school. A few aging homes stood
around the bare Common. Old women, capped and spectacled, still
peered beyond them through identical windows from which they
had watched Lord Percy's artillery rumble by on its way to Lexing-

ton, or had seen General Washington take command of the rebel army beneath the stately and now legended elm. Children played about the flat stones in the cemetery, under which lay the bodies of many former presidents of Harvard, weighed down with solemn Latin inscriptions. Even the children knew that the empty cavities on many of the tombs were places where leaden escutcheons had rested before they were prized out and converted into bullets for use by Revolutionary soldiers. Any one of them could have pointed out the place where President Langdon had stood, blessing the unkempt recruits who marched off to fight the British at Bunker Hill. Or he could have led one to Mrs. Craigie's house, where Washington had actually lived during his stay in Cambridge, and where Mrs. Washington had come, with coach and servants, to visit him on their wedding anniversary. A few wounded veterans, whom one regarded with reverence and listened to with wondering eyes, still lingered on in the flesh. Occasionally people might be found who regretted the late unhappy separation from the mother island, and who had seen, they vowed, no gentry in Cambridge since certain harassed Tory families, in 1776, set sail for the ageless serenities of England.

But the college they left, and which they had largely controlled, still slept on in the Indian summer of Federalism. Its enrollment was scarcely two hundred. Its annual income approximated a bare $45,000, half of which came from the students themselves, in fees. The Yard, or campus, President Kirkland had declared when he accepted office in 1812, resembled mainly an unkempt sheep-common. It was practically treeless, lacked regular paths, and was cluttered with crude privies, a brewhouse, and a woodyard.[2] This dignified gentleman, it is true, set about changing the least ethereal of these blemishes at once. But the trees he planted before the new set of "houses of office," as they were called, were still little more than saplings. Near by stood the raucous college pigpen, leveling its odors across the evening air. And at pig-killing time so great was the noise from this quarter that only the most stentorian professors

—·◄{ 2 }►·—

proved able to carry on, uninterruptedly, their methodical exposition of the classics.

Yet certain names later to be widely known were already associated with the college, although their bearers at this date were more rightly men of promise than of reputation. There were Edward T. Channing, the new lecturer in Rhetoric, who was exasperatingly precise about diction; Andrews Norton, the brilliant Professor of Sacred Literature; Edward Everett, the exponent of Greek culture, friend of Goethe and of Scott; and George Ticknor, the first Smith Professor of Modern Languages. Some of these men were fresh from German universities, filled with the ideal of a thorough scholarly discipline. They had studied the educational systems of Europe closely.[3] One of them, Everett, had come back convinced that, as compared with the mother country at least, "there is more teaching and more learning in our American Cambridge than there is in both the English universities together, though between them they have four times our number of students."

These young enthusiasts were devoted to their educational missions. And it was well that they were, for the Harvard library of a mere twenty thousand volumes seemed scarcely calculated to aid them to any real extent in their classwork or in their research, nor were their salaries of approximately $1,000 a year, unless augmented by the incomes of their wives, of very much service either. Of course, the tradition ran, Harvard professors were "considered to be partly paid in honor." But honor, unaided, could not buy books, the love of which was to drain the resources of many of them, Lowell included, for generations.

But come commencement week, the results of the perseverance of these and of similar professors were evident everywhere. During this period one might find a student walking aimlessly down some winding road, swinging his arms and talking fixedly to himself, rehearsing the Latin oration he was to deliver the closing day. Or if one strayed to the near-by gravel pit, he might find some other young scholar alone there, thundering his Ciceronian periods against the rugged sides of that retired amphitheatre.[4] Always these promising declaimers received a noisy welcome when they appeared on the stage. It may have been, as Lowell himself once implied, that the handclapping was meant to reveal, mainly, the audience's own self-satisfaction at recognizing the language in which it was being addressed. But this churlish suspicion mattered little. What counted was the fact that an accomplishment which both speaker and hearers esteemed was being displayed with a solemn grace before them.

For the natives, indeed, commencement at Harvard was the great holiday of the year. On the Sunday preceding, the minister would give notice to carry home the psalmbooks and cushions, and almost everyone would go out with something in his hands. That, wrote John Holmes,[5] was what really began the holiday, even if it did take place on the Sabbath. Monday the constable would mark out the places for the tents, proceeding as solemnly as if each was to be a grave. Tuesday afternoon the joists and boards and old sails would arrive and the actual tent-building would get under way, continuing far into the night. Then, Wednesday morning, before one had fairly accustomed himself to the sweeping array of canvas and color, the strident sound of trumpets began, and citizens would watch the company of light-horse prance up to the meetinghouse, escorting the governor. After him came a great procession of people, who very soon crowded the building to overflowing. Those who failed to find seats or standing room would wander down to the market place and the shows, and the day-long business of buying delicacies, seeing the exhibits, meeting friends, and of drinking rum and eating watermelon and Boston ice cream, was fairly started.

Perhaps most exciting of all—far more exciting, at any rate, than the Latin speeches of the pulpit-bound orators—were the strange displays to be seen in the many tents that circled the Common. All the features of an English fair were present, at a price within reach of everybody. Here, it seemed, had come all the wonders of the world; wonders that made even the Arabian Nights seem possible. Here the mummy unveiled her withered charms—still attractive in her three-thousandth year. Here were the ubiquitous Siamese twins, the flying horses that (even if they did require the aid of a man who turned a crank) actually left the ground, and also the Canadian giant who damaged his drawing powers by appearing at the tavern openly, for all to see, free of cost. And there was the great horse, Columbus, with the suspiciously thick iron shoes; the mermaid, so called, immersed up to her neck (but no further) in the trough of the town pump; and the dancing and singing dwarfs. Wisdom also, Lowell conjectured much later, may possibly have had her quiet booth there, a booth that might be entered without a fee. But even at that rate, he sadly added, she got never a customer the whole day long.

On a day like this the native characters of the place were compelled to forego the prominence they generally enjoyed.[6] Cambridge could count its quota of these picturesque figures. Everybody knew them and extended to each the deference proper to his station and talent. They were part of a world fast dissolving; yet for an interval at least, one felt, their status seemed fixed, in the cool shades beyond time. . . .

There was Lewis, the village brewer, for instance. An amiable Negro, he possessed a monopoly on the local trade in both spruce and ginger beer, and always he made a discount to his principal customers, the boys. He wheeled his entire stock in a white-roofed handcart, with a sideboard in front from either end of which dangled one of his mysterious and unpredictable bottles. It was somewhat risky to deal with him, for a customer could never be certain that the bottle he asked for would not explode in his face. But Lewis's manner was above reproach. He laid out three "sirs" with every glass: "Beer, sir. Yes, sir. Spruce or ginger, sir?" This mixture of flattery and service never failed to work. The purchaser was dilated with pride as well as with carbonic acid gas and went away, Lowell declares, with a double measure of contentment.

The village barber was one of the few settlers in the community who seemed of foreign birth. He was R., the Dutchman, whose shop was filled with curiosities as strange as the itinerant ones at commencement. Rumor alleged that he was immensely rich. How, otherwise, it was argued, could he afford to buy whatever rarity entered the town, for the simple purpose of embellishing his walls? Consider those walls for a moment. He had on them beaks of the albatross and penguin, and whale's-teeth fantastically engraved. There was a print of the head of Frederick the Great, and another of Napoleon. There were sea fights in plenty, but, chief of all, that of John Paul Jones and the *Bonhomme Richard,* dealing thunderous wreck to two hostile ships, the realism of the scene augmented by streaks of red paint leaping from each gun's mouth. Then there were the birds, foreign and domestic: a large white cockatoo that harangued at intervals in what its owner pronounced to be the Hottentot language, and canaries and Java sparrows mingling their notes with those of the more familiar robin, thrush, and bobolink. And when one tired of these merry diversions he could examine the display of Indian arrows, New Zealand war clubs, or the model of a sailing vessel that was suspended above the fireplace. R. might drench one's head with his odoriferous perfume, he might cut one's hair clean to the scalp during an inattentive moment, but whatever he did was done in character. It merely augmented the zest with which a young customer entered his shop.

The town could boast one authentic housepainter, or "white-and-yellow washer," and he, too, was an individualist. His own cottage, fresh-gleaming every June through grapevine and creeper, was his only sign and advertisement. All colors except white and yellow, indeed, were suspect with him. His fowls, his ducks, and his geese could not show so much as a single gray feather among them, and the blossoms that bordered his lot were the whitest of China asters and the most golden of sunflowers. "I fancy," said Lowell, "that he never rightly liked Commencement, for bringing so many black coats together." Yet all the housewives acknowledged his talents with the brush. Cruder hands might try their abilities on fences and the like coarse objects, but the ceiling of every home waited on the leisure of Mr. Newman.

It was a town that seemed somehow stable, one in which a child might grow to manhood and on into the eventualities of age and death untroubled by the strident forces that were changing so desperately that part of the country which lay beyond its ken. Judges might still arrest for contempt any man who visited their courts in shirt sleeves to witness the administration of his nation's laws. Though dead eleven years, Fisher Ames, the region's greatest orator, was still cherished as a prophet for declaring that our country "is too big for union, too sordid for patriotism, too democratic for liberty. . . . We are in the hands of the philosophers of Lilliput. . . . Democracy will kindle its own hell and consume in it."[7] Railways had not yet begun to make fluid a population that still cherished its provincialism, if not its isolation, and only one large omnibus that ran two or three times a day was available to lure the more restless townsmen toward the ampler diversions of Boston.[8] The sloop *Harvard,* owned by the college, still made its annual voyage to Maine, and brought back the wood that warmed and brightened the rooms of the scholars in winter.

James Russell Lowell was born in this town February 22, 1819, in a house that was already half a century old when his father acquired it. It was not only old, it was a place with a history. Built in 1767 for Thomas Oliver, son of a West Indies merchant, it had served as his residence until George III named him president of the Massachusetts Council, in defiance of the contention of patriots that this important office should be elective. On the morning of September 2, 1774, a number of property owners of the county waited upon Oliver and demanded that he resign his job. The "dapper little man" reluctantly did so, in words that Lowell was always fond of recalling: "My house at Cambridge being surrounded by about four thousand people, in compliance with their command I sign my name."[9]

Oliver left Cambridge immediately, and for good, and his home was seized for public uses. When the American army was stationed in the town, it served as a hospital for wounded soldiers. Later the property, comprising ninety-six acres, was confiscated and placed at auction by the state. The purchaser, Arthur Cabot of Salem, sold it soon afterwards to Elbridge Gerry, a signer of the Declaration of

Independence, governor of Massachusetts from 1810 to 1812, and Vice President under Madison until his sudden death in 1814. Four years later the homestead, with ten adjoining acres, was purchased by Lowell's father, the Rev. Charles Lowell, of Boston.

It was a square dwelling, Georgian in style, the usual brick abandoned for the wood with which New England abounded. There were three stories, the rooms were spacious, the hall that divided them spacious too. In brief, it was such a place as Lowell, had the choice been offered him, would have wished to be born in—would, indeed, have wished to die in. This latter desire, often deliberately expressed, was granted; die there he did, in the summer of 1891. But death came, at length, only after the village of his earliest recollections had changed for him into the shade of a memory. Yet the environment it represented was one that was to define his sharpest limitations and his most vigorous work. When he wrote in the light of its stubborn provincialism, he created material that is in many cases still read. But when he left it for broader spheres—either nationalistic or humanistic—the literary result proved all too often rhetorical, trivial, invertebrate, or dull. The Lowell that survives is the Lowell of Cambridge.

II

"I continue as juvenile as ever. I was passing a Home for Incurable Children the other day and said to my companion, 'I shall be sent there one of these days.'"
Lowell to his daughter, October 19, 1888.
New Letters, 326

JAMES RUSSELL LOWELL belonged to the eighth generation of the Lowell family in America. Its first representative, Percival Lowell (sometimes Lowle), had come over from Somersetshire in 1639, on the heels of the great migration to Boston Bay. He brought two sons and a daughter with him. A hardy gentleman of sixty-eight on his arrival, he settled in Newbury in 1642 and lived there until his death at the advanced age of ninety-four, surviving his eldest son, John, by almost two decades.

This son's first-born—also named John—was already ten years old when the family left England. He became a cooper by trade and an expansive family man. Before his death, in 1694, three wives had successively obeyed him as husband, and nineteen children had reverenced him as father. The fifteenth, Ebenezer, a cordwainer (or, in vulgar terms, a shoemaker), was the one who carried on the vigorous paternal tradition that is relevant here.

With Ebenezer's son John the family first began its long association with Harvard. He was graduated from the college, under "the great President Leverett," in 1721, and five years later took up his duties as pastor of the Third Parish at Newburyport. Twice married, like so many members of his hearty family, he lived on into the shadow of the Revolution, dying in the neighborhood of his church in 1767.

John's son, likewise christened John—the fifth of the name in the new world—received his bachelor's degree at Harvard in 1760. The family had evidently risen in prominence since the days of Ebenezer the shoemaker, for according to the rankings of graduates, which were based primarily on social status, he stood seventh in a class of twenty-seven. John turned to the law for a livelihood, and soon afterwards, in 1767, we find him identified with measures that were being taken to frustrate the encroachments of the mother country. During the early years of the war he moved from the family seat to the larger arena of Boston, and continued there his work in behalf of the rebel cause. After the Constitution was adopted, President Washington named him a judge of the United States District Court for Massachusetts. Further honors, including membership in the Corporation of Harvard College, fell to him before his death in 1802. It might also be added that, according to his son Charles (the father of James Russell Lowell), he "introduced into the Bill of Rights the clause by which slavery was abolished in Massachusetts." When that clause was passed, the son went on, John rose to his feet and exclaimed jubilantly: "Now there is no longer slavery in Massachusetts. It is abolished, and I will render my services as a lawyer gratis to any slave suing for his freedom if it is withheld from him." This declaration will be worth recalling when we come to consider his grandson's abolitionist work half a century later.

When Lowell's father received his degree from Harvard in 1800, the association of the family with the college had thus become traditional. He represented the third generation that had studied there. After graduation he traveled for three years in Europe, met the saintly English emancipator William Wilberforce, and on his return began his pastorate at the West Congregational Church in Boston. It was a position which he was to occupy, either actively or as emeritus, until his death three months before Fort Sumter was fired upon.

He was a kindly man, by anybody's standards. The brother of Francis Cabot Lowell (founder of the industrial city on the banks of the Merrimack bearing his name), he seems to have escaped completely the temptation of avarice and feudal domination that obsessed the mind of this master exploiter of elementary human rights. It is to be regretted that he did not set down his precise opinion of his

ELMWOOD

brother's activities in the furtherance of white peonage, did not pause to consider how futile the gospel of brotherhood might sound in a region where one's own kindred sweated young girls fourteen hours daily for the sickening pittance of $1.50 a week. But we do know that Charles Lowell was a conservative. He would never allow himself to be classed with those radical Congregationalists, the Unitarians. "I have adopted no other religious creed than the Bible," he wrote late in life, "and no other name than Christian in denoting my religious faith." "My child, my child, what is this I hear?" he once said to a young woman who had planned to come out for certain industrial reforms. The interview ended with a prayer that completely subdued the recalcitrant lady.

Though he was conservative in matters that might menace the financial eminence of New England, his heart overflowed in its sympathy for the indigent. He had, in fact, bought the home in Cambridge only after his parishioners had insisted that he retire and rest himself, at least partly, from the endless exactions of voluntary parish duties. His youngest son, James Russell, always thought of him as a New England Dr. Primrose, fortunately spared the ambitious wife of Goldsmith's story. He had brought with him to Cambridge a library of four thousand volumes, a collection that did not seem modest even when compared with that of the college itself. There he read silently, or aloud in a voice of "incomparable sweetness and effect," and from this association was to stem his son's earliest interest in the classics of recorded prose.[1]

From his mother, "Jemmie" Lowell acquired, equally early, an interest in poetry which never deserted him. Mrs. Lowell's paternal ancestry went back but two generations on this side of the Atlantic. She was Harriet Brackett Spence, and her grandfather, Robert Traill, had come over from the Orkney Islands. But at the outbreak of the Revolution he returned to his ancestral home, leaving behind him a daughter, Mary, who married soon afterwards. That he did not desert her because of any political differences of opinion is certain, for Lowell himself is authority for the statement that this proud lady was a loyalist to her death. Whenever July 4 came around, he declared, instead of joining in the general celebration she would dress in black and fast the whole day. Her only daughter was born in 1783. In 1806 that daughter married the Rev. Charles Lowell in Boston.

Jemmie was the sixth and last child of this union. Before him there had been Charles Russell, born October 30, 1807; Rebecca Russell, born January 17, 1809; Mary Traill, born December 3, 1810; William Keith, born September 23, 1813; and Robert Traill, born October 8, 1816. Of the family, only one, William Keith, was to die in his youth. He lived to the age of ten, and Jemmie's recollection of him was never distinct or important.

As the youngest of four brothers and two sisters, Jemmie was, rather naturally, a favorite with his parents. His father taught him weather-signs and all the various trees and birds. And as soon as he was old enough to travel, he began to take trips that often required a full day's absence from home. They would harness "September" to the chaise early Sunday morning and ride off to some neighboring village, where the Rev. Lowell would fill the pulpit of a colleague. There would be dinner afterwards, and much talk with friends of the host. These visits were of immense value to the boy. It was from them that he learned thoroughly the dialect and other characteristics of the then almost unmixed Yankee population of rural New England, a knowledge that was to make authentic the most vigorous poetry he ever wrote.

He noticed other things, too, on these excursions, things that no one who was born much later than he could hope to witness— notably the genuine deference which was paid his father as a minister. Boys doffed their hats and little girls dropped a curtsy by the roadside as he passed them. Nothing, Lowell declared much later, could he recollect as more delightful "than those slow summer journeys through leafy lanes and over the stony hills, where we always got out and walked. In that way I think I gained a more intimate relation with what we may call pristine New England than has fallen to the fortune of most men of my age." [2]

Jemmie was sent first to a dame school located near the river, in the neighborhood of what afterwards came to be termed Brattle Square. He had little definite to say, in later life, about this "Dame" or about the school itself. She seems, from what record does survive, to have been the principal *a-b-c* instructor for the town, but Lowell recalled much more vividly than her actual teaching the zest with which he left her guidance in the afternoons for the blacksmith shop that stood near his home. Here, it appears, he would be allowed to blow the creaky bellows as long as he pleased. Panting, he would watch the pent volcano's glow increase to a white heat, then stand aside to see the sledge disperse the iron from some plowshare or horseshoe in a swarm of vanishing golden bees.

If he left no wholly explicit account of what his life was like during these earliest years, he has been more than accommodating on the subject in his poetry. There, after the meaning of childhood had become distilled for him, he attempted to set down that meaning at some length, in statements that, when freed of their didacticism, still sound authentic and interesting.

He could recall many days of his childhood long afterwards, he declared. They were days that would linger always in his mind, as the mind's perfume when all other reality had departed. Thinking of them, in 1869, they seemed farther off than even Homer's age. The child he was had not loudened into the boy. Like Wordsworth—perhaps all too suspiciously like Wordsworth—he could remember those first sweet frauds upon his consciousness, blending the sensual with the imaged world. Life had not yet grown noisy, nor had rapture yielded to heavy-footed meditation. There was something secret, yet divine, he felt, in that faded panorama. "Primal apprehensions" it awakened in him even now, "blank forebodings" that fused all he looked on—the bird singing from the elm, the quick charm of the crocus in the sullen turf—with the flown ecstasy of vanished mornings.[3]

One spring stood out especially, above the many others that had come later. All night the surges of a southwest wind had boomed through the wallowing elms outside his window. When dawn broke, it seemed to have drifted up from the Gulf, so omnipotent was the sunshine which followed it. The bluebirds were singing everywhere, as they sang for him still in the green arbors of memory. And there were other days of different seasons: that autumn when he stood in the lane and watched the ash-leaves fall, balancing softly earthward without wind, upon the frosted ones that had dropped away earlier. And how marvelous winter was then, especially when first he tramped over the crusted ground past fence rails gray with rime, and on across familiar fields now gleaming and wholly strange!

And there were still further recollections, more palpable and ordinary, yet always zestful. There were the hidden chickadees singing at his side; the hungry and sober robins looking for cedar-berries; the birches, almost bare but hinting of foregone gentilities with a few saved relics of their wealth of leaves. Most exciting of all, perhaps, were those shortening days before winter had fully set in. He would listen to wagon wheels crunching through slippery ruts and wait restlessly for the ice to harden. How often, at this time of the year, had he sat in front of the fire at Elmwood before bedtime and tried each buckle and strap of his new skates! He would hurry out in the early morning to examine the glassy river. The marshes would be silver. High overhead a crow might be seen, flapping its wings against a glistening sky. Then suddenly a gull would plummet down and break the water. The time had not yet come for winter's finest sport.[4]

Meanwhile he was getting around to the beginnings of one of his most cherished traits: he had started writing letters. The earliest that survives is dated shortly before his eighth birthday. It is addressed to his brother Robert, aged eleven, who was away in school at Northampton. There was snow everywhere, it seemed, and when school was out he had found the family boy-servant waiting for him—with the colt, the horse, the sleigh, and the dog. He drove away to a party, "danced a great deal and was very happy." Afterwards, at home, he adds, "I read French stories." He had already begun to collect a library of his own, three books having just been given him in anticipation of his birthday.[5]

During the summer which followed, in 1828, his father took him on a visit all the way to Washington and Alexandria. There he spent several days with the Carroll family, relations of his mother's, who escorted him on a sightseeing trip to Mount Vernon. Fifty-nine years later that auspicious day returned to him in all its vividness. He led his own grandson to the same shrine and went straight to the key of the Bastille and to the honey locusts in the garden.[6]

When fall came he reëntered a second neighborhood school, in which he had apparently been first enrolled soon after learning his alphabet and his sums. It was kept by Mr. William Wells, an Englishman, who had failed in the publishing business in Boston and turned from it to the more modest responsibility of school-mastering. Mr. Wells had rented a house on Tory Row, the Fayerweather place, and there he sternly presided, equipped with his own edition of the Latin grammar and his rattan. His method of teaching was what Lowell, following Swift, has termed *a posteriori;* the birch, he contended, was the only classic tree. He believed in manly sports and a sound thrashing for negligent scholars, and young men preparing for Harvard attended his classes regularly. George T. Curtis, an older student in the school, once wrote of this gentleman's vigorous classroom manner. "Mr. Wells," he said, "always heard a recitation with a book in his left hand and a rattan in his right, and if the boy made a false quantity or did not know the meaning of a word, down came the rattan on his head. But this chastisement was never ministered to me or to 'Jemmy Lowell.' Not to me, because I was too old for it, and not to him because he was too young." [7] Curtis might have added that, in Lowell's case, at least, this instrument of discipline was probably seldom needed. His linguistic aptness was one of his most obvious talents, and apparently he had mastered the elements of Parson Wilbur's favorite language long before he enrolled at Harvard.

Meanwhile he had written another letter to Robert, the only other one known to have survived before his college days. It was dated November, 1828, and it contained, its author began by warning, some very melancholy news.[8] The family's horse was suffering from a lame leg, and he himself was troubled both with the ague and boils. Two classmates were also ailing, one with an undisclosed illness, another with a piece of glass in his knee. But with these announcements the recital of misfortunes stopped. He was going to have a new broadcloth suit, one he might wear every day in the week if he liked. Mother would even permit him to choose the buttons for it. She had given him three more volumes for his collection, Scott's new set of *Tales of a Grandfather*. He now had "quite a library." But the best information he reserved for a postscript: There it was November the second, and Mr. Wells had not once taken his terrifying rattan out of his desk!

He was, in truth, reading a good deal in these happy days, and being read to even more. Scott was a venerable, almost fabulous, contemporary to him, the wizard of the north whose works he never tired of poring over or, even in maturity, of recommending to children anywhere. He could conceive, he said, of no healthier entertainment for them. There were also the ballads, which his mother would sing to him. She seemed to know them all. The story even ran that the Spence in her name went back to that of the betrayed and lamented Sir Patrick Spens, who was lost with his lords on his stormy voyage from Dumferling Town to Aberdour. But best of all was the *Faerie Queene*. Night after night his eldest sister would sit by his bedside and unfold its marvels to him, until sleep merged the tapestry of its images with the fused wonder of his own dreams.[9]

He fed himself richly upon these dateless legends as the summers revolved, one after another, in a land that seemed always zestful and never disturbed. He grew taller, came to be known as high-spirited, yet proved always friendly, and his companions delighted in him. At the age of fifteen, in July, 1834, he duly went over to the college to stand the Harvard entrance examinations. He passed them readily and with credit, as three generations of Lowells had done before him.

III

"A University is a place where nothing useful is taught;
but a University is possible only where a man may get his
livelihood by digging Sanskrit roots."
Lowell, *Works*, VII, 192

THE president of Harvard when Lowell enrolled as a student
in the fall of 1834 was Josiah Quincy, a Federalist and a
Unitarian. He was serving his sixth year in an office that had fallen
to him after a distinguished career as congressman and as mayor of
Boston. Like many academic heads, he was interested in education
only incidentally; his principal concern was business and endow-
ment. But he entertained, as will soon appear, some rather positive
notions about student behavior. Although he wished, said his son,
to make the college "a nursery of high-minded, high-principled,
well-taught, well-educated, well-bred gentlemen," his manner with
undergraduates seemed scarcely calculated to achieve this end. It
is true that, for the first time in Harvard history, he addressed each
student individually as "Mr." He had also substituted real silver
stamped with the college seal for the baser metal that had formerly
been used in commons. He was a Bostonian of the "purest type,"
Lowell once remarked, remembering that since the town was first
settled "there had been a Colonel of the Boston regiment in every
generation of the family." But in the spring of 1834 his breeding
and strategy, and indeed his judgment, had failed him sadly.[1]

His blundering conduct really dated from the previous fall. At
their first meeting, the President had tactlessly greeted members of
the freshman class in words that harbored an ultimate insult. *If*
these young scholars demeaned themselves as gentlemen, he had
declared, he, as president, would treat them as such. That ominous
conjunction had rankled sorely. It was nothing short of a challenge,

and undergraduates have rarely been known to turn down a challenge.

They began, the winter of 1833-34, by staging unsanctioned bonfires in the Yard. Into the flames they tossed sticks of wood, amply loaded with gunpowder. The classicist, Dr. Beck, retaliated by requiring the first- and second-year students "to memorize a forbidding Latin grammar, and the Faculty as a whole decided to make a salutary example of a few prominent offenders." Injured class spirit thereupon rose to fever pitch. Brickbats began to sail through tutors' windows, furniture was destroyed, and the college bell began to be rung, jarring and ear-splitting, in the middle of the night. Spring came, and the proverbial antics of the undergraduates—restive under the best dispensation and the coldest weather—went on, augmented, as the season mellowed into burgeoning May.

Toward the end of that month, President Quincy gave up trying. With his surrender he abandoned one of the most sanctified traditions of academic life—the tradition that, no matter what the pretext, civil authorities should not be permitted to have anything to do with purely college affairs. Quincy turned over what evidence he could muster to the Grand Jury of Middlesex, with the plea that the chief window-breakers in the student body be tried and prosecuted according to the laws of the state.

"Then," in the terse language of Professor Morison, "hell broke loose." [2] The black flag of rebellion was hung from the roof of Holworthy Hall. Furniture and glass in the recitation rooms of other buildings were smashed, and the fragments were hurled out of the windows. Members of the junior class voted to wear black crape on their arms, issued a handbill dissecting the President's character, and hanged his effigy on the Rebellion Tree. A terrific explosion occurred in the chapel, and when the smoke had cleared away the phrase, "A Bone for Old Quin to Pick," was found to have been mysteriously scrawled on the walls. A certain committee of seniors printed a handbill which stated, cogently, their views on the real causes behind the uprising. The Overseers of the college replied with a forty-seven-page rebuttal. They went even further (as if this embarrassing necessity were not enough), depriving each member of the committee of his degree and sending others off to be quizzed by another Grand Jury at Concord. So many sophomores were turned out, in fact, that the class which finally was graduated in 1836 proved with a single exception the smallest to be awarded its degrees since 1809. The Harvard of Lowell's day was, in brief, a rowdy college, rather violent, undistinguished intellectually, except for a few professors, and presided over by an absent-minded, injudicious, and domineering executive. A successful life in politics had largely spoiled Quincy for his later duties. Undergraduates were children, he felt, but endowed with a persistence and sensibility (it soon developed) which seem to have defied both his calculations and his talents.

And yet Lowell was fond of the old man; more than fond, if we may trust a mature commentary he once wrote in the *Atlantic Monthly* regarding him. The fiery traditions of his incumbency had all died away, and apparently in the mind of his former student there remained only the amused recollections of his manner, during intervals at once placid and quaint.

Mr. Quincy, Lowell reflected in 1867, had many qualities calculated to win favor with the young—including that one which above all is sure to do it, indomitable pluck. With him the dignity was in the man, not in the office. He had some of those little oddities, too, which afford amusement without contempt, and which tend to heighten rather than diminish personal attachment to superiors in station. His punctuality at prayers, and in falling asleep there; his singular inability to make even the shortest offhand speech to the students; his occasional absorption of mind, leading him to hand you his sandbox instead of the leave of absence he had just dried with it; the old-fashioned courtesy of his, "Sir, your servant," as he bowed you out of his study- -all these idiosyncrasies tended to make him popular.

Changing from Mr. Wells's school to Harvard involved no very important adjustment on Lowell's part. He was already familiar with campus life. He continued for a while to live at his home,

which was only a twenty-minute walk from the Yard. The classroom procedure too, minus the ominous rattan, was largely managed
along accustomed lines. The textbook served as bible for professor
and student alike. One recited upon its contents each day and was
duly marked. The curriculum, except for seniors, was unvarying—
Latin, mathematics, and Greek being required of everybody. While
a freshman, Lowell also studied Tyler's *History,* but it was not until
his sophomore year that he was allowed to begin English grammar
and the modern languages. The junior year brought in Paley's
Evidences of Historical Christianity and Butler's *Analogy of Religion and Chemistry,* in addition to theme-writing and forensics.
The last year was more ambitious. Seniors dropped the classics and
in place of them took up natural science, intellectual philosophy,
political economy, and astronomy, along with a rather scattered
assortment of lectures on rhetoric, criticism, the Constitution, and
anatomy.[3]

Perhaps the two closest friendships Lowell formed during his
first year were with W. H. Shackford, a senior, and G. B. Loring, a
classmate. He carried on an extensive correspondence with both
men, during vacations and after Shackford had received his degree
and gone to Phillips Exeter Academy to teach.

With this older friend he was usually airing some opinion—
economic, literary, or moral. The first letter that survives (written
in July, 1835) contains his still remarkable theory about the railroad.
He had just heard of one contemplated between Boston and Portsmouth, a distance of sixty miles. The whole notion was foolish.
He was certain that there was not enough trade between Boston and
Portsmouth to support a railroad. Why, the tracks alone would cost
$700,000, and the engines $5,000 apiece, not to mention passenger
cars, baggage cars, and the like! "I do not believe," he concluded,
"that any of the railroads will prove very profitable." [4] After the
novelty had worn off, the passenger cars would certainly not be so
full as at first. He was voicing a conservatism that was to desert
him fully for but one period in his life.

Six months later his topic was books: He had just been given a handsome edition of Milton. Another present from a "paternal relation" was the English edition of Coleridge's works. He had himself purchased a volume of Beattie, another of the satirist Butler; he was indeed becoming, he said, an "editomaniac." He proceeded to talk of his favorites. *Hudibras* would always be among them, "an inexhaustible source of mirth from beginning to end." He was reading a life of Milton and had discovered that the latter's taste (as well as Cowley's) "was formed by reading Spenser. I am glad to have such good examples, for Spenser was always my favorite poet." He had also recently translated one or two odes from Horace.

He was aware that he ought to be attending to his college studies, but the temptations to read widely and write verses in Vergil's language were apparently too strong to curb. A new eight-volume edition of Shakespeare had been announced for the next month. He meant to buy it if he could possibly command the $14 it would cost.

He had already sent Shackford, however, at least one cheering report of academic progress. A few weeks after his sophomore year started, he wrote enthusiastically of Professor Channing, the Boylston Professor of Rhetoric. He liked him very much indeed, he said, "inasmuch as I sit where I can see his marks, and he has given me an '8' every recitation this term except once, and then he gave me '7.' I went up to ask him something so as to see whether I was not mistaken (as he makes a 6 something like his 8's) and I found on the paper exactly what I expected." [5] He was also getting along remarkably in German and added, in fact: "Mathematics are my only enemies now." The result of this diligence was that, in February, 1836, as a reward for excellence in his studies, he received a prize copy of Akenside's *Poems* bound in yellow calf and stamped with the college seal. It was the first, and the last, symbol of any particular intellectual distinction that the faculty saw fit to bestow upon him as a student.

It is difficult to trace Lowell's activities while Harvard was in session, for his letters (except those to Shackford) were naturally written almost entirely during vacation periods. We know, however, that before the end of his freshman year he had taken a room near the campus and that afterwards his interest in undergraduate life became much more pronounced. So active indeed was this interest that both privately and publicly, his second and fourth years, he was admonished for excessive absence from recitations and prayers, for general negligence in themes and attendance upon lectures, and for carving up the seats in classrooms. "14 prayers, 56 recitations, Whew!" was his comment on the college's statement for 1836. He had missed that many.

Yet there were compensations. In January, 1837, he was chosen secretary of the Hasty Pudding Club, a literary body that fancied light literature and kept its minutes in verse. And he continued to read widely in authors like Byron and Campbell, to write verses in the stanza form of Burns's "Mouse," to make periodic efforts to mend his ways by joining such bands as the "Anti-Wine Society" and by reading a chapter of the Bible every night. And he was known to study Cicero and Herodotus for hours at a stretch, uncompelled—out of a sheer, if temporary, fascination with their works.

Perhaps one reason for these fitful fevers of industry was a letter his father wrote him in May, 1837. Dr. Lowell and his wife were departing for Europe. Except for an older brother's chance supervision, Jamie, as he was now called, would be entirely dependent upon his own moral resources. And Dr. Lowell had already begun to have doubts about the stoutness of the fiber that held those ranging elements in check.

He set forth his parting lesson in great detail. Condensed, it read as follows: I wish you to write us once a month, making an arrangement with Robert not to write at the same time he does. You know the necessity for economy, and you know that I shall never deny you, but from necessity, what will afford you pleasure. I shall direct Charles to pay you half a dollar a week. If you are one of the first eight admitted to the Φ B K, $1.00 per week, as soon as you are admitted. If you are not, to pay you 75 cents per week as soon as you are admitted. If you graduate one of the first five in your class, I shall give you $100 on your graduation. If one of the first ten, $75. If one of the first twelve [sixty-five were to finish in his class], $50.00. If the first or second scholar, $200. If you do not miss any exercises unexcused, he added—tempting him on his weak side, his personal library—you shall have Bryant's *Mythology* or any book of equal value, unless it is one I may specially want.

It was all made plain, in coldly statistical terms. And following this appeared certain moral injunctions, much more warmly urged: Use regular exercise; associate with those who will exert the best influence upon you; say your prayers and read your Bible every day; make up your back exercises immediately and let the president know it; charge nothing without the consent of your brother Charles! Lowell's whole senior year stretched before him, to mar or to distinguish himself in as he willed.

And soon afterwards, in August, 1837, as if to buttress the good intentions of this letter, came another solemn communication from his friend Shackford. At Andover Shackford had been maturing rapidly, and meditating, as the process went on, upon the dense evils of undergraduate life at his Alma Mater. "It grieves me," he confessed, "to think of all those temptations to intemperance which exist at college; to think that many a young man comes from home uncontaminated, and with an abhorrence of drinking of all kinds, but after being inured to it by witnessing it for four long years, he comes forth, with an indifference (to say the least) to all excess. Scenes and habits are tolerated there which would be a total disgrace to any other class of men. What would be thought of a company of mechanics, or laborers, or even sailors, much more a company of gentlemen, who should go into some field and make the most uproarious noise, like a troop of bacchanals, and get drunk as fiddlers? Those young men who do so are the very ones who go forth to influence the destinies of the nation and who therefore ought to oppose such practices. This is a crying sin, and you, Jem, will think so when you get out of its vortex. The college faculty ought to rise up against such a disgrace on their discipline. Shame on them! I cannot think of these scenes without shuddering. Sorrow fills my heart when I see in my mind's eye those beautiful young men making beasts of themselves, their faces flushed, their voices raised to the highest pitch, and clothes almost stripped off." [6]

Then there was Emerson, the same month, addressing that very Phi Beta Kappa Society to which Dr. Lowell hoped, so tangibly, to see his son elected—Emerson, telling the young men, the American scholars, that the day of subservience to the cultures of Europe was closing; that they should rely on their own judgments, should cease to defer to the popular cry, should be godlike, self-trusting, leaders and inspirers of men, poets who should sing the rising glory of their radiant new land.

But all this advice, whether from parent, or friend, or from the transcendental enigma out of neighboring Concord, fell upon ears that were gayly unheeding. One's senior year, Lowell felt as it was beginning, was not a time to mend one's manners; it was a time to have the time of one's life. He had begun to keep a journal, it is true, and he was continuing his reading at a lively pace. Yet these interests were apparently much less significant to him than were his new opportunities as an editor of the undergraduate literary magazine *Harvardiana*.

Associated with Lowell on the editorial board of this publication were four men of unusual prominence: Rufus King, later an important Cincinnati attorney; George W. Lippitt, who was to serve for years as secretary of the American legation at Vienna; Nathan Hale (older brother of Edward Everett Hale), who distinguished himself in Boston journalism; and Charles W. Scates, of South Carolina, whose early death frustrated what might possibly have been the most brilliant career of the group.

Lowell contributed to this interesting monthly a total of twenty-four pieces: thirteen poems and eleven prose sketches.[7] In September, 1837, there were three—a "Dramatic Sketch" which comically echoed Shakespeare and Byron ("Is this a sonnet that I see before me, Its title toward mine eyes," etc.), an amusing book review entitled "A New Poem from Homer," and an "Imitation from Burns" which extolled the beauty of a certain lady's hair.

The following month he turned to the sentimental, and in "A

Voice from the Tombs" set forth a melancholy picture of the vast democracy of the grave and the story of a young betrothed maiden who was buried of a broken heart a week after her lover's death. When his own life is finished, the author concluded, let him have "no other monument than the regret of friendship—no other epitaph than a tear from the eye of love."

"Hints to Theme Writers" was a humorous complement to this solemn offering. "The first and grand requisite of a theme is, of course, to be three pages in length; for if it should be shorter then it is not a theme. The second requisite is that the canons of Lowth and Whatley [authors of the texts on Grammar and Rhetoric] be not violated; for if they are, then unsightly cabalistic marks will crowd the margin. . . . The first half page may always be easily filled with what may be called the ante-exordium. As to the exordium, we have an exquisite method of manufacturing one for every subject. . . . Keep by you a collection of proverbs, and when you begin to compose, say, 'It has been universally admitted among all nations and in all ages,'" etc. Then follows a specimen paper. After it he inserted another little piece extolling the music of the chapel bell of the college.

So his contributions went. Others appeared irregularly during the year. He would have nothing in two consecutive issues; then a burst of activity would fairly flood the pages of the next number with satire, moral pieces, sober essays, and sentimental or comic poetry. Under the fairly cryptic title of "Skillygoliana" (*skillygolee:* a poor thin watery soup), he celebrated campus activities from time to time in verse. Perhaps his liveliest piece was one he termed "A Pair of Black Eyes," which lauded the power of these charming organs to capsize the intentions of the wisest young men in the world. But he goes on to add, properly, in this work, that it is not the body that gives grace to a woman so much as the heart, and that many a penniless but sympathetic girl is more to be desired than others who languish in wealth.

Though he wrote most engagingly about black eyes, he achieved much more significance in a few comments about Emerson. By the spring of 1838 he appears to have got around to a sober reading of "The American Scholar," and even though his approval of its point of view was temporary, as will soon be seen, at this date he at least found one sentiment in the work to admire without restraint. " 'If there be one lesson more than another which should pierce one's ear,' " he quoted, " 'it is, *The world is nothing; the man is all.'* " And again, " 'Let a man not quit his belief that a popgun is a popgun though the ancient and honorable of the earth affirm it to be the crack of doom.' " "Better therefore," continued Lowell, "a thousand animal magnetisms, clothes philosophies, etc., should perish, than that our rush-light should be hidden under a bushel. This, to us, smacks of sound philosophy and the true dignity of human nature." Out of the welter of dispersed meditations and imitative effusions of which his pieces in the magazine give evidence, he was at last beginning, if dimly, to see himself in his relation to the world, to guess at the fact that if a person is even to begin to comprehend it he must set himself down solidly somewhere, must take his stand against its bewildering mutations. But that vision was soon to prove faint and evanescent, a wandering fire that his traditional conservatism quickly put out and, for an interval, repudiated.

Meanwhile he was reading a good many more books than most undergraduates ever manage to look into, and he was keeping at least a brief account of what he liked in them in his Journal. In the first volume, for example, may be found a list of books for 1838, many of which he seems to have got through before graduation. Carlyle's three-volume *French Revolution* is mentioned, along with Southey's *Thalaba;* Coleridge's *Poems,* in three volumes ("for the twentieth time or so"); Friar Bacon's *Discoveries; Wallenstein;* many poems by Joshua Sylvester and Du Bartas; Shelley's *Cenci* and most of his other poems; the *Merry Conceited Jests of George Peele;* three plays by Beaumont and Fletcher; Byron's *Manfred;* two volumes of Carlyle's *Miscellanies* and his *Sartor Resartus;* Bunyan's *Works;* John Ford's *Plays;* Mackintosh's two-volume *History of England* and his *Ethical Philosophy;* Tennyson's *Poems;* Norton's

Statement of Reasons; Vivian Grey; Locke's *Essay on the Human Understanding;* Chapman's *Bussy d'Ambois;* Webster's *Devil's Law Case;* Richter's *Works;* Cowper's *Task;* Daniel's *Defense of Rime;* Pope's *Letters;* Horace's *Art of Poetry;* Rabelais; Ludwig Borne; Fuller's *Holy and Profane State;* and finally the three "works" of Emerson that had thus far appeared. It was no mean list, by anybody's standards, though it was obviously unselective. It is important to notice further that three major transcendentalists —Coleridge, Carlyle, and Emerson—are prominently included in it.

Other things are worth noting, too, about this Journal. Lowell has begun systematically—insofar as he was *ever* systematic about anything—to record an alphabetical list of quotations from those authors who have impressed him. There are pithy remarks about "Art," "Biography," "Concealment," "Death," "Education," "Fate," and so on down through the other letters. Two hundred in all appear in the first of the volumes. In later volumes a similar collection of aphorisms may be found, but they are often Lowell's own. Taken together, they represent the beginnings of his conscious study of phrasemaking, an art in which he has had few superiors in American Literature.[8]

Young Lowell, however, was nothing if not versatile; the range of his interests, indeed, seemed at this time almost boundless. There was the matter of his friendship with certain classmates. They would write to each other like girls sharing secrets, would quarrel with each other with the petulance of young lovers. The case of George Loring is typical.

Loring had gone home to Andover for the spring vacation in April, 1838, and from that place resumed the correspondence which had developed during periods of separation since the two young men first entered Harvard. The burden of the first letter was petulant: I hardly know whether I should write you any more, because you charged me with writing merely in order to pass a pleasant hour, not out of real affection. Besides, we seemed wonderfully estranged last term, so estranged that I feared our friendship to be at an end. We both know the reason for this, so I will not set it down in a letter. After all our oft repeated vows and pledges, I thought nothing could separate us, and had promised to myself many future days of happiness, which should spring out of our friendship planted and cultured at our Alma Mater. It began when our hearts were warm, and if they *have* grown cold in so short a time by contact with the world, I think they might still have found sympathy in each other. I have waited patiently to hear from you. You used to say that you needed someone to whom you could reveal your secrets and lay open your thoughts and that you appeared to find such a person in me. Have you found a better, that you should wish to stop such intimacy? But perhaps I have said too much already about this *friendship* of ours—more than will be pleasant. Through fear that surfeiting may kill at once what starvation appeared to be destroying gradually, I will leave it.[9]

A good many more of these letters have survived, for Lowell apparently cherished all his correspondence. The literary Freudians could make much of a few of them. Those not particularly convinced of the critical validity of identifying love or affection with sex, however, will probably conclude that these letters are the quite normal accompaniments of masculine intimacy in a romantic age. The early Lowell was at moments intensely sentimental, though, at that, not nearly so given to the excesses of this failing as were some of his friends, who admired him and who at times even seemed jealous that he relished the companionship and the admiration of others.

That his friends were many and their esteem for him considerable was evident the early summer of his senior year. He was elected Class Poet of 1838. Apparently it was, if one may judge by his manner of celebrating it, an honor which he valued keenly. For at evening prayers he appeared in chapel a trifle late and in the best of spirits. Perhaps he was a bit flushed with wine from celebrating, during most of the afternoon, the prized distinction that had come to him that morning. The venerable Rev. Henry Ware had just begun, in trembling voice, the prayer service that had been faithfully observed through two hundred years of Harvard history. The president, "Old Quin," was seated beside him, surveying his boys. Poet Lowell, his face "richly suffused with the glow of youth," sat down near the front, then arose, turned to the audience and bowed, smirking, both to the right and to the left. The incident lasted for only a moment. He was pulled into his seat by a classmate, made one further effort to get up again, was restrained, and relaxed until the service was concluded. But "Old Quin's" eyes were snapping; they had missed nothing.[10]

The faculty wasted no time over this trivial but irreverent action. At its next meeting, June 25, 1838, by official vote, James Russell Lowell was rusticated to Concord. The decision to send him away was severe, at least so a number of his friends believed, and the chances are that this punishment would have been more modest had no further complaints been registered against him. The fact is that there were several others, all academically serious. His monotonous cutting of morning prayers was the talk of the campus; he was setting an evil example. President Quincy had had him in any number of times for "privates," or personal admonitions, and had solemnly exhorted him to mend his ways. Yet the effect of all this solicitude had been wasted. Finally there had been his indifference, in Mr. Francis Bowen's class, to Mackintosh's *Review of Ethical Philosophy* and to Locke's *Essay*. Mr. Lowell needed the ultimate discipline.

That discipline, applied, meant that—on penalty of forfeiting his degree—he must live in Concord until commencement, the last week in August. He could not read his poem at the class exercises. He could attend no farewell suppers. He could enjoy no vacation rambles with friends during the six weeks of freedom before graduation day. Instead, he must reside in the house of the Rev. Barzillai Frost, must study and recite to him regularly, and he must not return even once during the interval to the familiar delights of Cambridge. The compensations for this uncheering prospect were not catalogued. But among them was included the privilege of conversing with two already unusual residents of the village, Ralph Waldo Emerson and Henry David Thoreau. It was a rare opportunity which he might either grasp or miss according to the possibilities of his nature.

He faced the action of the faculty with philosophical resignation. There was neither complaint nor rankling, private bitterness, only a gradual, but at length most irritating boredom. Yet letters from friends kept him regularly informed about life at the college. The first of these that has survived, from Loring, reached him only a few days after he arrived at Concord. The two men had ended their quarrelings. Loring confessed that he had wandered about from place to place, almost like a dove that had lost its mate. Lowell had been the one person on the campus with whom he could sympathize. "But Concord is doubtless doleful enough, without any doleful notes from me. Does Mrs. Barzillai feed you well? I think there is no danger of your being downhearted, for you have always taken things as they come, and pretty coolly too. The senior class is in a dreadful quandary on account of what many call your *merited* suspension. I stoutly oppose this view." The question that faced the class, he went on, was this: Should the class exercises be held in Boston in defiance of the faculty, thereby allowing Lowell to read his own poem? It was a hard problem. What would happen, Loring surmised, was that a petition would be sent up to the Honorable President on Monday, requesting that a proxy be allowed to "operate" in Lowell's stead.[11]

Another classmate, Eben Wright, wrote him on the eve of Independence Day. This is a much more informing letter, bringing the news from the Yard up to date. The previous evening, it reported, the Faculty ("damn 'em") passed a vote that they would not allow Lowell's poem to be read on class day in the Chapel. Afterwards the class had a meeting for the purpose of choosing another poet. It was proposed that Lowell be allowed to name him, and that he should actually read Lowell's verses. Then someone said that he doubted whether anybody would consent to read publicly, as his own, what was really another's work. Later a resolution came up that the exercises be held in the Orthodox Meeting House in Cambridge, that Lowell appoint someone to recite the poem there, and that the faculty be invited to attend—if they could not consistently do so as a body, then let them be asked as individuals. A member objected that Cooledge, class orator, would be unwilling to deliver his oration in any other place than the college Chapel. The class promptly voted that Cooledge should be governed by its wishes, not it by his. And besides, practically everyone agreed that if the oration were delivered without the poem, there should be no one present; they didn't give a damn about hearing the oration alone! And a fund had been got up to pay for the printing of the poem. The list already contained the names of half the members of the class, and 170 copies were subscribed for.[12]

From his forced retirement, Lowell had already written Loring. The first note, highly self-conscious and literary, declared that Concord appeared to be "a pretty decent sort of place," that he had not composed a single line, and that he would probably take up smoking again "for very spite." He meant to do all he could to please the Rev. Frost, "since he does his best to please me and make me comfortable." He felt cursed queer, Lowell went on. He damned Concord; he damned everything. For one thing, everybody was calling him indolent. (As an aunt tersely put it, his trouble was simply "indolence and the Spence negligence.") "Damn everybody, since everybody damns me." Yet though he hadn't dug in the ground, farmer fashion, he had read a good deal, he felt, choosing the while both his books and his friends as he pleased.

July came round and advanced. Still, on the ninth, he was compelled to report that he hadn't written a line since he had been in "this horrible place." He felt as queer as a woman at her change of life. He was homesick. "I must go down and see Emerson, and if he doesn't make me feel more like a fool, it won't be because I don't think *him* one. Yet he is a good-natured man, in spite of his doctrines. He traveled all the way up from his house to bring me a book which had been directed to me *via* him." For the younger Concord celebrity he reserved only two meager sentences: "I met Thoreau last night, and it is exquisitely amusing to see how he imitates Emerson's tone and manner. With my eyes shut, I shouldn't know them apart."[13] The evidence seems to show that toward almost anything that concerned this young poet-naturalist—who, incidentally, became the author of some of the finest prose in English—Lowell kept his eyes shut, tightly and stubbornly, to the end.

The days of his confinement wore on, but they failed to mellow him. "If this town were in the same predicament with the cities of the plain, I doubt most exceedingly whether they'd find ten decent people to save the place." Thank heaven there were only four weeks more of it to put up with. But three weeks later, on August 17, he could report that he had added 250 lines to the class poem. It was not yet finished, alas, but it was nearly so. But, not being able to deliver it in person, he was beginning to regard its composition as a burden. By the following day, however, he had turned over to a printer a practically completed draft.[14]

Of course, one reason for the fits of melancholy at Concord was the character of Mr. Frost himself. In this gentleman's habitual reference to the college triennial catalogue, and in his general pedantry, Lowell may have found at least a few hints that suggested Parson Wilbur.[15] He could be boring or exquisitely comic, according to one's mood, and in sermons his unconscious talent for connecting lofty with absurd sentiments practically amounted to genius. They had been free, he once declared to his congregation, from the pestilence that walketh in darkness and the destruction that wasteth at noonday, but it was true that they had suffered some chicken pox and some measles. And there was his account, in another sermon, of his visit to Niagara Falls. He described the cataract with great feeling and eloquence. The mighty flood discharged its waters on a scale so broad and so grand that the imagination of man was staggered. That surging flood, he added climactically, forgetting his statistics in the torrent of his rhetoric, was "several feet deep." His major fault, said Lowell, was that he delighted too well in the sound of his own voice. When hearing lessons, his favorite diversion was in refuting Locke, with no Locke present to demolish the refutation. Lowell's early, yet considered, pronouncement upon him was one of the shrewdest he ever wrote: "He is one of those men who walk through this world with a cursed ragged undersuit of natural capacity entirely concealed in a handsome borrowed surtout of other men's ideas, buttoned up to the chin." Lowell left Concord as one leaves a prison.

Yet he left it with his ambitious poem completed, and the contents of that work, though not subsequently reprinted, are interesting to this day. It is mainly an indictment of the times, written for the most part in couplets. One of the first subjects ridiculed is Kant, the father of philosophic transcendentalism.

> Kant, happy name! change but the K to C,
> And I will wring my poem out of thee. . . .
> Cant be my theme, and when she fails my song,
> Her sister Humbug shall the lay prolong.

Afterwards comes *Sartor Resartus,* in which the clothes philosophers are advised to take to tailoring professionally:

> Lay down the goose quill then—take up the goose
> And put your talents to the proper use.

Next there is Emerson, whose salt he had eaten and whose little child he had danced on his knee at the very time that the poem was being written. It was the Emerson of the "Divinity School Address" whom he had in mind—the Emerson who, during the summer, had declared that the error of the clergy was in failing to realize that every man is divine, not merely Christ; that Christ, in fact, was not the son of God one whit more truly than was the least of those to whom he spoke. And all this had been said—the teachings of the entire faculty to the contrary—to the graduating class in theology! Woe to religion, bewailed the young versifier,

> When men just girding for the holy strife
> Their hands just cleansed to break the bread of life,
> Whose souls, made whole, should never count it loss
> With their own blood to witness for the cross,
> Invite a man their Christian zeal to crown
> By preaching earnestly the Gospel—down,
> Applaud him when he calls of earthy make
> That *One* who spoke as never yet man spake,
> And tamely hear the anointed Son of God
> Made like themselves an animated clod.

People wonder over these blasphemous doctrines, Lowell goes on, but are told that they must be true, since they represent the orator's own thought.

Women reformers are similarly castigated, and the graham flour addicts come in for their share of abuse, along with the bran and the diet fanciers in general. Afterwards he turns to the abolitionists,

> Those who roar and rave
> O'er the exaggerate tortures of the slave.

He confesses his sensitiveness to suffering, but he finds tedious the moralizing and tearful sermonizing of these zealots:

> I do blame the man who takes his place
> The self made benefactor of his race,
> Who in his zeal his neighbor's eye to free
> From motes that calumny can hardly see
> Dreams not that aught can shadow his clear sight
> Showing him all things in a jaundiced light,
> And in his care about another's sins
> On Satan's threshold breaks his own sweet shins.

Let the abolitionists but think of the noble Cherokees, driven from their lands, harassed by the white man. The nation's injustice to them was fully as great as is that of the South today toward its negroes.

The prohibitionists, finally, are meted out a special damnation. They are people who find poison in the bright juice of the grape, men who run stark mad in their indecent haste to cure sinners of their evil appetite. Such people are like those who would chop down all the apple trees to prevent the drinking of cider. Lowell dismisses them with a penetrating couplet:

> The worst intoxication man can feel
> Is that which drains the burning cup of zeal.

He ends his work with a reminiscent vision of the older generations of Harvard students. They were sane men. They drank their beer in abundance, but over it, even when most sentimental, they shed no tears about the status of the suffering Africans.[16]

The moral of the entire poem is tucked away neatly in this concluding observation. It was the work of a well-bred, conservative New Englander. From beginning to end it was orthodox, was safe, was the sort of thing his financially unharassed classmates would for the most part delight to hear spoken. But beneath the surface, and reaching, indeed, far back into the beginnings of his Harvard apprenticeship, was another quality whose fulfillment was unpredictable: it was Lowell's mental restlessness and curiosity. He was not at ease, wholly, in his comfortable but confining Zion. Brahmin he was in the main, no doubt, but a volatile Brahmin, unsure of himself. The influence of a strong personality might readily bend him wherever it willed.

IV

*"My pen has not yet traced a line of which I am either
proud or ashamed."*

Lowell to C. F. Briggs, February 18, 1846
Works, XIV, 148

SOMEWHAT chastened by his two months in the village, Lowell
returned to Cambridge the last week in August, 1838, and was
duly graduated with his class. One of his first acts thereafter was to
write a note to Emerson, apologizing fervently for his slurring
references to him in the Class Poem. The reasons for this sudden
recantation are not wholly clear. But they seem to have grown out
of certain remarks Lowell heard of, to the effect that it was ill-
mannered indeed for a young upstart poet to write cynically of an
older man who had treated him with every kindness and even
entertained him in his home.

In extenuation of his verses Lowell was plausible enough, and
thoroughly abject. He cited one of Emerson's own often emphasized
dogmas, that one should trust himself, should speak his own mind
always, no matter how sharply disconcerting his speech may occasionally prove to be to others. He really thought, he said, that he
was doing rightly. For he considered it as virtually a lie to hold
one's tongue as to speak an untruth. He would have written the
same of his own brother. "Now, sir, I trouble you with this letter
because I believe you a man who would think nowise the worse of
me for holding up my head and speaking the truth at any sacrifice.
That I could wilfully malign a man whose salt I had eaten and
whose little child I had danced on my knee—he must be a small man
who would believe so small a thing of his fellow." He hoped that,
if Emerson could offer the leisure, he would answer this letter and
put his correspondent at rest. Lowell hoped to be *acquitted* of all
uncharitableness; he did not think there was aught to *pardon*.[1] He

enclosed a copy of the poem, adding to it the hope that, as one honest man to another, he might continue to enjoy Emerson's friendship. His wish was granted. The two authors were at first not particularly intimate, as the collection of Emerson's letters makes plain.[2] But they were respectful and solicitous toward one another to the end.

Meanwhile, what should he do about a profession? There were law, divinity, and medicine, and, in a descending series, the countinghouse, to select from. His ranging abilities, he apparently felt, would serve him adequately in any one of them. Then, more vaguely apprehended, there was literature, if only he could hit upon some reasonably certain way of keeping himself alive while he produced it!

When autumn began, it was the ministry and his fitness for it that he was debating. He was convinced, he said, that no man ought to enter that work who has not experienced a special calling. "I don't mean an old-fashioned special calling, with winged angels and fat-bottomed cherubs, but an inward one. In fact, I think that no man ought to be a minister who has not money enough to support him, besides his salary. For the minister of God should not be thinking of his own and children's bread when dispensing the bread of life." If he did not suspect that he should some day make a great fool of himself and marry, he would enter the Divinity School tomorrow. But as he pursued this subject more fully in his mind, its appeal became dimmer and less interesting. Of course, he felt, he ought to stop giving so much of his time to the muses now; he should settle down to something tangible. But one special matter kept troubling him. He was convinced that he should write a dramatic poem on the subject of Cromwell. Those old Roundheads had never had justice done them. He was off, now, into a reverie about the open-hearted Cavaliers, and about Milton, Sidney, Hampden, Selden, Pym, and all the rest of the venerable fiery-eyed warriors and poets, speculating on their love for liberty and on their glorious trust in the arm of the Lord in battle. Irrevocably sunk in dust though they were, he would make them live again in his poem.

Meanwhile the notion of studying divinity had somehow got clean out of his mind.[3]

Two weeks later he set for himself a course of study in law. "I am reading Blackstone," he reported shortly afterwards, "with as good a grace and as few wry faces as I may." Yet his perseverance lasted a bare twenty days.[4] "Farewell, a long farewell to all my greatness," he wrote Loring. He had renounced the Law. Since he could not bring himself to like it, he was now looking out for a place in a store. He had had a great inward struggle over this problem, he declared, for his decision meant that he must expect to give up almost entirely all literary pursuits and turn to the making of money instead of rhymes. If only he could imagine himself as ever being able to love the Law, he would persevere. But "I am confident that I shall never be able to be on speaking terms with it." He was still thinking of the Ministry, had even considered Medicine. But both seemed worse than an attorney's career.

In nine days he was back at his law books, resolved to go on in the profession and to study it as well as he could! The man who unwittingly converted him this time was Daniel Webster. Wandering about the streets of Boston in a none-too-persistent search for a job, Lowell dropped in at court and heard the great orator pleading a case. The dramatic effectiveness of this scowling figure—who had been known to compel a judge to adjourn court merely by glaring at him and donning his hat—completely captivated the vacillating young Brahmin. So completely, indeed, did Webster's performance stir him that more than three months elapsed before desperation resulted in another report to Loring that he had "quitted the law forever."[5] He had meanwhile been substituting for his ailing brother Robert in the "counting room" of a Boston coal merchant, and he had also been writing verses as well as reading the legal commentaries. But his decision to give up the last-named drudgery was now final, he said. He meant it. Now, he wanted to know, about this business of lecturing at Andover. "Do they pay anything?" When should he come? Did they like abstract addresses such as he gave? He was going to speak at Concord shortly. "I hope to astonish them a little." The lyceum platform was beckoning to him, festooned with gold and adulation.

At Concord they gave him $4.00. "I wish they'd take it into their heads to ask me at Cambridge, where they pay fifteen dollars, or in Lowell, where they pay twenty-five dollars! What to do with myself I don't know." It was the ninth of March, 1839. The thought of business made him increasingly desperate; the prospect of law grew less and less dismal. But wouldn't people take him for a fool if he changed his mind again? This, however, he knew: he would never be happy in the countinghouse. For consolation he turned to his writing, began to publish a few pieces in the *Knicker-bocker Magazine,* and continued his desultory reading. But by May 20 he had finally made up his mind. He wrote Loring that the next day, without saying a word to anybody, he would "quietly proceed to Dane Law College [at Harvard] for recitation." He did so. And though, as the weeks proceeded, he successively liked the law, and liked it again, and was sick of it, and was resolved to learn it but not to practice it, and wrote much poetry in order to forget it, this time he at least stayed with it to the end. And as a reward, on the last day of August, 1840, he was able to report to his friend: "I took a degree of LL.B. on Wednesday, and never did a piece of parchment of the same size contain so many lies." [6]

Meantime, there had been a violent love affair. We know very little about this stormy incident in his life, for those who might have been informing have all shrouded it in vagueness. The young lady was "an intimate of the Lowell household," writes Greenslet;[7] or, in the words of Scudder, "she was one of the circle in which his family moved, and endowed with intellectual grace and great charm of manner." [8] Then, this biographer goes on, something he fears even to hint at "came between them." Lowell met her first in July, 1837. In a letter written in December, 1840, which previous editors partly suppressed, we learn that his compulsion toward her was "fierce and savage. It rose not like the fair evening star on the evening I first met her . . . but like a lurid meteor. And it fell as suddenly. For a moment I was dazed by its glare and startled by the noise of its bursting. But I grew calm and soon morning dawned." [9]

Morning, however, seems to have been much more tardy about dawning than Lowell implies. This "gale of possession shook the very foundations of his life," says Greenslet; or, to cite Scudder again, "it broke up the fountains of the deep of his own life." Whatever these tumultuous phrases may mean, it was a year and a half after the "gale" had spent itself before any serious interest in another lady appears in his letters.

But when it did appear this time it was fraught with the ultimate implications. Lowell has recorded his first meeting with the lady. He had gone up to Watertown on Saturday, November 30, 1839, to spend the week-end with a former classmate, William A. White. You ought to see White's father! he wrote Loring—the most perfect specimen of a bluff, honest, hospitable country squire one could possibly imagine. His mother, too, was a very pleasant woman. And his sister Maria was both pleasant and amiable; she "knows more poetry than anyone I am acquainted with." He hinted, in closing, at the only fault he was ever to acknowledge in her. She was more familiar "with modern poets than with the pure well-springs of English poesy." [10]

Maria White was a remarkable young lady, and one who matured much more surely than ever her suitor did, though he lived to be more than twice her age. Indeed it appears that, before her early death, she had grown so far beyond him as to be able, in her altogether quiet way, to lead him as one might lead a flighty boy who lacked both concentration and any sense of values or direction. Exactly where she did lead him—into what absurdities of reform, into what irrationalities of action—is another matter entirely. But the doubt can scarcely exist that his devotion made of him, with respect to her desires and attitudes, an ardent slave.

Maria had been educated at the Ursuline convent at Mt. Benedict, in Charlestown. The discipline she came to know there was strenuous: All the girls dressed in uniform—blue merino frocks, black silk capes and aprons, and straw bonnets trimmed in pink for the

THE FIRST MRS. LOWELL
(Maria White)
After a painting by William Page

summer. Sixteen of them slept in a dormitory, each with her trunk at the foot of her bed. They were aroused every morning by a sister reciting matins as she passed beside each bed and snatched off its covers. They dressed and went to the refectory, and while the older girls read to them from the lives of the saints, they partook of dry bread and mugfuls of milk.[11]

In 1834 the convent had been burned by a mob, enraged by the charge of a Cambridge girl, Rebecca Reed, that the nuns had attempted to make a Catholic of her. After this date, the details of Maria's education are vague, except for the fact that, in 1839, she is known to have begun attending Margaret Fuller's weekly series of educational "conversations"—along with the future Mrs. Hawthorne, the second Mrs. Emerson, Mrs. Theodore Parker, Mrs. George Ripley, and Mrs. Wendell Phillips. An intellectual sun in all its rounds could scarcely have shone down anywhere upon a more distinguished collection of satellites. Maria had imbibed, soon after her exposure began, two passionate convictions she was never to forsake —a belief in temperance (which actually meant abstinence), and an equally ardent belief in abolition. But at least she believed in *something,* with conviction that bespoke a passionate intensity.

Both passionate and sublimated this intensity appears to have been, if one may judge from Lowell's early remarks about Maria. May came. It was 1840, and he had reached his majority. She was beautiful, he wrote Loring, wholly pure and spiritlike. "She seems half of earth and more than half of Heaven." His ecstatic conception of her continued to grow as month followed month. By June it was more than he could bear. There had been walks in the moonlight —with stars and floating mist to transfigure her loveliness. There had been whispered conversations, soft and enraptured, when the unreal walk was over. There had been her "spirit eyes" luxuriously before him, and the rose she pressed into his hand as they parted. How could the heartless Goethe have merited the love of the child-like Bettina? he wondered. He resented all those who in the past had enjoyed a kindred rapture without deserving it; their worldliness was an offense to him. Thank God, it was not Maria who had raised the tempest in his soul three years ago, flinging up from its unplumbed bottom the foul and slimy weeds that had lain there! "A disappointment from her would I think have broken my heart." She had merged in his mind with all his rioting imagination had come to love. Before the summer passed, they were formally betrothed.

After that betrothal, their conduct became much more public and exemplary, and incidentally, it would seem, a trifle less ardent. He was still poor, the merest beginner in his profession; there was little immediate prospect of marriage. Only one thing intuitively disturbed him—a dream he had been visited with twice during the month in which their future plans had been agreed upon. In that unreal reminder, it seemed, he had seen her walking just before him, yet when he sought to overtake her she had vanished. "I asked a man whom I passed if he had seen her. 'Yes,' he replied, 'she has gone down the happy road.' Does this mean, George, that I shall love her and that she shall die?"

A few weeks later Lowell learned that his friends were curious; they were talking about Maria, were saying that she was transcendental. Did they really say this? he asked. Yes, it was true, she did indeed go beyond them. They could not understand a being like her. "But if they mean that she is unfit for the duties of life, they are entirely wrong. She has more common sense than any woman I have ever seen. Genius always has." Hear what she had written herself, in one of her glorious letters: "When I said that I loved you, I almost felt as if I had said, 'and I will espouse sorrow for thy sake,' for I have lived long enough and observed life keenly enough to know that not the truest and most exalted love can bar the approach of much care and sorrow." All this she was ready and able to endure. And by way of reciprocity for such open-hearted adulation, Lowell, in the autumn of 1840, had taken his place as a delegate to an antislavery convention in Boston.[12]

But one of Maria's earliest influences on him concerned his indecisive attitude toward his own poems. He should collect them and publish them in a book, she felt. Under the name "Hugh Percival," he had written a good deal for Mr. T. W. White's *Southern Literary Messenger,* and he was continuing his contributions to the *Knicker-bocker* and other magazines. Editor White even wanted him to turn translator (though without pay) and render a long poem of Victor Hugo's into English. This was in August, 1840. But he declined for a very sound reason. " 'Tis a bad habit to get into for a poor man, this writing for nothing. Perhaps if I hang off he may offer me somewhat."

The projected volume of poetry, under the title *A Year's Life,* made its official [13] appearance in January, 1841. In length, at least, the offering was fairly substantial: there were thirty-five sonnets and thirty-five other poems of varying extent within its 182 pages. The reader who knew a few phrases of German could have guessed the nature of its contents from the inscription upon its title page. *Ich habe gelebt und geliebet,* it declared, and of course the tribute was to Maria, who is described in the rhymed dedication as "the gentle Una I have loved, the snowy maiden pure and mild."

One need pause only briefly over this book. Of its seventy pieces Lowell retained only nine in his collected works. His favorite themes are his mystical joy in his new-found love and her perfection of both beauty and spirit. The bookishness that colored so much of his later work is modestly evident, and there is the typical romantic absorption with the theme of death, usually expressed in nebulous and ornate diction. His images are conventional and prettified. But one may find at least occasional evidence of the fact that he had looked at his own countryside and seen a few of its attributes precisely. The reviewer in *Graham's* noted another characteristic, praising Lowell as the herald of a new school, at once "humanitarian and idealistic." Two friends treated it sympathetically in the *Christian Examiner* and the *North American Review,* and there were other "important" and generally gracious notices in the *Boston Quarterly* and the *Messenger.* Fewer than three hundred copies were sold, but the right people were impressed. In the words of the dapper and widely traveled N. P. Willis, Lowell had become "the best launched poet of his time."

Probably no one was more pleased with the launching than were the members of that group of Lowell's friends who called themselves "the Band." The seeds of this relationship were apparently planted at Harvard, where Lowell, W. W. Story, John G. King, W. A. White, and Nathan Hale lived, declares Edward Everett Hale, "in the closest intimacy." White and King were cousins, Lowell and Story were both natives of Cambridge, and Hale had been an associate editor of *Harvardiana,* we remember, during Lowell's senior year. What was unique about the relationship was "the fact that four of these young men had sisters of nearly their own age, all charming young women, whose tastes, interests, and studies were precisely the same as their brothers', and whose complete intimacy and tender, personal, self-sacrificing love for each other was absolute." [14] So be it. The home of each was the home of all, Hale continues, and at parties they rescued each other, by secret signals, from bores or otherwise difficult problems. They exchanged books, staged house parties frequently, read aloud to one another, and sang Lowell's lyrics to the tunes of ballads or Elizabethan songs. Maria was always best at this.

Yet these things represented the diversions of their lighter hours. They were reformers too, and their indignation ran high when the woes of the enslaved African and the evils of wine were talked of. By a kind of natural superiority, Lowell and Maria, after their engagement, came to be known as King and Queen of the Band. It was New England's chastened version of the King and Queen of the May, with all the rowdiness that went with this ancient rite subdued to the debaucheries of an extra meal at 10:00 P.M., and with mother and father presiding at the table.[15]

The King and Queen, indeed, moved in such an exalted air, says Scudder, that their devotion came to have, by a paradox, an almost impersonal character, as if they were creatures of romance. Maria would pass James's letters about among the other less fortunate ladies, and even among the young men. "I never saw such perfect specimens of *love-letters,*" confessed one privileged male reader; "those in any novel you ever read are perfectly indifferent compared to them." Not silly, he went on to say, they were none-theless full of the fervor and "extatification" which one expected from the most ardent worshiper.[16]

The climax of the more serious interests of the Band Lowell himself recorded in the summer of 1842. The occasion was a proper observance of July 4, and it was staged in Watertown, Maria's home. He described the event itself, and the fervent acclaim that attended it. "Last Friday," he wrote two days later, "Maria presented a banner to the Watertown Washington Total Abstinence Society in the name of the women of Watertown. There were more than a thousand people present. The meeting was held on a beautifully wooded hill belonging to Mr. White. . . . Maria looked—I never saw any woman look so grand. She was dressed in snowy white, with a wreath of oak leaves and water lilies round her head, and a water lily in her bosom. There were a great many tears in a great many eyes when she presented her banner. . . . She said a few words in clear silvery tones. She told them that the banner came from their mothers and sisters, their daughters and wives, and that they must hold it sacred." The next day a great hard-handed, brown-faced farmer came up to tell Lowell that, though he loved his wife and would continue to love her until death, he had never seen a face like Maria's when she had spoken. Later in the day Lowell attended a dinner, and for ten full minutes addressed a crowd of more than three thousand, closing his remarks with the ringing peroration: "The proper place of woman—at the head of the pilgrims back to purity and truth." The sea of faces had not disturbed him in the least. He could have continued for an hour, he added, with perfect ease.[17]

He was a busy young man during the first few years after taking his bachelor's degree, though not by any means in the practice of law. He was given an office with the firm of Charles G. Loring, and in the fall of 1840 took up his residence in Boston. He remained a nominal resident of the city until the spring of 1842, when his mother's mental derangement led him to return to Elmwood to assist in looking after her. He prepared a temperance lecture, and gave it wherever he was asked.[18] He wrote out his opinion of Emerson—to others declaring his uncertainty, despite his lack of faith in the evidence of the senses, about the notion that man is truly divine in his nature;[19] to the sage himself, somewhat later, confessing frankly his love for him and the inspiration he had found in his works.[20] And, of course, his letters to Loring went on. When they did flow too slowly, in the fall of 1842, and when Loring in consequence became petulant again, Lowell wrote him what should have comprised an altogether sufficient explanation:

How can you imagine, George, that anything can ever change the warmth of my affection for you? The tendrils of the heart are like those of ivy; they cling the closer to what they have clung to long, and sustain what they embrace even after it has begun to crumble beneath them. My dear friend, I do not write letters to *anybody.* The longer I live the more irksome does the task of correspondence become. I have grown more philosophical with maturity, but mine is a philosophy which teaches me to rely upon the heart increasingly, every day, and to cherish more dearly whatever reminds me of my more inspired hours. The fact is, dear George, that I am working to found a new magazine and the business connected with it has harassed me beyond your imaginings. I have lacked the leisure to write to you in a happy spirit, and to my thinking a letter should not parade one's woes. I am doing an essay on the plays of Middleton. Within a few weeks I must go to New York on business.[21]

The magazine referred to was the *Pioneer,* and though its existence was brief, it was brilliant. Three numbers make up its complete files—the first one dating from January, 1843, the last one from March of the same calamitous year. Lowell's colleague in the enterprise was Mr. Robert Carter,[22] of Cambridge; their publisher, the firm of Leland and Whiting, of Boston. To all who had high visions of the rising glory of American letters, the prospectus these young men sent out must have proved heartening:

"The contents of each number," it read, "will be entirely original, and will consist of articles chiefly from American authors of the highest reputation.

"The Object of the Subscribers . . . is to furnish the intelligent and reflecting portion of the Reading Public with a rational substitute for the enormous quantity of thrice-diluted trash, in the shape of namby-pamby love tales and sketches, which is monthly poured out to them by many of our popular magazines—and to offer, instead thereof, a healthy and manly Periodical Literature, whose perusal will not necessarily involve a loss of time and a deterioration of every moral and intellectual faculty." [23]

The critical department, the prospectus went on, would be conducted with great care and impartiality. Satire and personalities would be sedulously avoided, yet opinions on the new books would be always candidly and fearlessly expressed. This magazine would be issued punctually, as scheduled, in the major cities of the union. It would be beautifully printed, and adorned with fine engravings. Terms were three dollars a year.

Perhaps the most important man of letters to read this prospectus was Edgar Allan Poe. He was residing in Philadelphia at the time it appeared, impecunious as always, ambitious himself to own such a magazine as Lowell described, but also interested in the appearance of one like it, no matter who might be directing its destinies. He wrote Lowell on November 16, asking whether the two might not reach some agreement which would establish him as a regular contributor.[24]

Lowell was overjoyed: Poe's letter, he said, assured him of the friendship and approbation of almost the only *fearless* American critic. Had Poe not written, he would soon have heard from this editor! He was given *carte blanche* for prose or verse, excepting only critical articles which contained violent personal abuse. "If the magazine fail, I shall consider myself personally responsible to all my contributors."

The result of this exchange was that Poe's "The Tell-Tale Heart" appeared in the first number. A Mr. A. T. Tuckerman, of the *Boston Miscellany,* had been considering this manuscript for his own publication, but something else which Poe published at this time appears to have offended him, and he rejected it. This change was altogether satisfactory to the author. If he had known the identity of the editor of the *Miscellany,* Poe wrote, he would not have offered him the story in the first place, and if Mr. T. should accept any writing by Mr. P., Mr. P. would at once query what twaddle he had been guilty of that it should have gained that editor's endorsement! [25]

Lowell himself contributed fourteen selections to the magazine— eight to the first number, five to the second, one to the third.[26] Illness, as will soon appear, cut down drastically the pace he first set for himself, and this illness was probably, more than any other single reason, the cause of the venture's untimely capitulation. But he won the support of other writers of importance, also—Jones Very, the transcendental poet; I. B. Wright, the art critic; and J. S. Dwight, who commented intelligently about music. And, in the later issues, Hawthorne's "The Birthmark" appeared, along with poems by Whittier and Elizabeth Barrett, and some critical notes on English verse, by Poe.

N. P. Willis reviewed the first number in words that, though characteristically supercilious, reflected accurately the taste of the decade. "J. R. Lowell," he said, "a man of original and decided genius, has started a monthly magazine in Boston. The first number lies before us, and it justifies our expectations, viz.—that a man of genius, who is merely a man of genius, is a very unfit editor for a periodical. A man of taste and common sense is worth twenty men of genius for any such undertaking. In the first number of the *Pioneer* are half a dozen articles which will fall still-born . . . yet they are articles of a very fine and elevated character." [27] Willis called this notice, privately, "the most judicious way of helping the magazine." The simple truth is that he damned it as thoroughly and as deliberately as any trivial but popular reviewer could have wished.

But Lowell, when this notice appeared, was already in New York, in attendance upon Dr. Elliot, the distinguished oculist who was endeavoring to cure him of ophthalmia. And Carter, back in Cambridge, was proving a poor editor and an even less competent manager. Lowell sent almost hysterical directions to him: Do not print nonsense, for God's sake. Print the history of Mesmerism. What do you mean by that notice of Emerson? The second number is full of misprints. Write an article on Japan. Where is Brownson's stuff? Lowell added that he could not read Carter's letters and answer them categorically, for the reason that he was compelled to undergo a treatment or an operation every day. "If I could see you for ten minutes I could arrange all." [28]

Yet all this frenzied directing proved futile. The March copies were eight days late, and the publishers, dominated by the usual motives, forced the two young men into a revision of their contract which was fatal to their hopes. By the original terms of this document, Lowell and Carter had bound themselves to furnish Messrs. Leland and Whiting with five thousand copies on the twentieth of each month, the consignment to be taken at a specified price. The penalty for failure was a forfeit of $500. When the March number reached them more than a week behind schedule, the publishers claimed their forfeit but offered to waive it if the contract should be altered to require them to take only as many copies as they could sell. This meant, of course, that the editors could no longer be assured of a stated monthly income, and could therefore obtain no credit with which to print.[29]

Well, that was that. Lowell had learned a good deal about himself and about the publishing business, and a good deal more about the taste of the people. The vogue for saccharine feminine twaddle and for ornate and very costly engravings still ran high; there had been no revolt against this tide in favor of the more serious literature in which he was interested. He had hoped to elevate the tone of his country's intellectual life, to foster what he fondly called not a national but a truly "natural" and universal literature. He would encourage free thought and disparage imitativeness. Instead, he had wound up with the task of explaining to his contributors why it was that he was unable at present to pay them as he had promised.

His explanation was both simple and disarming: the *Pioneer,* he sadly confessed, had left him more than $1,800 in debt.[30]

For a long time now—indeed, for several years before his own financial difficulties might be said to have supplied a personal motive —Lowell had been taking an interest in what his friends called "radical" ideas. Examined, this interest meant little more than that he was drifting into humanitarianism and that his thoughts were being focused, in particular, on the question of slavery in the South.

Everywhere about him a similar interest was evident and growing. Back in 1832 the New England Anti-Slavery Society had been formed in Boston, dedicated to the passionate and impersonal ideal of immediate emancipation for the Negroes. To the glowing visionaries who were directing this group (so enraptured by its promise, so blind to its meaning) Lowell had naturally listened, for he could scarcely have escaped listening. Arnold Buffum was its first head, William Lloyd Garrison its first secretary. During Lowell's college days its ranks had increased. The saintly Samuel J. May had joined them, then Karl Follen of Harvard, then Whittier, then the brilliant orator Wendell Phillips, and Lydia Maria Child and many others.

The clergy and the church itself was opposing this gathering whirlwind in vain. Phillips, in fact, was to reply to their strictures with a vehemence as outspoken as any which his followers would ever be compelled to tolerate. He looked about him at the Boston meetinghouses, at those godly spires that had been flung up by the early lovers of human liberty. Where was the pulpit of the Old South Church? he had asked. "Sustaining slavery as a Bible institution. Where is Park Street? Refusing to receive within its walls, for funeral services, the only martyr the Orthodox Congregationalists of New England have ever had. . . . Where is Essex Street Church? Teaching that there are occasions when the golden rule is to be set aside. Where is Federal Street Church? Teaching that silence is the duty of the North with respect to slavery and closing its doors to the funeral eulogy of the abolitionist Follen. . . . And I might ask, where are the New South and Brattle Street? *But they are not."* [31]

Such was, in part, the background against which Lowell's opinions were beginning to shape themselves. The fact that social feeling was strong against those Negroes who lived in the North did not matter.[32] What if they were forced, as in Hartford, Connecticut, to sit in church in pews completely boarded up, except for peepholes, so that white Christians should not have their feelings disturbed by the sight of them? What if they were generally kept out of New England's public schools? What, indeed, did it count—against the broad and intangible vision of fellowship which guided the movement—that two hundred aroused citizens of Canaan, New Hampshire, had actually, with twenty oxen, pulled the Noyes Academy from its foundations because a few colored boys had been allowed to study there?[33] Such items were trivial and incidental, while the general problem remained broad and compelling. For day after day, so rumor insisted, planters throughout the arrogant South were beating black men to death, separating them from their families, and yet insisting that their slave institution was "peculiar" to the region and that the world's conscience should in no way meddle with it. Two full centuries of Puritan indignation were being focused upon this problem.

The first symptom of Lowell's radicalism had appeared soon after he took his bachelor's degree. To Loring he wrote that he was fast becoming "ultra-democratic." Look at England! "I live in confident expectation of seeing the time when the people there shall wake up and heave that vast incubus, the Established Church, from their breast. Liberty is now no longer a cant word in the mouths of knaves and fools." According to recent dispatches, the Chartists were petitioning Parliament for the right to vote. Three hundred thousand attended a mass meeting at Manchester! A change was in the air, unmistakably. When they met there twenty years ago they were fired upon by the troops and we had the Peterloo Massacre. "It almost brings tears to my eyes when I think of this vast multitude starved, trampled upon, meeting to *petition* the government which oppressed them, and which *they* supported by taxes wrung out of their very children's life blood. . . . My dear George, there is no cant in all this." Of the extant parties, the abolitionists were the only ones with whom he was able to sympathize.[34]

Then, in November, 1841, Lowell had joined the Temperance Society, and shortly afterwards had proceeded to lecture his friend Eben Wright upon the latter's habits of drinking.[35] And, as we have seen, he had already served as a delegate to the antislavery convention in Boston. Moreover, in 1842, in January, Charles Dickens had visited the city. Greeted by half a dozen newspapermen on his arrival, cheered by mad throngs as he was driven through the streets, painted by an important New England artist, and entertained with his own stories at the theater,[36] he had at length been accorded an elaborate banquet. Lowell was invited, but he found it impossible, in conscience, to accept. The Boston Young Men, he wrote Francis Heath, then studying in Germany, were giving "Boz" a dinner. He was sorry to confess that his temperance principles would exclude him from attending. "I am sorry, because I proposed to have a dinner at which women should take the place of wine, and it was voted down by a very large majority."[37]

Late in the same year there had been the case of a fugitive slave, George Latimer, who was captured in Boston. Lowell was extremely concerned about this incident. The Supreme Court had recently decided that a slave was not entitled to a trial by jury. Latimer was lying in a Boston jail. What this meant was plain. A prison in the Bay State was being used as a "slave prison." The people were aroused; they demanded that Latimer be turned out. This was done, and his owner was sent back to Norfolk, Virginia, without his property. "The Norfolkians have had a public meeting," Lowell reported, "in which they threaten little less than an invasion and entire subjugation of the Northern states."[38]

Yes, he was becoming an extremist, even in his poetry, he confessed later to another friend. He had just completed an ambitious work, "Prometheus," a subject which in modern times had challenged the imaginations of Goethe, Byron, and Shelley; yet "you will find that I have looked at it from a somewhat new point of view. I have made it *radical,* and I believe that no poet in this age can write much that is good unless he give himself up to this tendency." What, after all, he continued, is the valid test of a good poem? He turned to answer his own question. "The proof of poetry is, in my mind, that it reduce to the essence of a simple line the vague philosophy which is floating in all men's minds, and so render it portable and useful and ready to the hand. Is it not so?" [39] It was an interesting, if venerable, theory. Applied in Lowell's case, as will soon appear, it meant that, practically, the poet should be a propagandist, fixing as best he might in metrical language the disordered emotionalism of his age. This interest, at any rate, was swiftly becoming his central objective in writing; "preaching," he called it in the *Fable for Critics.* His greatest merits and grossest defects as an artist are inevitably bound up with this conception of his relation as an author to his world.

"Prometheus" was one of the more ambitious pieces to appear in his second volume, *Poems,* which was brought out in December, 1843.[40] Few books more pervasively didactic in nature have appeared in American literature, and since Lowell was interested in the communication of practical attitudes, it seems only reasonable to examine his work primarily from this point of view. It was a stout offering of 279 pages, containing thirty-four pieces of varying length and thirty-seven sonnets. *A Year's Life* had fallen, practically stillborn, upon the unheeding American public, but since then its author had not been wasting his time.

His ostensible subjects are diverse enough. There is a tribute to Maria for settling his tumultuous spirit, as the moon's influence calms the sea. There is a commentary on the Poet, past and present. Formerly, he was a divine man, and was reverenced as a creator. Now, he is an empty rhymer. Let him shake off his lethargy, Lowell cries, and be ashamed no more to plead for Truth. Let him no longer defer to the silken proprieties. Let him cultivate the vision of brotherhood, and find his brother even in the evildoer. Speak out! The world will listen. Then there is an account of the heritages of men. The rich man's son inherits cares—the burning factory, the insolvent bank, the sated stomach that relishes only the most dainty fare. Not so the poor man's boy. His treasure is unpurchasable—stout muscles and a doughty heart, proficiency in all things useful. Both, moreover, are at length one in that vast democracy of the grave.

There is also "A Parable," suggesting Lowell's later and much more popular *Sir Launfal,* telling of a prophet who, looking for signs and wonders, found truth near at hand through an innocent act of his daughter's. Among the sonnets there are several other tributes to Maria, and half a dozen further poems on Wordsworth. The tenor of these latter verses is familiar. Wordsworth, a flower-like soul ordained to oppose Darkness and defend the Truth, has proved false to his high mission, says Lowell. He has mocked man's longing soul with lies. We behold in him the saddest of all sights—"an old man faithless in Humanity." Yet Lowell's hope for a better world remains unshaken. Another sonnet praises Wendell Phillips, prophet of that better world, for scorning fame and gold to stand with the weaker side, along with God.

The longest piece in the volume, "A Legend of Brittany," is both rambling and derivative. In it is recounted the tale of the seduction of a young girl, Margaret, by a young and formerly celibate Templar, Modred. After Modred learns that Margaret is with child he kills her, but her spirit returns to the church to win baptism for the infant, a rite which is duly performed by the "pale priests." It is the first poem in which one finds Lowell's moralizing tendency becoming vulgarly dominant: God blesses want with larger sympathies. Love enters most gladly at the humble door. The spirit can kneel before one only, as happy vassal and as king. Young hearts are free; the selfish world it is that turns them miserly and cold as stone. Love is blind, but only as Justice is. Art's fittest triumph is to show that good lurks in the heart of evil evermore. The unsuspicious eyes of honesty always pierce the thick mask of Falsehood. The world looks with Levite eyes upon the ruined maiden who is really more godlike than the most conventionally virtuous.

These meditations, and many more like them, interrupt to the point of frustrating an otherwise interesting, if secondhand, story. It is as if the poet lacked faith in his subject, felt that he must constantly reënforce it by conventional aphorisms of which his audience would approve. He has become a preacher without a pulpit, and taken humanity for his text. Poetry is now a means to an end.

Lowell's "Prometheus" added little to the conception of that figure as portrayed by Shelley. The fire-bringer is pictured as the Spirit of Liberty, who, defying Jove, prophesies an age in which Love shall triumph over brute strength and win Man back to an enduring peace. Then there is "Rhoecus," another story vaguely suggestive of *Sir Launfal,* in which—after fifty lines of moral meditation on the view that "God sends his teachers unto every age"— one reads of the Greek youth who meets a dryad, arranges a tryst with her, but, engrossed in a dice game later in the day, ignores her honeyed messenger, the bee. As a result, the youth loses his fragile love. He has scorned the least of nature's works, Lowell points out, and so has shut himself out from them all.

Similar admonitions recur in the other verses in the book. "He who would win the name of truly great must understand his own age and the next." This we are told in the poem on Cromwell. "Truth is eternal" is another view Lowell emphasizes. "Love," we learn elsewhere, "bides longest in a woman's heart." And in the "Stanzas on Freedom," first read at an antislavery picnic, all those New Englanders who refuse to strike out against slavery are indicted as the true slaves of oppression. Let them remember, the poet proclaims, that righteousness is always arrayed with the unfortunate and with the two or three who dare defy the hatred and scoffing of cowardly multitudes.

As for the technical defects of the book, Elizabeth Barrett (Browning) sensed them and stated them perhaps as accurately as anyone who read it. "If I ventured to make a remark in criticism of the new volume," she wrote Lowell, "it would be that there is a certain vagueness of effect, through a redundant copiousness of what may be called poetical diction (so that thoughts, images, and descriptions rather swim dimly in a golden mist than front the soul and eye with their individuality, cutting upon the sense forcibly and arrestingly)." [41] Her last sprawling sentence went to the center of his weakness, insofar as the values in poetry depend upon perception.

But the ambitious offering sold remarkably well. Within three months a third edition was called for,[42] and a separate printing was soon under way in England. For the first time in Lowell's career the prospect of making some money by his writing seemed imminent. Necessary and welcome though this prospect was, in many ways, it was also fraught with permanent evil to his future. For his success appears to have confirmed him in his worst tendency as a writer—the tendency to indulge in pompous and often entirely irrelevant moralizing. He was to contend with it for the remainder of his life.

V

"I know more of the history of Ancient Rome than I do of that of America."
Lowell to E. M. Davis, July 24, 1845.
Works, XIV, 132

LOWELL'S primary interest during the year 1844, before marriage at the end of it sublimated all previous excitements, was the *Broadway Journal,* edited by a friend, Charles F. Briggs, whom he had met during his illness in New York. Almost as soon as his own magazine had come to grief on the shoals of a Boston publisher's materialism, he had turned to assisting other men of letters in their efforts to ride out the perilous tide. First there had been Poe, who had projected his ambitious *Stylus* to appear the following July. Lowell, at Poe's request, had solicited a contribution for it from Hawthorne. But when July had come round its editor-to-be lay sick and poor in Philadelphia, begging his friend Rufus Griswold for a loan of $5.00, and desperate over his wife's fatal illness.[1] Briggs's prospects, however, seemed definitely more promising, his plans more deliberately and carefully laid. Even the recent death of his daughter was a calamity, Lowell pointed out, which would enrich his talents for his work. Made wiser by his present affliction, he now had the best right to pass judgment upon the merits of the poets. After all, his consoler went on, are not the greatest ones those "who give us something to lean upon in our sorrow, and something yet to look forward to in our deepest joys and our amplest successes?"[2]

Maria shared James's enthusiasm for the forthcoming *Journal,* and on December 12 wrote Briggs in some detail about it. The two lovers had but one misgiving: its proposed name was inelegant. "James told me to express his horror to you at the cockneyism of such a title. The *Broadway Chronicle* [an earlier choice] chronicles the thoughts and feelings of Broadway, not those of the New England people whom you seem willing to receive somewhat from. Should not a title have truth for its first recommendation? Do you write for the meridian of Broadway?" Such a thought she seemed quite unable to entertain. Though he was living in another region, his eyes must surely be looking homeward, away from the godlessness of Manhattan. "I think you write from a sturdy New England heart, that has a good strong well-spring of old Puritan blood beating therein, with all its hatred of forms and cant, of fashion and show." Let the name express the man truly, she urged. He must forgive her frankness. She would not like to appear unwomanly to him, but frankness seemed to her as truly a woman's right as a man's.[3] Briggs finally dropped "Chronicle" for "Journal," but left the curse of "Broadway" unamended.

Maria had sent this letter for a good reason: James was too busy correcting proof to write to anybody. He was at work on his first volume of prose, *Conversations on Some of the Old Poets*. It was published the last week of the year, 1844, and dedicated to his father. Five pieces, which Lowell never thought sufficiently well of to reprint, comprise its contents. There are two on "The Old Dramatists," and others on Chaucer, Chapman and Middleton.

The prefatory note to the reader is oddly apologetic. On three different occasions Lowell declares that the work was done in great haste, that writing and printing proceeded simultaneously, that he therefore entirely lacked the chance to make revisions, or to obtain from some loving friend the criticism he doubtless needed. He especially regrets the fact that "the more refined eye of a woman" was not available to chasten his pages. No reason for this desperate hurry is suggested.

He points out, further, that no effort at all was made to give the conversations a dramatic turn. "They are merely essays, divided in this way to allow them greater ease and frankness and the privilege of wandering at will." [4] Moreover, he implied, let it not be objected that many of the topics discussed seem only remotely related to his stated subject. If they should appear foreign, "I can only say that they are not so to my mind, and that an author's object in writing criticisms is not only to bring to light the beauties of the works he is considering, but also to express his own opinions upon those and other matters."

Only in the light of this last point of view can the intention of the *Conversations* be understood. Lowell's "own opinions" dominate the book; his stated subjects obtrude, as he later complained of Masson's subject in his *Life of Milton,* merely as occasional visitors. They are brushed aside for much more burning issues—the issues of the moribund church in New England, of a vital morality, and, of course, of abolition. Another important question, that of the essence of poetry, is faced chiefly in terms of these absorbing equivalents.

There is the essay on Chaucer, for instance, wherein these several interests converge: "Piety is indifferent," says Philip, one of the characters, "whether she enters at the eye or the ear. There is none of the senses at which she does not knock one day or other." "All things that make us happy incline us also to be grateful," John replies. "I would stamp God's name, and not Satan's, upon every innocent pleasure, upon every legitimate gratification of sense, and God would be the better served for it." Then Philip again: "The Church needs reforming now as much as in Luther's time, and sells her indulgences as readily. There are altars to which the slaveholder is admitted, while the Unitarian would be put forth as unclean. If it be God's altar both have a right there—the sinner most of all—but let him not go unrebuked." We bandy compliments and compromise with sin instead of saying to it sternly, "get thee behind me." Religion, he feels, has come to be esteemed as synonymous with the Church. As a matter of fact, "the Church has corrupted Christianity." Philip agrees: he will never enter a Church from which a prayer goes up for the prosperous only, and not for the oppressed and fallen. Yet we should not despair. Error is the offspring of Blindness, not of Wilful Sin.[5] Chaucer, meanwhile, had been left far behind—five centuries behind, in fact, in the dark age of irrelevance and long-settled issues.

This book sold well; better, indeed, than the two preceding

volumes of poetry put together. There were two American editions and another in England, and less than three months after it appeared, Lowell reported to Briggs that his publisher, John Owen, of Cambridge, owed him $300 in royalties.[6] At least two reasons for this success are fairly evident. One is that during a decade that was to crown its activities with the European revolutions of 1848, Lowell had come out in print with an open advocacy of the principles which informed those movements. He was championing what he termed the oppressed classes as completely as any writer in the country. The second reason was literary in nature. He was, ostensibly if not actually, reviving a tradition which no important native author before him had consistently respected—the tradition of Elizabethan drama. Coleridge, Lamb, Hazlitt, and De Quincy had already written about it enthusiastically in England, but it remained for Lowell, three decades later, to suggest its values for Americans.

It would be pleasant to think that one reason for the haste which attended the writing of the *Conversations* was Lowell's impending marriage, but the evidence is wanting. The marriage took place at Elmwood, December 26, 1844, and after a day at home, and another day or so in New York, at the dazzling New York Hotel, the two arrived in Philadelphia and took lodgings at the home of a Quakeress Maria had met the spring before, Friend Parker. Soon they were intimate with other members of the Society of Friends, drawn together by a common hatred of slavery. Their circle of acquaintances was further enlarged to include "the swell of fashionable society" when a well-to-do kinsman, Dr. Elwyn, called and began to prove very attentive. Maria wrote Mrs. Hawthorne that they were allowed all the privacy they desired, but that company was available at any time they wished it. Financially, they seemed wholly free of worry. *Graham's* was paying Lowell $30 for each poem. Soon the *Broadway Journal* would be sending him checks. He was also able to predict $150 a year in royalties from his books. And further, he was receiving—with a few pangs of conscience for accepting it—still another $10 a month for articles in the *Pennsylvania Freeman*.[7] God was in his heaven.

Winter passed, fraught with felicity and with many interests. The only cloud on the horizon appeared to be certain developments that were going on in the office of the *Journal*. Briggs wrote Lowell late in February that he had associated two men with himself as editors—Poe and Henry C. Watson, a music critic. Lowell was doubtful. "I think," he said, "that there should never be more than one editor with any proprietary control over the paper. Its individuality is not generally so well preserved." Briggs refused to be disturbed. "Poe," he wrote—not aware of that gentleman's camel-like talents for crowding—"is only an assistant to me and will in no way interfere with my own way of doing things." Briggs went on to explain that he was often away on business and needed some name "of authority" to assist him. As for Watson, he was the only musical critic in the country. Poe had left the New York *Mirror*, N. P. Willis, its co-editor, having proved "too Willisy for him." Unfortunately, however, Poe "has mounted a very ticklish hobby just now, Plagiarism, which he is bent on riding to death." Briggs thought that the best policy would be to let him run down as soon as possible by giving him no check.[8] The editor could not foresee that, before he did "run down," Poe was to run *over* not only Lowell himself, but Lowell's fast friend, Longfellow.

In May, with the weather more clement, Lowell and his wife decided to return to Elmwood; they had left it in the first place chiefly because the bitter New England winters were proving a menace to her always unpredictable health. Their return was by way of New York. Once there, they settled in a third-floor apartment. With them in the home were Lowell's aging father; his mother, now mentally far gone, and his sister Rebecca, a "queer" spinster who never recovered from an unhappy love affair, but who still managed the practical accompaniments of housekeeping.[9] Lowell's reputation as a writer, in its most palpable form, soon followed him there. Mr. Edward M. Davis wrote him in July requesting an outline for a course of reading. It was a hard question. Very few scholars, Lowell informed his young admirer, ever think of such a thing as a course of reading after their freshman year in college. They are constantly having books thrown in their way, and they select what they need by a kind of instinct. He went on to comment upon his own case. He has read *something* in probably every branch of knowledge. He has read a great many out-of-the-way books, yet has passed over others with which almost everybody is acquainted. "I have read books on magic and astrology, and yet never looked into a history of England. All that I know of it I have acquired by reading the biographies of men whose lives *were* the history of England." He wrote further, and significantly: "I know more of the history of Rome than I do of that of America."

Having proved himself, as he confessed, wholly unqualified to make suggestions, Lowell turned to the luxury of throwing them out, in abundance. Read the Reviews, he said; they will keep you abreast of modern literature. Read Nichol in Astronomy, Lyell in Geology; read Michelet's *History of France* ("it is now being published and is, I think, a good one"). He advised an emphasis upon history in particular. There were Hume and Smollett for England, Robertson for Scotland, Niebuhr and Gibbon for Rome, Mitford for Greece, and Bancroft for America. Read always with a modern eye. If you do, you will see the masses always struggling with a blind instinct upward. "All history shows the poverty and weakness of Force, the wealth and power of Gentleness and Love." He recommended his own last article in the Boston *Courier,* which would probably be reprinted soon in Garrison's *Liberator.* He had been impelled to write it after reading an account of the four fugitive slaves who were captured near Washington. "I think it has done some good." [10] The watchers over Israel should never sleep, the implication ran, while the cause of freedom can be served through any agency.

Watching over Israel—which meant, to Lowell, that the supporters of slavery must never pine from neglect—was indeed precipitating some stubborn differences with his friend Briggs of the *Broadway Journal.* Briggs had begun his solicitation for articles in all kindness. "I would like to make a contract with you," he had said. "Furnish me with a column or two of prose once a week." Lowell might suit himself as to its contents. Let him not demur on the score of indolence, "for there is no such stimulus to execution as a sure reward." Briggs would compensate him adequately.

Lowell took the editor at his literal word regarding the subject matter of his contributions. His first article, he confessed, was really half Maria's, a remark which should sufficiently indicate the nature of its theme. He was willing to have it freely altered. "I wrote it only in the hope of doing some good."

Briggs appeared doubtful, highly doubtful, about the good this well-meant piece would accomplish for his fledgling magazine. In content, it was a letter upbraiding a congressman for his vote in support of the annexation of Texas. Such a vote meant war, Lowell contended, and—worse than war—the extension of the limits of southern power. Editor and author began to argue. "Your satire," wrote Briggs, "bruises instead of cutting the flesh, and makes a confounded sore place without letting out any of the patient's blood." Tactfully, he went on to say that he would use as much of the contribution as he could, but that there were certain expressions which it was not safe to make public. He added his regrets that so much time had gone into the framing of the piece, but consoled Lowell with the reflection that the exercise of writing it would prove useful in drawing off so much of his superfluous zeal. "I shall think better of you for knowing that you can feel so strongly and write so harshly." But why not do something on Philadelphia, its art, its academy, its abominable white doors, or its watery oysters? If he *must* treat abolitionism, let him do so in rhyme; everybody would read him then.[11]

A full year passed before Lowell realized the wisdom of this last suggestion. Its immediate effect was to fill him with a sullen, if disciplined, resentment. In his letter Briggs had spoken of "the unity of evil"—the problem was everywhere, and ultimately unsolvable; it was inherent in the nature of man. This being so, why harry one's soul over a minor and trivial phase of it? Lowell was quick to reply. Briggs was worse than a "philanthropic eunuch." Lowell admitted that, since all these sore boils with which God had

—◦◦⊰{ 63 }⊱◦◦—

smitten the social fabric sprang from one disease, it was idle to apply external remedies merely to one of them, leaving the others to grow up uncared for. But this was not the philosophy which governed the abolitionists. They knew a prescription for all human evils: it was "the application of Christianity to life. We cry out most loudly against slavery, because that seems to be the foulest blotch, and it is easier to awaken the attention of the worldly and indifferent to that than to any other." This interest once excited, the citizens— by some miraculous transfer of solicitude—might safely be left to themselves. For Truth, let Mr. Briggs remember, "is like the stalwart Paddy at the gate of heaven—if she has been able to get her finger even into the crack of the door of a man's soul, there is never a fear but she will make her whole body follow." Lowell deplored, infinitely, the spectacle of the poor harlots of Broadway, flaunting their unblessed bodies up and down that sinful thoroughfare. But was it not better, granting the one-sidedness of abolitionists, to be explicit and constant in their testimony against one sin than silent in regard to all? [12]

Mr. Briggs was unconverted, but his recalcitrance seems to have mattered little against the accumulating disadvantages of editorship. He had tried, the month before, to make arrangements with another publisher, convinced that the one he was working with was already treating him shabbily. Simultaneously, Poe had gone on a "drunken spree" and decided that his employer was handling *him* with a similar unfairness. So while Briggs looked around for someone else to put out the magazine—temporarily leaving the *Journal* to its own fate—Poe issued it independently and, in the main, as it was scheduled to appear. Briggs was indignant, but he was nonetheless completely frozen out.

Lowell's reaction was characteristic of his nature. "Poe," he wrote, by way of consolation, "is wholly lacking in that element of manhood which for want of a better name, we call *character*." As he suspected, he went on, "I have made him my enemy by doing him a service. In the last issue of the *Journal* he has accused me of plagiarism and misquoted Wordsworth to sustain his charge."

Lowell cited the evidence, which was conclusive in his favor. This man, he continued, merely wished to kick down the ladder by which he rose. After this odd statement—odd because Poe's reputation was established before Lowell even began to publish—he drifted into a description of his own true nature, and a lament over the way that nature was misapprehended by the world. He could not, he declared, appear in society as he really was. He must always be introduced as "Lowell, the poet," which made him sick. Not comprehended even as a person, how could he hope to be comprehended as a poet, especially by a critic like Poe? "I cannot understand the meanness of men. They seem to trace everything to selfishness." [13] It was a sad story, and it recorded the end of his friendship with the erratic genius from Virginia. Gone forever were the "My dear Mr. Poe," "My dear Mr. Lowell," and other polite salutations. Henceforth there would be only "Sir"—with surly overtones and poorly veiled damnations—as the two men consigned each other's good names, by turns, into the limbo of stupidity and discredited talents.

On the last day of the year 1845, Maria bore her husband their first child—a daughter, Blanche. The event interfered with his writing, to a degree, but it did not affect his moral convictions. He was still as ardent as ever on the subject of slavery, this time concerned with the kind he could actually witness. How difficult it was for one to avoid the curse wholly! "I never see Maria mending my stockings or our maid bringing the water for our shower bath, without hearing a faint tinkle of chains." Yet how could he escape this torture? "Maria laughs went I propose to learn darning, and Ellen flies into open rebellion and snatches the pail out of my hand when I would fain assume half of the old Israelitish drudgery, and become my own drawer of water." But in one resolve, at least, he was settled. "I do not believe," he declared, "that children are born into the world to subject their mothers to a diaper despotism, and to be brought down to their fathers after dinner, as an additional digestive to the nuts and raisins." No, not that, definitely. He was attending to the infant indiscretions of Miss Blanche himself. And as a result, the baby—by something resembling an inspired reciprocity—had come to regard her father as "the personification of the maternal principle." [14]

Yet all this time—while the Lowell whom his friends knew was gayly changing the diapers of Miss Blanche, and glowing pardonably over her fresh morning spirits—the Lowell whom history has chosen to remember was busy with elaborating the first deliberately held convictions of his life. He was writing the articles for the *Pennsylvania Freeman* and the *National Anti-Slavery Standard* which, beginning within a month of his marriage, were to epitomize his thinking for more than two full decades. He never saw fit to collect them, and one who examines their contents can guess his reason. But those essays which he produced in hurrying sequence and with passionate assurance between the years 1845 and 1850 are indispensable to any serious student of his career.[15]

They abound in plain speaking; Lowell gave no quarter, nor did he ask it. There is little, if any, effort to argue his case, little setting of reason against reason. He had no use for such a tedious procedure, having confessed formally to a certain "impatience of mind" which made him contemptuously indifferent about debating any matter, once it had become a belief with him. His appeal was, rather, to what he called the "moral principle," and having invoked its sanction, he was content to proceed from it directly.

Almost as soon as his honeymoon began to wane, he turned his clouded meditations toward Texas. There were factions in the Union which seemed to him desperately bent upon making it a state. "The advocates of slavery," he wrote, "will find that they have not advanced a single step even if they succeed in annexing Texas. Slavery is but the weaker for its seeming triumph. Every success of wrong is a step toward its annihilation. What if five or six score of men come to Washington and say that the institution of domestic slavery shall be extended and perpetuated? How stands the case then? When the question is asked, *Shall slavery be fostered and strengthened?* a few pitiful political hacks and time servers answer Yes! But is slavery thereby made the stronger? Before making up our minds, let us count the votes on the other side. The voice of God, speaking through the divine instincts of our nature, says No! The indignant conscience of every good man in the country says No! Justice turns away her mournful face and says No! Religion presses the cross closer to her heart and says No! Freedom looks up with the young light of hope and says No! Every feeling of our common humanity rouses itself in the soul and in the heart and says No! We are reconciled to the slaveholder's majority of twenty-two." [16]

Yet neither God, nor Justice, nor Religion, nor Freedom, nor all the other gleaming virtues together could dampen the vigor of his hot indignation. Two weeks later he was busy again, disparaging the South in terms of the "Prejudice of color." What could be more ridiculous, he inquired, than "a patent of nobility founded on no better distinction than an accidental difference in the secreting vessels of the skin?" He went on to clarify his objectives: "It has always seemed to us that abolitionists could in no way more usefully serve their holy cause than by seeking to elevate the condition of the colored race in the free states, and to break down every barrier of invidious distinction between them and their privileged brothers."

Then in July, 1846, he paused to consider "Daniel Webster." His article begins with a quotation, citing the news that Webster's son, Edward, has arrived in Boston for the purpose of recruiting a company of soldiers for the Mexican War. Lowell was already disillusioned with Webster and out of sympathy with his followers. "Among the thousand-and-one so called great men of this so called democracy, Daniel Webster always excites in us the most painful feeling of regret. A man who will die without having disburdened the weary heart of humanity of one of its devouring griefs!" He turned to the familiarities of his rhetoric. "What has freedom to thank Daniel Webster for? What has civilization? What has true conservatism, which consists in bringing the earth forward and upward to the idea of its benign Maker? In one word, how is God the better served, how are heaven and earth more at one for His having bestowed upon this man that large utterance, that divine faculty of eloquent speech?"[17]

Lowell reviews the major incidents of Webster's career, sneering at every effort of that statesman to compose the country's sectional differences. Finally, he declares, "Webster has sent his son (a youth who has just about brains enough to be conveniently come at by a cannon ball) to Boston to recruit a company for the Mexican War, as if his subservience to the slave power had not already amply atoned for his federalism in the last war, and richly earned for him the title of patriot, as it is understood in America. Shall not the recording angel write *Ichabod*[18] after the name of this man in the great book of Doom? What voice of one enfranchised man, what saving testimony of a single great truth made clearer, shall plead for a reversal of the decree?"

These articles kept appearing, as the decade of the forties spun itself out in the fabulous delirium of the Gold Rush. Lowell was not interested in California, but the hysteria which attended its exploitation found fit equivalent in the words that poured forth from Elmwood, flooding his already too distracted nation. "Shall we ever be Republican?" he asked in the spring of 1848. "However it may have been in theory," he said, "it has never become practically understood that governments are intended solely for the advantage of the many. What difference does it make whether an aspirant for office cringe to a president or a king, whether he bribe the mistress of some anointed majesty with gold, or the sovereign people with fawning and sophistry? As far as our national government is concerned, we do not deserve the name of a free people. Whenever there has been the least danger of its expressing the great idea which nominally underlies our institutions, slavery has put her bloody hand over its mouth. She has gone on from usurpation to usurpation, till we have forgotten that we ever intended to be free. She has taught us to cringe and falter and equivocate. She has been the source of every political evil that has befallen us. She has not allowed us a single statesman, but hordes of shufflers and trimmers. Is it not a degrading fact that a man's being known is enough to prevent his having any hope of the presidency? The two great parties are equally corrupt. They would vote for the Devil—provided he were a slaveholder. It is because slavery has made our great intellects blind that we are ruled by our little ones. . . . We produce great speakers by the score but never a great doer—except of mischief." [19]

The next month he looked over the likely presidential candidates and paid his respects to the American party system. There was Zachary Taylor, the Whig nominee. General Taylor's claims may be very shortly summed up, he wrote: He is a general, a slaveholder, and nobody knows what his opinions are. There is a good deal of strength in these qualifications, no doubt. "As to his having employed bloodhounds in the Florida war, we think he displayed both wisdom and humanity, for it was a service much better suited to bloodhounds than to men. To those who raise objections on the score of his slaveholding, it is answered that he is a mild one, and that he was born and bred to it. Should it ever unhappily chance that any of his partisans find themselves in the larder of his majesty of the Cannibal Islands, they will have the satisfaction of knowing that they will be chewed mildly, with a due regard for the claims of humanity, and by a person born and bred to the occupation." [20]

He turned, with more appetite, to John C. Calhoun. "Exciting Intelligence from South Carolina" reported the threat of secession from that state. How ridiculous and unreal the threat seemed, when contemplated beneath the still green luxuriance of Elmwood! "How utterly childish is the scarecrow of Mr. Calhoun's pumpkin-lantern rebellion! As an attempt to scare the rest of the Union it is absurd, but what shall we say of it as a scheme to intimidate manifest and irretrievable Destiny? We have all heard it said often enough that little boys must not play with fire, and yet if the matches are taken away from us, and put out of reach upon the shelf, we must need get into our little corner and scowl and stamp and threaten the dire revenge of going to bed without our supper. The earth shall stop until we get our dangerous plaything again." [21]

Lowell also took up, in later pieces, other figures of earth. "The politician, the merchant, the clergyman, each in turn found that it would not do to be an abolitionist." To be specific, there was Mr. Clay. The unpardonable thing about the great apostle of compromise was that he wanted to compromise what was basically a moral question. He talked of the white race as a superior one. "He takes the case out of the court of conscience, where alone it can be decided absolutely and without appeal, and puts it at the never ending litigation of political economy." This would do for Mr. Clay.

There were those who spoke of "Compromise"? [22] "Slavery being an acknowledged evil, the very permission for it to exist was at first a concession and a surrender. This was called a compromise. Then slavery desired to extend itself and treachery allowed it. This was called a compromise. Again the monster felt the pains of hunger, and Texas was thrown to it. This was called a compromise. Now, affairs have thriven so well that Freedom sits an outcast and a beggar at the gates of her own ancestral dwelling. And this is also called a compromise. Better strangle at once that 'bird of our country' of which our orators are so fond of talking, than let her go on hatching eggs of all manner of unclean birds." [23]

What principle informed this utterance? It was one as ageless as human testaments could reveal. "All history is the record of a struggle, gradually heightening in fierceness, between reason and unreason, between right and wrong. Of what good is it that we can put off the evil time a century, which is but a day in the history of the human race. . . . Our legislators might as well try to stay Niagara with a dip-net, or pass acts against the law of gravitation, as endeavor to stunt the growth of avenging conscience. Do they think that the Union can be stuck together with mouth glue, when the eternal forces are rendering it asunder? There is something better than expediency, and that is Wisdom, something stronger than compromise, and that is Justice." [24]

Then there were Lowell's remarks on Webster's famous "Seventh of March" speech. To the abolitionists that speech was both vulgar and insulting. It was "the effort, not of a senator representing

Massachusetts, but of an advocate holding the brief of State Street. It is a matter of debate in the newspapers whether or no Mr. Webster is sustained by the public sentiment of Boston. It seems to be forgotten that the distinguished senator represents an undivided half of the Bay State. He has remembered that he was the delegate of Boston, but has apparently forgotten that Bunker Hill and Concord have also their share in him."

What was wrong, specifically, with this address in the Senate, an address which had stated so plainly that the limits of slavery had been set by God's laws, not man's; that the territory west of Texas was unadaptable to large-scale cotton planting? Three things in particular about it represented, to Lowell, a disgraceful truckling to enemy interests. One was Webster's declaration that he would favor compensating the southerners (after the English practice) for the slaves who might be emancipated. Another was his willingness to support any properly conceived plan of colonization for the liberated Negroes, a plan which, he knew, would avert a race problem in the South of overwhelming proportions. Finally, there was his flat and pointed remark about the value of the abolitionist societies. "Sir," he had shouted, "I do not think them useful. I think their operations for the last twenty years have produced nothing good or valuable." He confessed that wholly well-meaning people supported them; he would not impute gross motives to their leaders. "But I am not blind to the consequences of their proceedings. I cannot but see what mischiefs their interference with the South has produced." He went on to show how, before the abolitionists began the most vigorous phase of their agitation, in 1835, the cause of emancipation was freely discussed and often strongly supported in Virginia and in other southern states. Yet what happened after that date? "The bonds of the slaves were bound more firmly than before, their rivets were more strongly fastened." And Lowell, incidentally, could thank his own strenuous articles of the past five years for helping to bring the condition about.

Yet although these views of Lowell's were extreme, it would be unfair to him to imply that they were held in isolation. In taking his stand he had broken irretrievably with the point of view of Boston and Cambridge Brahminism. He had broken, even, with his own father, whom he still cherished deeply, though as a Dr. Primrose and a harmless sexagenarian, a kindly old man who was always affectionate, blissfully unaware of the real problems of the age.[25] But though he had lost many friends of his Harvard days, he was by no means alone. Behind him was the same body of sentiment which was opposing the admission of Texas into the Union, and which, in the House of Representatives, was solidly indorsing the Wilmot Proviso. Lowell was an officer of fully respected talents, indeed, in a vast army of Righteousness which, led by God, was crusading for a more godly world.

William L. Garrison was certainly a major general in these forces. Since 1831 he had been assailing the slave system in language that harbored an ultimate arrogance. In his view, the most humane slaveholders were no better and no less terrible than the monsters of Greek mythology; they were "tyrants, murderers, thieves, and criminals." [26] Did the government sanction slavery? Then he and his followers would be no-government men, passive yet militant in repudiating their allegiance to it.[27] "Accursed be the American Union," proclaimed the *Liberty Bell* (a Boston publication) in 1845. And the following year, Lowell's friend Edmund Quincy had declared to a correspondent, in stirring capitals, that the only hope for America lay in "The Abrogation of The Present Pro-Slavery Constitution and the Dissolution of the Existing Slaveholding Union." [28]

Abolitionism, Calhoun had said, "originated in that blind fanatical zeal which made one man believe that he was responsible for the sins of others"; it reflected the same madness which, two centuries before, in New England, had tied to the stake the victim it could not convert. With the same point of view, its champions continued to publish their judgments of the South. The South was "one vast brothel," declared the Rev. George Bourne. Atrocities occurred there constantly: hogs were allowed to devour Negro babies before the eyes of frantic but helpless mothers. Pious masters who were really "Baptist cannibals" battered their Negroes with clubs, branded their arms and foreheads, shot them in the legs, bashed in their front teeth in order to simplify the problem of identifying them. Slave girls were forced to work during the pains of parturition; one, it was charged, gave birth to a child on the bare ground and lay helplessly by while a ravenous sow devoured it.[29] Members of the black race as a whole "are overworked, underfed, wretchedly clad and lodged, and have insufficient sleep. . . . They are often made to wear round their necks iron collars armed with prongs, to drag heavy chains and weights at their feet while working in the fields, and to wear yokes, and bells and iron horns. . . . They are often kept in the stocks day and night for weeks together, made to wear gags in their mouths for hours and days."[30]

Others were contending that all southern slaveholders were kidnapers and men-thieves, inasmuch as they treated Negroes as property; that all of these masters kept the instruments of murder —the dirk, the pistol, the bowie knife—constantly at their pillows at night, and "a troup of bloodhounds standing sentry at every door." This condition, they went on desperately—this "burnished steel ready to drink the lifeblood of outraged innocence"—branded all slaveholders as murderers.[31]

Then there were the young southern white women. The were reared in a haremlike seclusion, and thus became quite easy prey to the colored attendants in their homes. As a result of such widespread miscegenation, young southerners almost invariably visited the North when the time came round for them to look seriously for wives. Only by making these melancholy pilgrimages could they find mates who were without vitiated constitutions, the remains of their attachments to their fathers' Negroes.[32]

Finally there was the Methodist Church, *South*. Its bishops were "slave-breeders." Likewise, "slave-manufacturing preachers" upheld their institutions of "man-stealing, lewdness, and cruelty." One southern minister was charged with selling his daughter to a neighboring planter for service as a concubine. And after the general conference of Methodists failed to condemn slavery in 1836 and 1840, one abolitionist leader termed the meeting "a conclave of incarnate fiends," in which every "intelligent communicant" was worse and more infamous, in God's eyes "than the common prostitute, the pickpocket, or the assassin." This church, it was added, was "more corrupt than any house of ill fame in the city of New York." Was proof demanded? The reply set forth that, within the denomination, fifty thousand females were "inevitably doomed to lives of prostitution" under the penalty of scourging and death.[33]

As for Lowell himself, he was not allowed to deploy his convictions through the decade of the forties without receiving at least one chastisement, a chastisement written by an author who was more than his master in any literary field. Edgar Allan Poe, the year before his death, picked up a copy of the *Fable for Critics,* read it through, and wrote out his opinion, not merely of the volume itself (which he misapprehended) but of the personality of its author. Lowell he described, quietly and truthfully, as "one of the most rabid of the abolition fanatics. His fanaticism about slavery is a mere local outbreak of the same innate wrong-headedness which, if he owned slaves, would manifest itself in atrocious ill-treatment of them, with the murder of any abolitionist who should endeavor to set them free. A fanatic of Mr. Lowell's species is simply a fanatic for the sake of fanaticism, and must be a fanatic in whatever circumstances you place him."[34] A shrewder appraisal of Lowell in his thirtieth year could hardly have been written.

VI

*"I am the first poet who has endeavored to express the
American idea, and I shall be popular by and by."*

Lowell to C. F. Briggs, December, 1848
Works, XIV, 201

M
Y true place is to serve the cause as a poet." So wrote Lowell,
in June, 1846, to Sydney Howard Gay, new editor of the
National Anti-Slavery Standard. He was continuing, of course,
to work for that cause in prose, and had even contributed, at the
invitation of Dickens, four anonymous articles to the London *Daily
News.* Leaving these pieces unsigned was the result of deliberate
strategy: "If it became generally known that they were written by
a professed abolitionist, it would give them a taint in the delicate
nose of the public." [1] In them he recounted the struggles of "that
devoted little band who have so long maintained the bleak Ther-
mopylae of Freedom," predicted that the future would rank them
with the world's saints and martyrs, and defined the struggle now
heightening in America as one "not between Northern and Southern
States, but between barbarism and civilization, between cruelty and
mercy, between evil and good." [2] Yet despite all this eloquent
support of Goodness and Virtue, Lowell was still restless. One
spring of his genius had not yet been tapped, and the pressure to
release its pent energies was stifling him. There would be a "squib"
of his in the current Boston *Courier,* he soon informed Gay. "I
wish it to continue anonymous, for I wish slavery to think it has as
many enemies as possible." That squib was the first of the *Biglow
Papers,* the most lively verse he was ever to produce.

The first series of these papers comprises nine satires of varying
length. Numbers I–V appeared in the *Courier,* the next four in the
Standard. The series was published in book form the fall of 1848. [3]
Something more than two years elapsed, then, between the beginning

and the end of this witty, if uninformed, attack against the South and the causes of the war between the United States and Mexico.

Lowell portrays three characters in the work, each representative of a facet of what might be termed the New England mind. By no means does he attempt inclusiveness here. The mind of Daniel Webster and even the mind of men like his own father are allowed to go unrecognized. Yet within the limits he defines for himself he achieves a remarkable variety and a consistent humorousness. For all his characters are, in the Jonsonian sense, possessed by humors and conceived on a flat surface.

There is Parson Wilbur, of Jaalam, Massachusetts, to begin with. Writing in dialect as he did, Lowell felt that he "needed on occasion to rise above the level of mere *patois,* and for this purpose conceived the Rev. Mr. Wilbur, who should express the more cautious element of the New England character and its pedantry." Then there was young Hosea Biglow. An unlettered rustic, Hosea was nonetheless drawn to represent the "homely common sense" of his region, vivified and heated by conscience. The parson, Lowell explained further, "was to be the complement rather than the antithesis of his parishioner." Finally, there was Birdofredum Sawin. "I invented Mr. Sawin for the clown of my little puppet show. I meant to embody in him that half-conscious *un* morality which I had noticed as the recoil in gross natures from a puritanism that still strove to keep in its creed the intense savor which had long gone out of its faith and life." [4] This is Lowell's academic way of implying that Sawin is a rascal, and that, being one, he naturally fell into the ways of the southern planters. He epitomizes further his country's blind faith in manifest destiny.

The first of these papers took the form of a letter from Mr. Ezekiel Biglow, of Jaalam—he was Hosea's father—to the editor of the Boston *Courier.* It enclosed a poem by his son, along with a note announcing the circumstances under which it was written. Hosea, it appears, went down to Boston the week before and saw a recruiting "Sarjunt" strutting around the town, with twenty rooster's tails stuck in his hat and enough brass bobbing up and down on his shoulders

HOSEA AND THE "CRUETIN SARJUNT"
by Howard Pyle

to make a six pound cannon ball. He had two other fellers behind him, drumming and fifing like mad. One look at Hosea convinced the "Sarjunt" that the bumpkin lad from the backwoods would make an easy victim.[5] He tried to lure him into enlisting for the cause against Mexico.

Hosea was riled. He came home, but even there his indignation continued to boil. After going to bed, confessed his father, he heard the youth thrashing around his room like a short-tailed bull in fly time. What Hosea was doing, it developed later, was writing a poem about the insulting officer and the army he served. The next morning he took his verses to Parson Wilbur to obtain scholarly criticism. The result was the first of the Papers.

"Thrash away," said Hosea, addressing the "Sarjunt." In substance, he went on as follows: You'll toot until you're yeller before you git ahold of me. Your flag is rotten. Those dreadful southerners always make us blow the bellows of their discontent. They are overreaching negro drivers. See what a thundering wedge they are clearing, through the "Vartu" of the North. The North's "Vartu." Let it speak.

It spoke of war. As for war, it was murder. There you have it plain and flat. "If you take a sword and draw it and go stick a feller through, government aint no answer for it. God will send the bill to you." Why did the agitators want California? The answer was plain: To make of it another slave state. He had come to this conclusion, after long and careful figuring: Every inhuman act injures the whole human race alike. Moreover, go home and ask Nancy whether she thought him simpleton enough to join up. Her answer would be plain to anybody not a fool. She wanted him for home consumption.

He invited his reader to have a look at the militant editors who were supporting the war. One wouldn't catch any of them enlisting in the army! And consider Massachusetts, even! She was kneeling, like the other states, before the unhallowed altar of servitude. Let the Bay State speak out, he cried, clanging the bells in every steeple. Let her proclaim to the South this message:

I will not help the Devil make man the curse of man:
I am a tyrant hater and the friend of God and Peace.
I prefer separation to a forced and unholy union of them thet
God has no ways jined.

So argued Lowell's first "squib" in the long war of blind and always growing sectional vituperation.

His second, more lively in motive, followed discreetly after it.[6] It was a note from Mexico, from Private Sawin, who *had* enlisted with the Massachusetts Regiment; unlike Hosea, he had been taken in by the sergeant's glitter and fanfare. Well, the army has proved a great disappointment, he confessed to the folks back home. Ninepence a day—his compensation—seemed rather a cheap wage for murder. For relaxation, he started to walk off to a fandango the other day, but the sentinel ran his bayonet—that one pronged pitch fork—clean through Sawin's clothes, jest as if he wuz an enemy.

Maybe the family would want to know about this country down here. It was the meanest place any skunk ever discovered. The food was trash. The land swarmed with every kind of varmint. The soldiers had been told of the delicious fruits of Mexico. The only fruit Sawin had found was prickly pears. And the bugs! They were as big as year-old elephants. The mosquitoes sounded like horns and fairly stabbed him in the legs. Scorpions and land crabs had gnawed his feet, and yellow fever was everywhere.

Birdofredum had found out another thing. Back home the flag-waving orators told him that Mexicans weren't human beings, but a kind of orang-outang people. Actually they were not much different from his own fellow-soldiers. Yet here he was, scrouging them out of their own property, or, as old Caleb Cushing had put it, sheltering them under the eagle's pinions. The truth was, Sawin confessed, he would desert now and strike out for home if he weren't afraid of being snake-bitten before he got there. And let him add this: the officers were certainly a changed set.

Our ossifers aint wut they wuz afore they left the Bay-State;
Then it wuz "Mister Sawin, sir, you're middlin' well now, be ye?
Step up an' take a nipper, sir; I'm dreffle glad to see ye";
But now it's "Ware's my eppylet? here, Sawin, step an' fetch it!
An' mind your eye, be thund'rin spry, or, damn ye, you shall ketch it!"

But there was no use complaining now. Sawin had enlisted for the duration.

Lowell appended to this letter a scholarly communication from Parson Wilbur. In content it was largely an attack on the "my country right or wrong" doctrine. It has been argued by some, the Parson points out, that the Lord has prospered our armies; therefore He favors our cause. "This opens the question, whether, when our hands are strengthened to make great slaughter of our enemies, it be absolutely and demonstrably certain that this might is added to us from above, or whether some Potentate from an opposite quarter may not have a finger in it, as there are few pies into which his digits are not thrust. Would the Sanctifier and Setter-apart of the seventh day have assisted in a victory gained on the Sabbath, as was Cerro Gardo in the present war?"

The Parson goes on to excoriate those clergymen who have supported the conflict, calling them not fishers but "shooters" of men. He reviles the feckless indifference of the people for condoning it because it appeared to be popular. "One might imagine America to have been colonized by a tribe of those nondescript African animals the Aye-ayes, so difficult a word is *no* to us all." A mouth filled with the national pudding, or watering in expectation thereof, is wholly incompetent to utter this refractory monosyllable. Wilbur concludes with a vigorous aside against democracy and President Polk. By what College of Cardinals is this God's-Vicar of ours elected? he asks. His answer is direct. "By the sacred conclave of Tag, Rag, and Bobtail, in the gracious atmosphere of the grog shop. Yet it is of this that we must all be puppets."[7]

Number III is the briefest of the first collection; Lowell declared that he wrote it in a single sitting. Its title, "What Mr. Robinson Thinks," refers to a statement by this gentleman, a Whig, that he expected to support Caleb Cushing, a brigadier general in the Mexican War, for governor of Massachusetts. His opponent was George Nixon Briggs, who was running for reëlection. Briggs was successful, thanks in part, it appears, to Lowell's help; for this poem, Greenslet implies,[8] was likely the most popular of the series.

First there was Guvener B. He stayed at home, looked after his folks, and avoided meddling in other people's potato patches:

> But John P.
> Robinson he
> Sez he won't vote fer Guvener B.

My, wasn't that terrible! exclaimed the poet. He guessed they would all have to come round and support the candidate of thunder and guns, since Mr. Robinson had made his decision public. As for Gineral C., he was a dreadfully smart man. He had been on all sides that had preferment to give. He was consistent too, always loyal to one party—himself.

General C. believed in war. What did God make us rational creatures for, he was asking, if it wasn't for glory, plunder, and blood? True, they used to get along nicely up there in Massachusetts. Darkened by old ideas, they still thought Christ was agin war and pillage, and that epaulets were no special marks of a saint. But apparently they were wrong, for J. P. Robinson was saying that that kind of thing's an "exploded idee"! Always, he argued, people have got to take their country's side; they must coöperate.

Parson Wilbur called such talk lies, just so much *fee, faw, fum.* He said, too, that rum and ignorance were back of all these perorations about manifest destiny. Moreover, he had never heard of any of the apostles ever rigging themselves out in swaller tail coats and marching in front of a drum and fife.

> But John P.
> Robinson he
> Sez they didn't know everythin' down in Judee.

It was simply too bad for Mr. Robinson. Rumor has it that the unfortunate gentleman fled to Europe to escape the sound of his name in the streets, only to hear a child in an adjoining room of his Liverpool hotel chanting the vindictive refrain. He wandered on to Malta, but there again another voice in innocent merriment sang out in his presence the now quite legended curse.[9] The poet had branded him for life—and after.

In explaining his point of view in these verses, Lowell (as Wilbur) assumed the extreme position of the New England moralists—the point of view made famous by Emerson's "I will not obey it, by God" reference to the Fugitive Slave Law, and by Thoreau's bald statement to the effect that a government which countenanced human servitude was one to which he would accord no loyalty. "We are inhabitants of two worlds," Lowell wrote, "and owe a double, but not a divided, allegiance. In virtue of our clay, this little ball of earth exacts a certain loyalty of us, while, in our capacity as spirits, we are admitted citizens of an invisible and holier fatherland." But what if a conflict should occur between the claims of these grim contenders for the mastery of our souls? The meaning of Lowell's answer was unmistakable. "There is a patriotism of the soul whose claim absolves us from our other and terrene fealty. Our true country is that ideal realm which we represent to ourselves under the names of religion, duty, and the like."

The *Biglow Papers* are uneven in quality, and occasionally, when Lowell elects to treat an obscure item in politics and fails to give it any general significance, they seem positively flat. Number IV is an example.[10] It purports to be a speech by one Increase D. O'Phace, and was provoked by Mr. J. G. Palfrey's refusal to vote for a Whig candidate for the speakership. The selection is relieved by a few homely reflections on the manner in which office affects men, once their choice is assured. There are some philosophers who think, says the orator, that a faculty is granted men the moment they have need of it. Such people contend, for instance, that the tail of the monkey suddenly sprung from his vertebrae when he found himself falling from a tree and became frightened. Similarly, it appears, our representatives have a way of sprouting collars the moment they get down to Washington. Afterwards, in the poem, Lowell satirizes an equivocating speech by a typical demagogue. Polk comes in later for the usual amount of ridicule, and Palfrey is finally denounced by the orator for voting independently, as his moral convictions had prompted him to do.

"The Debate in the Sennit," No. V, is one of the sprightliest of the series. Lowell had a villain of stalwart proportions to attack, and in assailing him, his wit was unfaltering. That villain was John C. Calhoun; the point of ridicule, Calhoun's views on the Negro question. Whenever that issue is touched, wrote Lowell, as Wilbur, "he sets up his scarecrow of dissolving the Union." His fault may be very simply stated. "Mr. Calhoun cannot let go the apron string of the Past." He continues to hide his face in her lap, though the Future holds out her arms to him.

"Here we stand on the Constitution, by thunder," begins the gentleman from South Carolina in his speech. Human rights, Lowell represents the Senator as saying, had no more place on the Senate floor than the man in the moon. Freedom's keynote was slavery. It was a divine institution. Calhoun did not believe in oppression; he believed in the superiority of race. There was slavery in the North of the worst sort—it was white slavery, the slavery to heartless employers and to wages. Agitating this question further would brew anarchy. Southern negroes were happy. The South, in fact, was the last fragment of Eden left on this earth. And as these sentiments were spoken, Lowell pictured Dixon H. Lewis, Jefferson Davis, Colquitt, Jarnagin, Wescott, of Florida, and other senators from the section hanging on Calhoun's words and agreeing, like automatons, to every sentiment he uttered.

These rhymes were preceded by a sample of the Parson's moralizing, and they were followed by another, more passionately urged. Alas, we are told, we have no right to interfere. "If a man pluck an apple of mine, he shall be in danger of the justice; but if he steal my brother, I must be silent. Who says this? Our Constitution, consecrated by the hallowed consuetude of sixty years, and grasped in triumphant argument by the left hand of him whose right hand clutches the clotted slave whip." Justice says—*Speak!* The Past says—*Speak!* Nature through her thousand trumpets of freedom cries—*Speak!* The still small voice of the Soul says— *Speak!* But, alas, the Constitution and the Honorable Mr. Bagowind say—*Be dumb!* "There is a point where toleration sinks into sheer baseness and poltroonery." The conflict he viewed as a great wrestling match between a few blind Southerners on the one hand and Christ and the Nineteenth Century on the other. "I must confess my fears for the gentlemen from the South." [11]

"The Pious Editor's Creed," Lowell's first Biglow Paper to be published in the *Standard,* is "a satire upon the code of this person, who believes in humbug and cant, and whose main guide is self interest." The type of editor he especially reviles is, naturally, the one who defended the Mexican War. These verses today seem considerably less interesting than does a note by the Parson which accompanied them. Despite a certain borrowing from *Sartor Resartus,* three of its paragraphs embody some of Lowell's most consistent prose. Wilbur's subject is the newspaper, the weekly journal, which brings to him, every seventh day, its account of that mysterious puppet show men call the world.

"Hither, to my obscure corner, by wind or steam, on horseback or dromedary-back, in the pouch of the Indian runner, or clicking over the magnetic wires troop all the famous performers from the four quarters of the globe. Looked at from a point of criticism, tiny puppets they seem all, as the editor sets up his booth upon my desk and officiates as showman. Now I can truly see how little and transitory is life. The earth appears almost as a drop of vinegar, on which the solar microscope of the imagination must be brought to bear in order to make out anything distinctly. That animalcule there, in the pea-jacket, is Louis Philippe, just landed on the coast of England. That other, in the gray surtout and cocked hat, is Napoleon Bonaparte Smith, assuring France that she need apprehend no interference from him in the present alarming juncture. At that spot, where you seem to see a speck of something in motion, is an immense mass-meeting. Look sharper, and you will see a mite brandishing his mandibles in an excited manner. That is the great Mr. Soandso, defining his position amid tumultuous and irrepressible cheers. That infinitesimal creature, upon whom some score of others, as minute as he, are gazing in open-mouthed admiration, is a famous philosopher, expounding to a select audience their capacity for the Infinite. That scarce discernible pufflet of smoke and dust is a revolution. That speck there is a reformer, just arranging the lever with which he is to move the world. And lo, there creeps forward the shadow of a skeleton that blows one breath between its grinning teeth, and all our distinguished actors are whisked off the slippery stage into the dark Beyond.

"Yes, the little show-box has its solemner suggestions. Now and then we catch a glimpse of a grim old man, who lays down a scythe and hour-glass in the corner while he shifts the scenes. There, too, in the dim background, a weird shape is ever delving. Sometimes he leans upon his mattock, and gazes, as a coach whirls by, bearing the newly married on their wedding jaunt, or glances carelessly at a babe brought home from christening. Suddenly (for the scene grows larger and larger as we look) a bony hand snatches back a performer in the midst of his part, and him, whom yesterday two infinities (past and future) would not suffice, a handful of dust is enough to cover and silence forever. Nay, we see the same fleshless fingers opening to clutch the showman himself, and guess, not without a shudder, that they are lying in wait for spectator also.

"Think of it: for three dollars a year I buy a season ticket to this great Globe Theatre, for which God would write the dramas (only that we like farces, spectacles, and the tragedies of Apollyon better), whose scene-shifter is Time, and whose curtain is rung down by Death." [12]

Number VII may be briefly dismissed. It is a letter, purportedly written by a candidate in reply to certain inquiries from Hosea. The ardent young man particularly wanted to know the gentleman's stand on war. The candidate proved an obvious straddler:

> Ez fer the war, I go agin it,—
> I mean to say I kind o' du,—
> That is, I mean thet, bein' in it,
> The best way wuz to fight it thru;
> Not but wut abstract war is horrid,
> I sign to thet with all my heart,—
> But civlyzation *doos* git forrid
> Sometimes upon a powder-cart.

In Number VIII Lowell returned to his amiable friend Birdofredum, and his wit revived with his account of that character's wanderings. Fate had not dealt kindly with Private Sawin. "I spose you wonder ware I be," the letter began. He couldn't tell exactly, at least not about the whole of him. When he left home, he had two legs. Now he owned but one. The doctors had decided, after a wound, that the other was kind of mortifying and sawed it off. His sole consolation was that whiskey couldn't get into the wooden stump they gave him as a substitute. So he was always partly sober, which was helpful.

Also, Sawin had lost an eye. The one that was left, though, was still good enough to see all the pay he'd likely ever get for his misfortunes. There had been other calamities, too—his left arm shot off, and the four fingers of his right hand. Also about six ribs were broken; he couldn't be exactly sure. Speaking of ribs reminded him of the one he left behind—his wife. If the Parson saw her, Sawin wished him to make up some story to the effect that he would be getting an annual pension someday, and, besides, he wasn't as expensive to keep as he used to be.

He was forced to add that his expectations of plunder had not been realized. When he joined up he thought that Mexico was a regular Promised Land, flowing with rum and water, a place where one could dig gold as easily as potatoes back home. That was what those speechifying buzzards in Boston told him. The truth was that his whole share of the spoils wouldn't come to a V spot. Mexico was an all-fired buggy hole. One day you practically died of thirst, the next the rain virtually drowned you. The only piece of property Sawin was bringing away was a case of shaking fever. At least he was "some great shakes" there! The soldiers had won victories, but while the glory for them flooded the generals, it trickled out completely before the men got a taste of it.

> We get the licks—we're just the grist thet's put into War's hoppers;
> Leftenants is the lowest grade thet helps pick up the coppers.

Sawin went on, army-fashion, to damn his officers; they enjoyed the banquets, he must be satisfied with the aroma from their dishes.

But he had hit upon a plan: He would run for office. And when his opinion on any issue was demanded, he would cite his war record and display his wooden leg. If that wasn't enough, he would cry "One Eye Put Out." He would like to run for President, but a certain misfortune seemed to disqualify him: he was not a resident of the South. He closed his letter by listing his account with the "Bank of Glory." The credit items, including service under Colonel Cushing, totaled a neat 100. Balancing that figure were his debits: 1/675 of three cheers in Faneuil Hall and elsewhere, an evening of band music, a uniform, and one homecoming dinner ran this side of the ledger to 76. His chance of a pension counted one. As for the remaining 23, that was charged to the privilege of drawing the long bow for the rest of his natural life. The communication from Wilbur ends with a penetrating indictment of the system of indirect taxation that was used to finance the war. "If we could know that a part of the money we expend for tea and coffee goes to buy powder and balls, and that it is Mexican blood which makes the clothes on our backs more costly, it would set some of us athinking." [13]

Sawin's next letter was the last of the first series. He reminds Wilbur that in his preceding note he had spoken of running for office, maybe for President. Well, he has changed his mind, is withdrawing in favor of old Zachary Taylor. He gives his reasons. Taylor is the most popular candidate. He has been into many a saloon seeking to know the public sentiment of the country, and there, he finds, the patrons are uniformly endorsing the General. Only think of his qualifications! He has no platform. He is tied by no previous pledges. He's a Whig, but not "ultry." This fact makes him practically a Democrat, since followers of both parties are bent upon a single objective—squeezing Uncle Samuel's purse. Lowell, through Sawin, proceeds indirectly to ridicule the arguments against Van Buren, the Free Soil candidate, showing them to be ignorant and trivial prejudices. Van Buren's son, they say, used to "cuss and swear." One of his followers, a few years back, tried to make Sawin sign a temperance pledge. That settled it, Sawin exclaimed. He always takes "the side that isn't took by them consarned teetotallers."

From that point he shifted into a lively account of his adventure with a family of southern Negroes. He had come up, recently, upon a certain Pomp and his children. They were hoeing a field; apparently no one owned them. Sawin got the drop on the family and proceeded to march them all toward the nearest town. He could sell them for a tidy sum, he felt certain. But when noon came he grew tired, and his wooden stump began to chafe his leg. Having no idea what ill will the pis'nous brutes bore him, he stopped to rest, removed his leg, lay it beside him, and took a few drinks of whiskey. What did the Parson think that rascal Pomp was doing all this time? He was sneaking up behind Sawin, coming closer and closer. Suddenly, before he could wink, Pomp snatched the wooden member and ran behind a tree with it. Until that moment Sawin hadn't believed that an alligator could be so destitute of humanity.

Pomp's fuzzy-headed children had got behind trees too, it seemed. Finally, Pomp called out to Birdofredum: He must throw away his gun and pistols, or the entire family would cut and run, taking the stump with them. Sawin had to submit. The black-hearted monster marched him off to his fields and worked him there all summer. He even demanded to be taught to read the Bible. And when fall came and the crop was harvested, the ungrateful wretch kicked his white benefactor out of doors. Did the parson wonder that Sawin was now opposed to setting free such renegades as that? [14]

The arguments that inform these racy pieces are well worth summarizing: The "dreadful" South caused the war. Southerners are overreaching Negro drivers, whose corruption is so great that it has even begun to menace that sublime citadel, the Vartu of the North. War—all war—is murder, and God will hold those who support bloodshed between nations individually responsible for their acts. The purpose of the South in fomenting the present conflict is to extend the boundaries of slavery. Those editors who indorsed its cause (which was, incidentally, that of the national government) are guilty of thievery. Let Massachusetts, at least, arise and defy the common enemy; even secession is preferable to a forced and unholy union with slave breeders. We should remember that when the dictates of the state clash with those of one's private conscience, one is fully warranted in defying the state. The real villain in this Mexican struggle is John C. Calhoun. His trouble is that he clings to the Past, a stubborn enemy of Christ and Progress.

Then there was the reality of war itself. Stripped of its glamour, what was it like, what did it mean? It meant living in a vile country. It meant being subject to strictest discipline. It meant poor food, monstrous mosquitoes, scorpions, and yellow fever. It meant submitting to arrogant officers and the killing of innocent human beings. Finally, it meant the loss of legs, arms, fingers and eyes; in short, permanent misery. Yet all this was accompanied by no assurance of reward.

These papers have naturally made a good many people indignant. What is surprising is the fact that the gentleman who appears to have resented them most was the late Justin H. Smith, a distinguished historian of the Mexican War and a member of the Massachusetts Historical Society. Lowell, he says, made fun of our uniform and of what he called the "strutting" of the recruiting sergeant, "ignoring the fact that a soldierly costume and bearing are seen in every well ordered army." Again, it was unfair of Lowell to present a character like Sawin, who enlisted for mere personal gain; for in the case of a national conflict, personal gain should never be considered. Probably Lowell, too, very soon came to regret that he had called our dead American soldiers "compost," as he had actually done in one reference.

Most remarkable of all Smith's rebuttals is the one which deals with the casualties suffered by Mexico, casualties which to Lowell, we recall, constituted plain murder. Such a view, replies his critic, is merely begging the question. "A large percentage of the officers opposed to us did not linger on the field or did not linger long, and the fighting was mainly done by Indian privates and corporals."

These men, as everyone ought to know, are racially indifferent to pain. Bullets can't hurt them. Moreover, they had experienced nothing to make life pleasant or worth enduring, if we except the sight of religious processions and an occasional debauch with pulque. Consider, on the other hand, the shining prospects which death held out for them. "As fanatical Roman Catholics, they felt sure of paradise." And (like the generality of mortals) they knew that death was inevitable. This being the case, "they did not object very much, as in fact they had no reason to do, against facing it in the ranks." [15] Every American bullet that was successfully fired would seem, to this scholar, to have carried a blessing with it! His moral indignation is fully as great as Lowell's, though directed against an opposite evil. The humor of the *Biglow Papers* he apparently never once tasted.

A saner view of the whole complex problem would seem to suggest that these poems ought to be looked upon primarily as propaganda. They represent the work of a man who, despite his Harvard training in the humanities, had become too blinded by his zeal to see either the slavery issue or the war with Mexico in realistic or historical terms. Regarding anything like a first-hand familarity with the institution, Lowell of course knew next to nothing. As a boy, he had visited Washington, Alexandria, and Mount Vernon with his father. There he was merely a tourist. Later, when a Harvard student, he had gone to see his good friend Scates, in Charleston, South Carolina. There he had been an amiable guest, a gay young Brahmin who liked to dance, to pun, and to talk pleasant nonsense. Lowell's information about the South was thus drastically limited and derivative. After his marriage he did read the Congressional debates on slavery, but he had no frame of personal experience within which these utterances might be judged.

The actual complex history of the Mexican Question cannot be discussed here.[16] Perhaps it is sufficient to remark that those who have studied it deeply have traced its cause to a boundary dispute between the two governments, Mexico claiming the whole of Texas after it had been admitted into the Union. Yet settlers from our older states had meanwhile gone there seeking homes, for the same basic reasons that others were seeking them in the Great Northwest. The charge that the South wanted the whole of the territory extending to the Pacific for the purpose of "lugging in" more slave states was made only after this immigration was well under way, and made, moreover, by the irresponsible propagandist, Benjamin Lundy. His were the arguments which misled John Quincy Adams, William Cullen Bryant of the New York *Evening Post,* the editor of Philadelphia *National Gazette,* and a number of other persons influential in shaping public opinion. Lowell was simply one of the thousands who took the truth of his statements for granted.

VII

"I know of nothing more depressing than to look one's old poems in the face."
Lowell to J. T. Fields, March 23, 1869.
Works, XV, 195

THE YEAR 1848 has been called Lowell's *annus mirabilis,* and, by almost anybody's standard, the term is just. He published *The Biglow Papers* then, as we have seen, but that work was only one of the several to absorb his interest during this crowded twelvemonth. Along with it, in almost dizzying sequence, came his second series of *Poems,*[1] *A Fable for Critics,* and *The Vision of Sir Launfal.* The rapidity with which the presses reeled off so many divergent pieces proved, before the interval was out, almost more than his abundant energies could keep abreast of. A number of the selections he printed at this time had been written and published in periodicals, a fairly great while before. Yet the world's general approval of them would seem to date from this period.

What was he saying to that stubborn populace which had, at length, begun to lend him a wholly respectful ear? In one mood he was transmitting to it a message; a message, he felt, which it was sorely in need of. The burden of it was simple enough, but, like most simplicities, appeared in danger of being forgotten. He coated it in the title, *The Vision of Sir Launfal,* openly risking the suspicion of certain readers that the hero who bore this name in legend would scarcely have recognized himself beneath Lowell's well-intended and chastened narrative. The older Sir Launfal, the Launfal of the medieval *lai,* it will be recalled, was a man who never entirely lost sight of the elementary requisites of his sex. He was a very passionate and very normal young person. Led to leave Arthur's court through the discourtesy of Queen Guinevere, whom he had scorned, he fell in with the irresistible lady Triamour and relished with her certain timeless and altogether incalculable favors. During this blissful interlude, moreover, he proved neither hot-gospeler nor advocate of any other satisfaction that might be labeled as celestial in character.

This traditional concept of the hero held no interest for Lowell. In the first part of his poem—the plot of which its author admitted to be wholly his own—Launfal is portrayed merely as a snob. This section is introduced by a "Prelude," [2] which, largely didactic in tone, celebrates the widely quoted rarity of a day in June. On such a day as this, Sir Launfal, "a maiden knight," quite properly remembers the keeping of his vow, and, in a dream, sets forth to find the Grail. Outside his gate he meets a leper, but, bent upon his quest, he tosses him gold and passes on. The leper is indignant. The poor man's crust, he says, when given from the heart, is better than the most priceless treasure, when a bare sense of duty prompts the latter and richer prize. But Launfal rides on, into darkness and rain, and into that sympathyless vacuity which is the world, seeking the elusive chalice. Years pass, and before we hear further from the knight he has turned gray. Through his hair the wind makes a harp and sings in dreary monotone a chorus whose burden is "shelterless, shelterless." When he again approaches his palace, he finds that another lord has inherited the earldom; his raiment is unavailing against the barbed air. Then, amidst reveries of summer hours, the voice of the forgotten leper: "For Christ's sweet sake, I beg an alms. . . ."

"And Sir Launfal said, I behold in thee an image of Him who died on the tree." He was no longer scornful. He gave him not gold, now, but a drink from a frozen stream and one mouldy crust, for the coarse brown bread was all he had. But though meager, we recall, the gift was spiritually complete; it became for the leper wheaten bread and red wine, constituted for him the ultimate communion. Behind this dream hovered Lowell's overt message that what counts is not our gift but the heart that goes with it. The poem is still deservedly popular with children.

Then there were other messages in verse, and in verse, moreover,

view of poetry as a medium
ne's age may find fit language
n. The second series of *Poems*
There were, to cite an instance,
ive Slaves near Washington."
New England's native air, he
our fathers when we tempo-
e craven, while Pity's burning
We are traitors to humanity.
owe allegiance to the State—
to God. God works for all.
of geographic latitude. Signs
roken are already evident, as
raoh. " 'Tis ours to save our
eace and love." If we delay,
om our listless hands.
ain throughout the volume.
Present Crisis," with its an-
ne for Freedom, a thrill of
ching breast. Once to every
on which side he shall stand,
d or Evil. May his people
remember that though Evil prosper, Truth alone is strong. Perhaps at times the Deity does indeed seem careless, with Truth forever
on the scaffold, Wrong forever on the throne.

> Yet that scaffold sways the future, and behind the dim unknown,
> Standeth God within the shadow, keeping watch above his own.[3]

It is easy to be a hero. Let the fathers of 1620 inspirit us. The
Mayflower was launched not by cowards but by iconoclasts. New
occasions teach new duties. The door of the Future is not to be
opened with the blood-rusted key of the Past.

Other poems—many, many others—might be cited as further
evidence of the insistent didacticism of the book. The tendency
crops out unpredictably in verses on subjects that seem innocent of

any moral occasion. Even "The Oak" must bend to serve his purpose, and "Miles Standish" is made to return to denounce New England's compromise with the slaveholders. "Lord! all thy works are lessons," he writes in the former poem. "Cause me some message of the truth to bring."

The Lord, it would seem, was freely obliging. Yet the burden of that message proved so heavy as to stifle Lowell's perception of almost every less exalted object. It rendered his imagery slight and blurred; he was too busy preaching to look about him sharply at anything. The fact is that despite all his fervent talk on the subject of poetry, he seems to have come to respect it only occasionally as a valid art form. He is not interested in writing it primarily for its own sake. It must be made to serve a purpose; its values for him are now instrumental and utilitarian. Not worthy of an independent status in this world, it must lean upon Rock of Ages—upon that Higher Truth, of which, along with the Soul, Lowell always spoke with assurance.

In his other work, the *Fable for Critics,* Lowell returned to a more congenial vein—the vein of humor mixed with interesting judgments of his contemporary authors. The volume is discursive, slow in getting started, highly self-conscious in parts, but, when edited, its comments are usually sound, though often vague. He introduces the book with a facile series of rhymed paragraphs to the reader: He is not worried about its sale, he says. "For there is not a poet throughout the whole land but will purchase a copy or two out of hand, in the fond expectation of being amused in it, by seeing his betters cut up and abused in it. Now, I find, by a pretty exact calculation, there are something like ten thousand bards in the nation." Of course, this being true, he could not be expected to notice them all. But let those who are omitted take comfort. He will consider every one in the future, if the need demands it, "at the rate of one author to each new edition." [4]

After several pages of talk about Phoebus, the ardent wooer, and Daphne, who leapt inside a tree trunk to escape this god's attentions, the reader is introduced to a donkeyish lad who became a critic. This lad, "our Hero," went finally to college, where he continued to read, widely but carelessly. He was awarded his bachelor's degree, having become by this time haphazardly versed in a great deal of undigested knowledge. The obvious future for such a person was that of book reviewing. He took to this hack work, though generally blind to the significance of the authors he pretended to judge. Like most critics, moreover, he was a dull person socially, drier at teatime than any toast he ever buttered. He was as fond of dates as an Arab, and a stickler for punctuation —in short, the kind of figure whom Addison and Steele had satirized more than a century before in "Tom Folio" and "Timothy Tittle."

This critic, in the presence of Apollo and the muses, attempts to entertain his audience with a poem. They stop him, and later he is sent to fetch a flower for the god. Then comes Mr. E. A. Duyckinck, editor of the *Literary World*. This gentlemen is followed by a small, bespeckled versifier named Damon, who is cursing a certain reviewer for disparaging his work. Apollo welcomes them and gives Damon some good advice: Let the poet do his writing conscientiously, in his garret, and not bother with its public reception. Stay out of literary quarrels. If his poetry is valid, no critic really can injure it.

Mr. Duyckinck then presents Apollo with an unsalable book, and as they sit there meditating the villainies of the literary world, Tityrus (Rufus) Griswold appears, leading—shepherd-fashion and with the entrepreneur avarice of anthology editors the world over —his flock of native American authors. The critical estimates of Lowell's contemporaries really begin at this place, after twenty-three sluggish pages have been used in getting the *Fable* started.

Emerson naturally comes first. Each of his rich words is like a nail to hang a trophy upon. His prose is poetic, though his verse is like prose. It is piled up, unorganized, lacking in form. But Emerson's is a Greek head with Yankee shoulders, a combination of the mystic Plotinus and the skeptic Montaigne. His gospel is inspiring but vague. He should be compared to Plato, not to Carlyle, who is more burly but far less rare.

Lowell turns next to the other transcendentalists. With Thoreau he is, as almost always, surly. Thoreau is an imitator of Emerson, with a finger in the seer's every pocket. "Fie, for shame, brother bard; with good fruit of your own, can't you let neighbor Emerson's orchards alone." Then there is Alcott, calm as a cloud, an eloquent talker, never perplexed by facts. Indeed, he is a great talker, but when he takes up his pen he is hopeless. He is as bad as the mystic Orestes Brownson, who is always pleasantly contradictory and who, when a choice is forced upon him, invariably selects the wrong side. It is worth noting that Emerson is the only one of this school who wins the critic's approval, and that even in his case the approval is somewhat guarded.

In another category Lowell notices N. P. Willis, the author of *Pencillings by the Way* and a celebrated foreign correspondent. His pet phrases and over-ornamental diction remind one of a bull with a ring in his nose. He is not deep, but then to ask for depth is perhaps unfair; his beauty is in this very shallowness. He is an innate cockney; his pieces are like champagne with foam on it. An impetuous writer, his work spoils with deliberation. He is the sort of fellow who might well have cracked jokes with Ben Jonson, provided the barmaid were always near to enliven his wit. He is the topmost bubble at present on the wave of the Town.

Next there is Theodore Parker, an independent theologian, the dissidence of dissent. He has been read out of the orthodox church, but the fact has not daunted him in the least. And what learning he has mastered! Confucius and William Pitt, Shakespeare and Machiavelli, and many, many others are at his tongue's end. He can discuss the Bible or the Koran with equal thoroughness. A good transcendentalist, he believes that all men *may* be inspired. It is hard to tell of what his creed consists, though it's certain his faith in Parker is unshakable. Moreover, his speech "smacks of the field and the street." It is something uncommon to meet a man like that anywhere.

Lowell then leaves the New England galaxy to range for a while at random through less confining pastures. He turns to William Cullen Bryant, who is described, in a well-known passage, as being "as quiet, as cool, and as dignified, as a smooth silent iceberg that never is ignified." He is smooth, but he can kindle no warmth or enthusiasm. Lowell recommends him for summer reading exclusively. Moreover, he says, let us stop comparing him with Wordsworth. That poet is better than our whole tuneful herd together. A fairer similarity would be with Cowper, without the latter's craziness. And Whittier (to look again hurriedly toward Mecca)? His faults are about identical with certain ones Lowell was later to notice in himself. He can't distinguish between inspiration and mere enthusiasm. He has been true to the Voice—that meteor which has guided all good abolitionists. For this he deserves full praise. Hard language, as he or any other emancipator uses it, is good, and wholly warranted. Perhaps he is merely guilty of driving in his message of brotherly love with Thor's blunt mallet, rather than with David's pebbles.

A number of minor authors are treated in the poem, with an amplitude naturally less interesting to later ages than to Lowell's own. There was R. H. Dana, Jr., for instance. Dana, a friend of the critic, escapes with only mild censure. He is a fine writer of sea narratives and should not allow himself to be distracted by his ambitions as a poet. Next comes John Neal, of Maine, who lacks balance, whose conceit of his own talents prevents his cultivating them with proper judgment. Neal once boasted that within twelve years he had written the equivalent of fifty-five duodecimo volumes,[5] and Lowell seems to have diagnosed his weakness accurately. Later he treats another minor but once vigorous author, Fitz Greene Halleck, a native of Connecticut but now one of the Knickerbocker school. He is capable of wit, Lowell has heard; there is a genial manliness about him; but the odds are that he is better as a person than anything he has written.

For Margaret Fuller, the transcendental and oracular feminist and friend of Emerson, Lowell reserved some unusually direct strictures. He seems never to have forgiven this tart lady for a statement she made in a review of his 1844 volume: Mr. Lowell's "interest in the moral questions of the day," she had declared, "has supplied the want of vitality in himself; his great facility at versification has enabled him to fill the ear with a copious stream of pleasant sound. But his verse is stereotyped; his thoughts sound no depth, and posterity will not remember him." [6] For a while he debated whether to include her, "because she has done me an ill-natured turn." "She is a very foolish conceited woman," he added in this letter to Briggs, "who has got together a great deal of information, but not enough knowledge to save her from being ill-tempered." But the temptation to avenge himself was strong. "Even Maria thinks I ought to give her a line or two." [7]

What he finally wrote had a good deal of truth in it, but not all the truth; it was astringent throughout. She is a self-centered woman, forever stressing her peculiar resemblance to Minerva. Now that she has been abroad, she will probably be worse than ever.[8] She is habitually taking old ideas and transmitting them as her own by saying them over in her Sibylline manner. She can confuse the simplest issue by mixing it with her infinite egotism. One thing she owns completely, however, as both native and genuine. It is her spite. At this point in the verse, Lowell pictures her as coming up to Phoebus and declaring that, since the day of her birth, she has lived cheek by jowl "with the infinite soul." She represents herself, further, as having introduced to America the greatest achievements of western civilization—to wit, Shakespeare, Bacon, the Bible, and her own works.

Lowell's treatment of Poe is written in his favorite manner; it is catchy, quotable, and largely vague. Poe is three-fifths genius and two-fifths sheer fudge. He talks like a book of iambs and pentameters. Some of his work is certainly superior, but in it the heart seems squeezed out by the mind. After these brief remarks he turns to chide Poe for his attacks upon Longfellow as a plagiarist. Lowell makes no attempt to refute this charge; he merely praises his Cambridge neighbor's loving kindness. Longfellow, he says, is charitable to a fault. His immortality as an author is assured. His personal life, moreover, is quiet and wholly chaste.

Fenimore Cooper is rebuked almost as severely as Poe. Lowell begins with a reference to the later Cooper, the militant critic of American institutions. He has written six volumes, it is charged, to prove to the world "he's as good as a Lord." Admittedly, this man has drawn one fine character—Natty Bumppo—but he has done nothing but copy him ever since. As for his women, they are, all of them, "as sappy as maples and flat as a prairie." But he has been courageous in lecturing his countrymen, especially since those lectures have cost him a great deal in unpopularity.

For Irving, Lowell has nothing but praise. His humor is grave and sweet; he is Addison and Steele combined, yet he is unique. So it goes for Hawthorne. His genius is shrinking and rare. His frame is robust, but his character is sweet. Nature, seeking to outdo herself, mixed some of the finer-grained stuff of women in his temperament. The result was a full and perfect man. Holmes merits a similar accolade, though practically all of his remembered work was written long after the *Fable* appeared. As a wit, he is matchless, and in the writing of lyrics appears already far better than Campbell.

Lowell himself is the last important author to be treated. He is striving to climb Parnassus,

> With a whole bale of *isms* tied together with rhyme
> He might get on alone, spite of brambles and boulders
> But he can't with that bundle he has on his shoulders,
> The top of the hill he will ne'er come nigh reaching
> Till he learns the distinction 'twixt singing and preaching.[9]

It was the sanest comment of the entire book. The tragedy is that he so rarely respected it. The poem continues with further strictures on our lesser poets for imitating the English. Afterwards, the critic who was treated in its early pages returns to Phoebus, bringing with him a thistle, which he calls a lily. Apollo thereupon moralizes upon the decay of poetry and the pettiness and ignorance of reviewers. Margaret Fuller (as Miranda) interrupts to correct his views, and the last lines picture the god in a hasty flight from this oracle's presence.

It is a lively and amusing volume, one that, for students of American literature, at any rate, has lost little of its original appeal. Of course, it is encumbered with the critic's own strutting asides and elaborate self-consciousness, and as has been implied, it is an unpardonably long time in getting under way. Yet it represents a fairly complete mustering of the important writers of Lowell's age. He knew his American contemporaries well, even if he did appear to be much less informed about his English and European contemporaries than was Poe. As for the quality of his judgments upon his fellow authors, two facts are readily evident. One is that his criticism is vague and impressionistic. To say that Poe is three-fifths genius and two-fifths fudge is to say nothing very definite about him, and to call Hawthorne a genius shrinking and rare is scarcely to root out the quality of that author's peculiar talent. The second fact is that the figures who are most generously treated are those who tended to respect the Harvard tradition. Longfellow and Holmes are unstintedly praised, though, as suggested, the latter had in 1848 achieved no real importance as a writer. Emerson, over at Concord, *had* done so, and he is given a sanction which was denied the other transcendentalists. Moreover, Emerson knew the art of social diplomacy, while Thoreau had apparently not bothered to study it; he had, in fact, completed his rather notorious Walden Pond experiment only shortly before the *Fable* was written.[10] For those authors whose orbits moved in spheres outside the geography of New England, Lowell has little praise to bestow. He is completely kind only to the innocuous Irving, who liked respectability as much as did Lowell himself. The poem, in brief, reflects mainly the bias of Lowell the Cambridge graduate. He was still a conservative in his literary preferences, which, for better or worse, had by no means kept pace with the militant stridings of his mind through the more turbulent field of American politics.

VIII

"After hearing them for some time, he said—'Gentlemen, this is the first time I was ever East of the mountains. I had always heard a great deal of the Eastern people and had intended to visit New England before I returned home. But, gentlemen, you have changed my mind. If you are good specimens of the Yankees, by God I don't want to see any more of 'em!' ...I had never before any adequate idea of the barbarism of these Western people."

Lowell to Edmund Quincy, June 12, 1848.
New Letters, 27

HIS FOUR books so recently out, Lowell began to read of their merits in letter after letter that fairly showered his "celestial study"[1] at Elmwood. Oliver Wendell Holmes proved one of his most enthusiastic correspondents. Perhaps his judgment wasn't of much value, he declared, but he thought the *Fable for Critics* capital—"crammed full and rammed down hard—powder shot—slugs—bullets—very little wadding, and that is gun cotton and all crowded into a rusty looking sort of blunderbuss barrel as it were—capped with a percussion preface—and cocked with a title page as apropos as the wink to a joke." There was a vast deal of fun it it, a force and delicacy in the critical diagnoses. The comments on Carlyle and Emerson, for instance, were subtle enough for Duns Scotus. What he said about Margaret Fuller was *too* good! May the author live a great many years longer to whack pretension, to praise without jealousy, and to separate the sham from the real.[2] So it went for *Sir Launfal*. A little book, with "not much more thickness to it than to a consecrated wafer," one might still get more nourishment from it than from many a whole loaf. It appeared somewhat crude in spots, and Holmes didn't think dandelions and Baltimore orioles "belonged" in a poem with such a distant and romantic setting. But the picture of June was rare and bold, though the Leper's speech reminded him a little too much of some of his "transcendental friends." Yet these demurrers were all trivial, he confessed. The *Vision* abounded in many beauties.[3]

Longfellow was similarly responsive. Some of the *Poems* he found "very striking, often soaring to the sublime." *The Biglow Papers* were "very droll," the *Fable* was "full of fun and with very true portraits," as seen from the comic side.[4] And from less civilized areas, from far-off Ithaca, New York, a young Presbyterian poet-preacher wrote "to relieve his thoughts" by saying to him "what I have said to many in the past year . . . that I consider Mr. Lowell the truest poet of the land." How Lowell's recent note about his own little volume has inspirited him! "Now I have a letter that I can wear over my heart as autograph chain-armor to protect my sensitiveness."

This writer, Mr. H. W. Parker, went on at length to record his personal history, a history enacted, he felt, so tragically remote from the shining center of America's cultural life. "There was nothing literary and congenial in the atmosphere around me, until I went to college." There, at Amherst, he did get through a good deal of reading. "But thus far my life has been spent in Ithaca (at the head of this lake), Amherst, and Auburn; and there is hardly one person of true culture to ten thousand in this region." Naturally, he found what Lowell had written a great comfort. He had read through the poems, the *Fable,* and *The Biglow Papers* twice this year. "Your 36th sonnet in the First Series *wonderfully* expresses me." [5]

And in a kindred tone of mingled deference and gratitude Mr. Ben Cassiday, of Louisville, was swelling the chorus that seemed to reverence no bounds of either section or creed. Mr. Cassiday was an emancipator, but a southerner who had scant sympathy for the technique of the abolitionists. He regrets that so able an artist as Lowell has elected to associate himself with "the most ultra of the sect." The slaves, by his prediction, will gain their freedom within five years, but it must be accomplished by the states alone. "Foreign effort will crush it or retard it." As for certain of Lowell's lyrics, "I read and reread them with renewed comfort." Some of these works were lost on his western people, because civilization there was eminently utilitarian and crude. He found this crudeness in other places also. "I have spent the greater part of this summer among the mountains of Virginia, where the earth seems literally 'drowned in beauty,' but among the most ignorant and unlovely of all the back woodsmen of America." [6]

These servile tributes to Lowell and New England from authors in other regions kept on for another two decades. They are melancholy to read. One does not mind the praise they contained, for it was usually sincere and innocently meant. What seems regrettable, and so often contemptible, is the fact that, nearly always, along with the praise went the sentimental complaint that the writer's own environment was hostile to him, that he was misunderstood, that there was nothing about it to inspire him. Southern writers were especially culpable in this regard—Paul Hamilton Hayne (*before* the war, as will be shown) and Sidney Lanier, in particular. Somewhere in the neighborhood of Boston, they seem to have felt, they might go, if privileged, and become wholly free from the difficult personal problems involved in their craft. The view was part of that flabby derivativeness that was blinding them fatally to the literary material lying at their own doors. It accounts for a great deal that is worthless and secondhand in the work of the early poets of the South. The example of Walt Whitman, after 1855, and later of Mark Twain, in prose, might have taught them a great deal, but the sad fact is that it taught them next to nothing. These two were men who ignored or forgot New England, but who in so doing—to quote Wendell Phillips in an altered context—"remembered themselves into immortality." Into an immortality, it seems only fair to add, that is proving much more vigorous than that which one can claim for most of the products of Brahmin culture.

Meanwhile, there was a literary problem involving another poor but important author who had cared very little, in his latest years, for either Lowell or the tradition which had nourished him. Edgar Allan Poe had died, tragically, in October, 1849. Lowell's first reaction was one of sympathy and pity. "I know only a single item of news which you will be interested in hearing," he wrote W. W. Story. "That is the lamentable end of poor Edgar Poe. He was picked up in the streets of Baltimore staggering under *delirium tremens,* and taken to the Hospital, where he died. Sad enough, and a man of real genius too." [7]

This innocently reported bit of news later involved Lowell in a good deal of correspondence. Back in February, 1845, he had done for *Graham's* a biographical and critical account of Poe, one of a series called "Our Authors." Now the harrassed Dr. Rufus Griswold—who found himself named as Poe's literary executor and charged with the task of publishing a four-volume edition of his works—began to write Lowell desperately for help. The proceeds from sales were to go exclusively to Poe's unfortunate mother-in-law, Mrs. Clemm. Wouldn't Lowell assist by bringing his sketch of the dead poet up to date? "It will be of very great advantage to Mrs. Clemm." Willis intended to make into an article what had generally been written about Poe by other critics. Griswold was willing to say in a note to Lowell's sketch "that you are to be held responsible for nothing else in the volume." [8]

The following months, as the labor of editing mounted, Griswold's resentment of his subject mounted with it. He allowed one statement to escape which explains to a considerable extent the general severity of his "Ludwig" article for Greeley's *Tribune*—especially such comments as, "Poe exhibited scarcely any virtue in either his life or his writings." [9] "Poe," he confessed in this note to Lowell, "was not my kind—I was not his—and he had no right to devolve upon me the duty of editing his works. He did do so, however, and under the circumstances I could not well refuse compliance with the wishes of his friends here [in New York]. From his constant habit of *repeating himself,* and from his habits of appropriation, particularly in the *Marginalia,* it is a difficult task; but I shall execute it as well as I can, in the short time that is allowed to me—that is, in *three weeks.*" [10] Reflection had not led him to regret his earliest remarks on the unfortunate poet's career. "I wrote a very hasty notice of Poe for the *Tribune* the moment I heard of his death. A part of it is quoted in the last Home Journal. Though badly done, I think it essentially just." A postscript to this letter requested copies of whatever reviews Poe had published of Lowell's own works. "If you will make any suggestions upon the subject, indicating what you would have reprinted, it will save me labor and greatly oblige me. . . . Any wish of yours will be an absolute law to me."

The essay on Poe with "a few alterations and omissions," was reprinted, as Griswold desired. As usual, Lowell is a long time working around to his subject. He must first talk of the fact that America has no literary capital, to conform to its political one. "Our capital city, unlike London or Paris, is not a great central heart from which life and vigor radiate to the extremities, but resembles more an isolated umbilicus, stuck down as near as may be to the center of the land, and seeming rather [to the good abolitionist!] to tell a legend of former usefulness than to serve any present need." The critic then declares that Poe was graduated from the University of Virginia "with highest honors," though it is only fair to remember that the "facts" for this sketch were sent Lowell by Poe himself. Then follows another long exhibit of Lowell's own talents. Proceeding from the thesis that "no certain augury can be drawn from a poet's earliest lispings," he amasses evidence from Shakespeare, Pope, Collins, Chatterton, Byron, Wordsworth, Coleridge, Cowley, and Milton, to establish his point. This done, he returns to Poe.

"Mr. Poe," he declares, "had that indescribable something which men have agreed to call genius." Then he qualifies. Poe did not reveal evidence of the "highest" genius. In 1845, however, Lowell still had been hopeful on this score. He may yet achieve this illusive quality, he said, by "zeal, industry, and a reverence for the trust reposed in him. . . . Mr. Poe has two of the prime qualities of genius, a faculty of vigorous yet minute analysis, and a wonderful fecundity of imagination." Lowell then differs with Poe in his view that the object of poetry is the creation of Beauty. Then, hedging again, he reminds his reader that perhaps "it is only in the definition of the word that we disagree." He adds that his subject is a conscious artist, that his writings have the merit of form. As for his style, it "is highly finished, graceful, and truly classical." [11]

But all this was for the public, and it dealt with Poe the writer, not with Poe the man. That he lacked "character" in this latter capacity was a view which Lowell never surrendered. Late in life, when asked for his views by George Woodberry, one of Poe's biographers, he could recall that Poe was short in stature, that his complexion was a clammy white, that his head was fine, his eyes dark, and his temples broad. "His manner was rather formal, even pompous, but I have the impression he was a little soggy with drink—not tipsy—but as if he had been holding his head under a pump to cool it." [12] Poe, at the interview referred to, had apparently felt a kindred disappointment. Lowell "called on me the other day," he wrote his friend T. H. Chivers, "but I was very much disappointed in his appearance. He is not half the noble looking person I expected to see." [13]

It was their only meeting, and it seems to prove, despite the fortuitous condition in which "poor Eddie" appeared at the moment (leading him, Mrs. Clemm implied, to "speak unkindly" [14] to his guest), that the ways of the two men's worlds were not to be reconciled by any ritual of manners. It may suggest, as well, a further truth which neither author appears to have perceived consciously: that the harmonious literary capital which Lowell had sighed for is, perhaps for the better, an impossible dream in a land so divergent as America.

All this while, there had been a lively discussion going on about the *Anti-Slavery Standard* and Lowell's relation to it. For more than a year his contributions to this weekly had been unfaltering and vigorous. In its pages, as has been seen, he had pressed his views with a militancy and wit against which no honest abolitionist could cavil. Every relevant public question, and every candidate for office, had been praised or damned according to the emancipator's code, and Lowell had done much to win for the publication a large, if erratic, following.

Yet its directors had suddenly grown troubled. They were in financial straits again, and they decided that a shake-up in the editorial policy of the magazine was imperative to its continuance. To that end, in May, 1849, it was agreed that Lowell's annual salary of $500 should be cut in half—that it be divided, in other words, with another correspondent, Edmund Quincy. In return, Lowell would be expected to contribute only half as often as before— every fortnight, that is, instead of once a week.

Wendell Phillips, secretary to the directors, informed him officially of the change, after the editor, Sydney H. Gay, had already broken the news in a personal note. Lowell's work had fulfilled their most sanguine expectations, Phillips wrote, but "deferring to our narrow means," the present proposal must be made. "I must earnestly hope that you will consent to it. Do not let me lose the charm of your name, the attraction of your style and the value of your criticism on the various events of the cause. I entreat you to stay with me. In a word, we *want* and *can't* spare you and won't take *no* for an answer. You must not find it in your conscience to offer it." [15]

Back of this letter was a series of minor differences which, taken together, had begun to assume fairly major proportions. More than a year before, Lowell had informed his friend Briggs, bluntly: "I do not agree with the abolitionists in their disunion and non-voting theories. They treat ideas as ignorant persons do cherries. They think them unwholesome unless they are swallowed, stones and all." There is Garrison, for instance, our leader. His trouble is that he "is so used to standing alone that, like Daniel Boone, he moves away as the world creeps up to him, and goes farther *into the wilderness*. He considers every step a step forward, though it be over the edge of a precipice." That he was a great and extraordinary man, Lowell admitted. The fact is simply that "there never has been a leader of reform who was not also a blackguard." [16]

Then there had been the confession, two months later, of his doubts about contributing to the magazine at all. "It is not the place for me. It *fags* me to deal with particulars. The tendency of my mind is too reflective. I can interest myself in general ideas (such as include the particulars), but weary of their application to the present." And the personal appeals of escaped slaves, of those brothers he was pledged to protect and also to aid—how deeply they were draining the reservoirs of his devotion to them! He was positively "beflead" with runaway slaves who wished to buy their wives from their owners, he wrote Gay. "They cut and come again. I have begun to fancy that polygamy is not unusual among them. What can I do? We, in principle, deny the right of compensation. But if a man comes and asks us to help him buy a wife or child, what are we to do? I cannot stand such an appeal. So, when I have money I give something; when I have none I subscribe, to be paid when I have. And I never can tell whether they are speaking truth or not." He mentioned a bootblack who worked for the Harvard students during the school year, but who left regularly each vacation and posed in other towns as a runaway slave, tearfully bent upon raising money to buy his wife's freedom. And all the while he had left one already, as free as a bird, back in Cambridge! [17]

But the heart of his differences remained the one he had mentioned the year before in his comment upon Garrison. "You know," he replied to Gay's announcement of the committee's action, "that I never agreed to the Dissolution-of-the-Union movement, and simply because I think it a waste of strength. Why do we not separate ourselves from the African whom we wish to elevate? from the drunkard? from the ignorant? At this minute the song of the bobolink comes rippling through my open window and preaches peace. Two months ago the same missionary was in his South Carolina pulpit, and can I think that he chose another text or delivered another sermon there? Hath not a slaveholder hands, organs, dimensions, senses, affections, passions?" Even slaveholders are human. "The longer I live the more I am convinced that the world must be healed by degrees." [18]

He wanted to say this to the committee, however, as plainly as he could: If its members *"wish* me to write once a fortnight, I am willing to do it. But if they only make that proposal to break my fall, I should choose to decline." To Gay, he wanted to add that he had all along entertained the idea of turning back his salary to him as resident editor "in case my income were increased from any other quarter." But let him never mind this unfulfilled ambition. The time for cherishing it was past.

He stayed on as associate editor for another full year, until May, 1850. Then it was proposed that he become corresponding editor— that is, that he write merely "now and then" for the magazine. Gay was assigned, again, to tell him the news in all gentleness.

Lowell was disgusted. "My dear Sydney, a kick in the breech may be either symbolical or actual, may be either bestowed with a velvet slipper or a cowhide boot; but it is, after all, a kick in the breech." He had apparently offered, the month before, to resign, since his views in opposition to dissolving the union were still resented by certain members of the committee. This time he had been taken at his word. "Instead of saying 'I resign,' a better form would be the passive 'I am resigned.' And so I am." But he wanted Gay to tell his committee something else: For every poem of his—except the exclusively antislavery ones—which was ever printed in the *Standard* he could have got four times the money they had paid. "This I wish them distinctly to understand, that they may not imagine that I came to them with my hat held out for an alms." [19]

He continued as correspondent desultorily, for still another year, until he sailed with his family for Italy. His views on slavery, and upon those who would compound with it, did not change. ("I should like to tack something to Mr. Webster—the most meanly and foolishly treacherous man I ever heard of—like the tail which I furnished to Mr. John P. Robinson." [20]) In his *Biglow Papers,* it will be recalled, a character had actually recommended disunion, the putting asunder of the alliance between "them thet God has no ways jined." [21] Yet that was merely armchair talk, merely "philosophical radicalism," not the real thing. Besides, it was Hosea who had said it, not the author. Now the leaders of the cause to which he had given so amply of his energy wanted to go further, were clamorous to pursue the logic of antislavery to its desperate end. That end proved, to Dr. Lowell's son, quite too gruesome to contemplate. His latent Brahminism cooled his head.

Meanwhile, late in 1849, he had published again, this time a two-volume edition of his collected *Poems*. The job of proofreading was quite losing its novelty for him. With the appearance of this book naturally came certain new resolutions, resolutions that embodied a broader and far less doctrinaire ambition in the troubled field of literature. He wrote out his views in a letter to Briggs which states excellently his own conception of his earlier work, and his plans for the future.

His poems hitherto, he said, had been a true record of his life, and he meant that they should continue to be. They had reflected a regular and natural sequence. "First, Love and the mere happiness of existence beginning to be conscious of itself; then Freedom —both being the sides which Beauty presented to me—and now I am going to try more *wholly* after Beauty herself. Next, if I live, I shall present Life as I have seen it. . . . I have preached sermons enow, and now I am going to come down out of the pulpit and *go about among my parish*. . . . Certainly I shall not grind for any Philistines, whether reformers or conservatives. I find that Reform cannot take up the whole of me, and I am quite sure that eyes were given us to look about us with sometimes, and not to be always looking forward. . . . I am tired of controversy." [22]

What was his home life like during these strenuous times? He was still occupying his third-story apartment at Elmwood, and he was naturally receiving a good many guests. One of them, Fredericka Bremer, who visited in Cambridge during the Christmas season of 1849, has written of the occasion with a disarming insight and accuracy. In December a friend accompanied her from Boston to the home on Tory Row, where she had been invited to stay. She was already enthusiastic about Lowell's works.

"There I have been now a week," she wrote on the fifteenth,

"and shall remain yet a week longer; they *will* have me stay and I am willing to stay because I am well off to my heart's content in this excellent and agreeable home. The house and a small quantity of land which surrounds it belong to the father of the poet, old Dr. Lowell, a handsome old man, universally beloved and respected, and the oldest minister of Massachusetts. He planted all the trees round the house, among which are many northern pines. The whole family assembles every day for morning and evening prayer around the venerable old man; and it is he who blesses every meal. His prayers, which are always extempore, are full of the true and inward life, and I felt them as a pleasant refreshing dew upon my head, and seldom arose from my knees with dry eyes.

"With him live his youngest son, the poet, and his wife; such a handsome and happy young couple as one can hardly imagine. He is full of life and youthful ardor; she is gentle, as delicate, and as fair as a lily, and one of the most loveable women that I have seen in this country, because her beauty is full of soul and grace, as is everything which she does or says. This young couple belong to the class of those of which one can be quite sure; one could not for an hour, nay half an hour, be doubtful about them. She, like him, has a poetical tendency, and has also written anonymously some poems, remarkable for their depth and tender feeling, especially maternal, but her mind has more philosophical depth than his. Singularly enough, I did not discern in him that deeply earnest spirit which charmed me in many of his poems. He seems to me to be occasionally brilliant, witty, gay, especially in the evening, when he has what he calls his 'evening fever,' and his talk is then like an incessant play of fireworks. I find him very agreeable and amiable; he seems to have many friends, mostly young men. Among his poems, the witty and satirical are the most popular; as, for example, his *Fable for Critics,* in which, in a good humored way, he has made himself merry with the poets and poetesses of New England [*sic*], only one of whom, Margaret Fuller, is severely handled. His satirical, political, fugitive pieces have been very successful.

"As one of his merits, I reckon his being so fascinated by his little wife, because I am so myself. There is a trace of beauty and taste in everything she touches, whether of mind or body; and above all, she beautifies life. Among other beautiful things which she has created around her in her home, I have remarked a little basin full of beautiful stones and shells, which she herself collected; they lie glittering in water clear as crystal, and round them is a border of coral. Pity it is that this much-loved young wife seems to have delicate lungs. Her low weak voice tells of this. Two lovely little girls, Mabel and Rose, the latter yet at the mother's breast, and an elder sister of the poet, one of the worthy and the good, constitute the remainder of the family." [23]

The tragedy behind this amiable exterior Miss Bremer may have sensed, but, if so, her awareness of it was not recorded. The elder Mrs. Lowell was confined to an asylum, was lost to the family, was apparently not even mentioned by them. There had also been the poet's first child, Blanche, whom he had cherished so completely, had ministered to with such unstinted care. She had died in March, 1847, at the age of fourteen months. Mabel, his second, was born half a year later; she was the only one of his children to survive him. Next there was Rose, born in July, 1849. Six weeks after Fredericka Bremer visited the family Rose, too, was dead. He would have no funeral for her, Lowell said to Gay. "My father only made a prayer, and then I walked up alone to Mount Auburn and saw her body laid by her sister's. . . . Dear little child! she had never spoken, only smiled." [24] Eight weeks later his mother died. Of his own generation there were left, now, Charles Russell, his oldest brother; Rebecca, who still managed the house; Mary, who had married Samuel Putnam in 1832; Robert, also married and away from home; and his father, broken, almost completely, with grief and with the inevitable infirmities of age. Of his children, then, only Mabel, aged three, was living when Maria bore her husband his last child. It was an only son, christened Walter.

They were both tired when the spring of 1851 came round, and Maria was not only tired but weak and ill. Lowell had written Gay several months before of his plans to go abroad when summer came, if he could sell some land to pay their expenses. The land in question his wife had inherited from her parents; it had thus far been kept intact. "How long we shall stay I know not, but the farther I can get from *American* slavery the better I shall feel." In a later note he spoke more definitely and more enthusiastically of their plans. In Italy, he had heard, people could live like princes "on fifteen hundred a year." They were going to travel on their own property. "That is, we shall spend at the rate of about ten acres a year, selling our birthright as we go along for messes of European pottage."[25] They sailed July 12, 1851. With them were Walter and Mabel, a nurse, and (as guardian against the already too familiar hazards of infancy) a milch goat.[26]

IX

*He [Michael Angelo] is the apostle of the exaggerated, the
Victor Hugo of Painting and Sculpture."*
Lowell, *Works*, I, 246

DURING this first fifteen-month stay abroad, Lowell wrote
few letters that have survived, but he kept a Journal that reflects with fair accuracy the ideas which engaged him during this
interesting trip. Their yield for the reader who is curious about the
complexities of the human intellect is scant, and lacking in nourishment. Perhaps it would be unfair to expect any considerable rich-
ness in them in the first place. He was tired of controversy, had
uttered to exhaustion the dogmas of his abolitionist circle, and he
badly needed a change of environment. He shed his coat of moral
rectitude without effort, although the operation bared the essential
shallowness of his mind. It left him with little to rely upon, except
the recollections of his varied reading and his talent for amusing
observations of foreign temperaments. Deprived of a Cause, and of
a Cause's urgency, he became discursive, flabby, and essentially tedious in his prose. Only his friends, it seems, could read with continuing interest what he wrote formally; only his reputation as an
author could justify its being printed at all.

He had gone to the Old World for the same basic reason which
had prompted Washington Irving to go there, more than two decades before him: The United States comprised a great nation, admittedly, and the natural scenery of the country was incomparable;
nevertheless, our culture was young. Europe, on the other hand,
"was rich in the accumulated treasures of age. Her very ruins told
the history of times gone by, and every mouldering stone was a
chronicle." This Irving had frankly declared, and Lowell in a
similar mood complained in his Journal: "What we always feel the
artistic want of at home is background. It is all idle to say we are

Englishmen, and that English history is ours too." What made this argument meaningless, he went on, was the fact that history can signify little to those who have dissociated themselves from the regions in which it developed. This barrenness was reflected everywhere in our arts. "Surely, in all that concerns aesthetics, Europeans have us at an immense advantage."[1] He would go there, then, to recapture, as well as one could, the still radiant glories of a world that had hitherto been revealed to him only vicariously, through books. He would substitute for this unsatisfying medium the reality of direct experience.

He sailed on a clipper ship, the *Sultana*. It was a beautiful vessel, one that taxed his credulity to believe "that such a wonder could be built of canvas as that white many-storied pile of cloud that stooped over me or drew back as we rose and fell with the waves." For five weeks they were at sea. It was a tedious voyage, so tedious, he said, that "I no longer wonder at the cruelty of pirates." The random visits of whales that rose suddenly to the side of the ship and said *Pooh,* and meditations upon the fact that Progress was robbing the world of its old enchantment—these things alone served to free the interval of an otherwise unalloyed monotony.

As refuge, during the Atlantic stretch of the journey, he relieved his mind of its accumulated erudition. Allusions to the great authors of the past—who are lugged into the record by a truly talented circuitousness—struggle to pad it with an appropriate dignity, however they may retard its narrative interest. Montaigne, Ulysses, Dr. Faustus, Don Juan, Tannhäuser, the French Revolution, and Longfellow's travel book, *Outre Mer,* are called into service for a fourteen-line comment on the sea serpent, while references to Thor, Marco Polo, *The Tempest,* Milton, the City of Lok, Dante, El Dorado, Prester John, Thomas Browne, and Herodotus crown another page that is devoted to the mysterious interest which the world held for early travelers.[2] With the lament that each year robs the earth more and more of its poetry, he leaves the Atlantic (Part I of his Journal) for that more historic body of water, "The Mediterranean." It is here that, apparently for the first time, he takes note of any companion on the voyage. It is the chief mate, and he describes him in detail, noting especially his hearty sympathy with that "manly metal," iron. Afterwards, a brief tribute to the cleanliness of an English inn at Malta brings him to the heart of his work, the section devoted to Italy.

"Italy" is introduced with a discourse upon Fielding and *Jonathan Wild*. Next comes Goethe, after him Ovid, and then Pepys, Mrs. Grundy, Ulysses, and Montaigne.[3] The irony of the several pages which contain this self-conscious display of erudition is that Lowell, while hammering his reader with it, is developing the thesis that to travel and tell what you have "actually seen" is a most difficult job. "In ninety-nine books out of a hundred does not the tourist bore us with the sensations he thinks he ought to have experienced, instead of letting us know what he thought and felt?" It requires him five pages to get around to his first observation about the country, and it was one he had doubtless arrived at before he sailed: Italy's charm is that she gives the traveler cheaply "what gold cannot buy for him at home, a Past at once legendary and authentic."

His next statement of importance is a revised version of his first: "There are two kinds of travellers,—those who tell us what they went to see and those who tell us what they saw. The latter class are the only ones whose journals are worth sifting." The reader, by this time, has been furnished with one other detail about Italy. "Is it not the chief charm of the land, that it is changeless without being Chinese?" Lowell, from this point, deletes a good deal of the material he had originally written. Our next glimpse of him is dated April 20, 1851—nine months after he sailed. He has devoted seventy-five hundred words to his announced subject, Italy. The student who has read them is repaid with the information just noted—that the best travel books are rich in direct observation, and that Italy is both a changeless and a legended land. No argument about the mid-nineteenth century being a more leisurely age than the present—and therefore more tolerant of discursiveness—can justify such flabby composition. The truth is that, although Lowell had the urge to write, he had simply nothing to say at the time.

The Journal admittedly improves after this point, though for a reason perhaps too obvious to need naming. It contains several lively comments on the Italian temperament. There was the people's instinct for bargaining, for instance, a characteristic which appeared universal among them. "They do not feel happy if they get their first price. So easy a victory makes them sorry they had not asked twice as much, and, besides, they love the excitement of the contest." One would think that millions were at stake—instead of some two-cent earthern pot, or trinket—to judge from the flying offers and counter offers, the protests and denunciations that rend the mild air constantly in the shopping districts. "A single turnip is argument enough with them till midnight." But it was a game, and both contestants delighted in it; nor would either, Lowell adds, have been happy without it. Elsewhere he remarks, "if I were asked to name one universal characteristic of an Italian town, I should say, two men clamoring and shaking themselves to pieces at each other, and a woman leaning lazily out of a window, and perhaps looking at something else. Till one gets used to this kind of thing, one expects some horrible catastrophe; but during eight months in Italy I have only seen blows exchanged thrice."

The impetuosity of these people led him to certain reflections about his own countrymen. Perhaps even they could profit from an occasional fit of temper. America, he said, seems a land without thunderstorms. Our nation is materialistic, and in proportion as the commercial instinct dominates, do we not also become dispassionate and incapable of electric emotions? Men cannot live by intellect alone. Brain is always to be bought, but passion never comes to market. "On the whole, I am rather inclined to like this European impatience and fire, even while I laugh at it, and sometimes find myself surmising whether a people who, like the Americans, put up quietly with all sorts of petty personal impositions and injustices, will not at length find it too great a bore to quarrel with great public wrongs." [4]

Considered more specifically, the Journal contained several interesting comments upon certain institutions and heroes of the country.

Like almost every literary visitor of this period, Lowell set forth his opinion of the Catholic Church. "Suppose," he said, paraphrasing Keats, "that a man in pouring down a glass of claret could drink the South of France, that he could so disintegrate the wine by the force of imagination as to taste in it all the clustered beauty and bloom of the grape, all the dance and song and sunburnt jollity of the vintage." This is what the great poets do for us, and it is what the Catholic church does for religion, "feeding the soul not with the essential religious sentiment, not with a drop or two of the tincture of worship, but making us feel one by one all those original elements of which worship is composed." [5] This was the one church, it seemed to him, which had been loyal to both the heart and the soul of Man, that had clung to her faith in the imagination, and that refused to "give over her symbols and images and sacred vessels to the perilous keeping of the iconoclast Understanding." It is the one poet among all the churches. It wisely provides for the childish in men.

Holding these views, he naturally found St. Peter's an unforgettable sight. He linked it best in its noonday silence and solitude, "when the sunlight, made visible by the mist of the ever-burning lamps in which it was entangled, hovered under the dome like the holy dove goldenly descending. Very grand also is the twilight, when all outlines melt into mysterious vastness, and the arches expand and lose themselves in the deepening shadow. Then, standing in the desert transept, you hear the far off vespers swell and die like low breathings of the sea on some conjectured shore." And there were the occasional illuminations of the cathedral, which he went to see with a never-waning rapture, and contemplated until his mind could endure no more unless he withdrew for a troubled while to cool his eyes with darkness.

But it was not all St. Peter's and illuminations in Rome; there were, as always, the beggars, and the trifling laborers, and the works of Michael Angelo, who had misconceived the true nature of art. Macaulay, Bayard Taylor, Mark Twain, and practically every literary traveler in Italy has come away with his indignant story about the beggars. Lowell decided that beggary was an institution in the country. These rascals had escaped the curse of Adam, for, though often in the best of health, they regarded every day as one of freedom from all secular labor. Their mendacity was sanctioned by the Church. And to so many did this sanction extend that it seemed impossible for a stranger to say who *might not* beg in the city. The practice seemed to be "a sudden madness that may seize any one at the sight of a foreigner." Lowell began to feel wary even of cardinals, after seeing so many elegant hats come off in his presence to the accompaniment of prayers for alms. Once he attempted to confuse a begging friar. The good Catholic asked for a subscription for repairing his convent. "Ah, but I am a heretic," Lowell interrupted. "Undoubtedly," replied his wholly complacent visitor, "but your money is perfectly orthodox."

Then take the laborers. One of them while on the job will trail a small wheel barrow up to another who stands leaning on a long spade. "Arriving, he fumbles for his snuff box, and offers it deliberately to his friend. Each takes an ample pinch, and both seat themselves to await the result. If one should sneeze, he receives the *Felicità!* of the other; and, after allowing the titillation to subside, he replies, *Grazia!* Then follows a little conversation, and then they prepare to load. But it occurs to the barrow-driver that this is a good opportunity to fill and light his pipe; and to do so conveniently he needs the barrow to sit upon. He draws a few whiffs and a little more conversation takes place. The barrow is now ready; but first the wielder of the spade will fill his pipe also. This done, more whiffs and more conversation. Then a spoonful of earth is thrown into the barrow, and it starts on its return. But midway it meets an empty barrow, and both stop to go through the ceremonial once more, and to discuss whatever new thing has occurred in the excavation since their last encounter. And so it goes all day." [6] Lowell's sense of humor was omnipresent, and such a practice amused him, but how its wastefulness rankled within his thrifty New England soul!

Then there was the world's most acclaimed sculptor-painter, Michael Angelo. "Shall I confess it?" he asked. This man seemed to him, "in his angry reaction against sentimental beauty, to have mistaken bulk and brawn for the antithesis of feebleness. He is the apostle of the exaggerated, the Victor Hugo of painting and sculpture. I have a feeling that rivalry was a more powerful motive with him than love of art, that he had the conscious intention to be original, which seldom leads to anything better than being extravagant. The show of muscle proves strength, not power." These, he said, were his second thoughts, though, when coolly considered, they somehow appeared both niggardly and unjust. There was the dome of St. Peter's, for instance. But then there were so many domes in Italy; they seemed to be the *goitre* of architecture. So heavy they were, so lacking in grace! His mind wandered to St. Mark's, in Venice, which contained the only light dome he ever saw. Still the interior effect of St. Peter's was noble. Yet for both outward and inward impressiveness, he said, give him a Gothic cathedral.

His thoughts trailed off, became blurred, and on the subject of cathedrals they remained inconclusive. But the fact that he disapproved of too much originality, of too violent a repudiation of conventional forms, was evident three years later in his comment on Whitman. He, too, had mistaken brawn for real strength. The kind of thing which he writes "wont do," Lowell declared to the friend who became his literary executor, C. E. Norton. "When a man aims at originality he acknowledges himself consciously unoriginal, a want of self respect which does not often go along with the capacity for great things." [7] Whitman's case reminded him again of the great Florentine who "cocked his hat a little wee bit too much." Eight years later his critical opinion on this matter remained unaltered. Of Whitman's *Leaves of Grass* he wrote then: "It is a book I never looked into farther than to satisfy myself that it was a solemn humbug." It was an "evil" volume, he went on; he would "take care to keep it out of the way" of students at Harvard.[8] This was a view that embodied one of his most consistently held convictions about the arts. At his intimate intellectual table he preferred to dine with such easy, graceful, and polished gentlemen as his good Brahmin friends back home. The Mark Twains, the Melvilles, the Whitmans—and the Angelos—must wait in his outward rooms.

His activities and personal problems in Italy are a good deal more engaging than his thoughts. The family's first stop of any importance was in Florence, where they stayed from late August to the end of October. He has left little record of this interval, although we do know that, just before departing for Rome, he received news from Elmwood which distressed him greatly. His father had been stricken with paralysis.[9] His first impulse was to return home at once with the entire family. Yet, on reflection, such an act appeared both futile and dangerous—futile because, once there, he would be helpless; dangerous because a crossing so late in the year might permanently destroy Maria's too uncertain health. They had gone to Italy in the first place, she implied in a letter to Mrs. Frances Shaw, because the necessity had become for her the ultimate one of either "life or death." [10] Lowell wrote his father immediately. "I should never have left home," he said, "if I had not thought that you wished it, or rather wished that we should have been abroad and got back. . . . I find nothing abroad which, having been seen, would tempt me away from Elmwood again."

In the capital, later news proved even worse. There was no hope of Dr. Lowell's recovery. "The dear Elmwood that has always looked so sunny in my memory comes now between me and the sun, and the long shadow of its eclipse follows and falls upon me everywhere. It is a wonderful satisfaction to me now to feel that that dear Father and I have been so much at one and have been sources of so much happiness to each other for so many years." What could one do but try to remember the past, now that the present had grown cheerless, utterly?

The mild Italian winter set in, and he became reconciled to his familiar, Sadness. And soon word that was much more encouraging reached him from friends back in Cambridge. Dr. Lowell was much improved. Lowell began to visit the sights, to take long walks in the always shining sun, to observe the strange agelessness of the country. As has been implied, he was not wholly pleased by what he noticed. "Add malaria and the idea of desolation to an Illinois prairie, and you have the Campagna." He went to a Christmas service. "I stood," he declared, "among the undistinguished faithful, and it being a fast, there was such a smell as if Weathersfield had been first deluged and then cooked by subterranean fires. I stood wedged between some very strong devotees (who must have squandered the savings of a year in a garlic debauch) in abject terror lest my head should be colonized from some of the overpopulated districts around me."[11] But he studied the painters with considerable diligence. Of the more prominent ones, he wrote a friend, "I can now distinguish the style and motive almost at a glance. Sometimes I make a particular study of a particular artist, if any gallery is especially rich in his works. Life is rather more picturesque here than with us, and I find that I am accumulating a certain kind of wealth which may be useful to me hereafter."

And there were private theatricals in which he took part, along with other visiting Englishmen and Americans. He was especially pleased to make his debut on the stage in the rôle of Shakespeare's Pyramus, and later in that of Bottom, the weaver. He wrote the prologue for both performances. Maria was happy too, relishing the simple pleasures of the consumptive, finding each day one of renewed, if transient, delight as it broke over the hills she would live to see no more. "Day after day and week after week of sunshine we have had, and they tell us that winter is nearly over and the spring will soon be here." And what a contrast this season was to the bleak and enduring frigidities of New England! The oranges hung on the trees where they had the protection of a wall to shelter them, and the carnations bloomed continually. In Florence, even last autumn, the crocus had flowered everywhere—"whole fields purple with their delicate wings and looking like butterflies who had mistaken their season and come out of the ground before their time."[12] For neither of them, though neither could know it, would there ever be another interval like this. They were the perfect days of Launfal's Vision.

The illusion they had woven was rudely shattered, almost before its vividness was over. Their only son, Walter, had grown and thriven "finely"; [13] he had begun to cut his teeth, had learned his *a-b-c's,* and was already showing a remarkable affection for his father. "He is the fairest boy that ever was seen," Lowell wrote, "and has the bluest eyes and is the baldest person in Rome except two middle aged Englishmen, who, you know, have a great knack that way. In a word, he is one of that countless number of extraordinary boys out of which the world contrives afterwards to make such extraordinary men." [14]

But the world, in this case, was to want the opportunity. Maria recounted to Mrs. Shaw, in early July, a story that had by this time become familiar with her. "The baby," she said, "was remarkably well and running around all day in the garden, but that very night he was taken ill, and after nearly a month's intense solicitude and anxiety all was over.... I am tired of broken promises, and dare not think of a future for Mabel. She is well now, today, but I have no certainty for tomorrow." [15]

That quiet, intense, and patient spirit was crushed by this last catastrophe. Four children she had borne her husband, in pain and with ever-augmenting sacrifices of her health. Now, of that four, only one survived. Of what could a mortal be certain on this earth? She might find consolation in the latest doctor's doubtful diagnosis, which declared that not tubercular germs but only an irritation was discoverable in her lungs. She might even welcome, fitfully, the cheerful moods that are peculiar to victims of her then incurable disease. But the fire of her necessity had gone out. Espousing sorrow for her husband's sake had become at length an inevitable condition against which it appeared now altogether futile to contend. They traveled on into Switzerland, into England, Scotland, and Wales. On the ship that sailed from Liverpool, the thirteenth of October, 1852, they found as companions both Thackeray and Matthew Arnold's friend, Clough. But the stay in Italy had matured them both, and had saddened one of them, forever. The Old World had not fulfilled its glad promise. Its illusion of happiness and restoration had gone to pieces.

X

*"I am obliged to you, however, for calling my attention to
a part of this book [Leaves of Grass] of which I knew
nothing, and I will take care to keep it out of the way of
the students [of Harvard]."*

Lowell to the Reverend W. L. Gage, December 7, 1863.
New Letters, 116

LOWELL'S thirteen-day crossing to America was greatly enlivened by the companionship of his two English acquaintances. For Thackeray his esteem was to remain cordial to the end;
with Clough it was soon to develop into a close friendship. The
former went on to New York, to begin his lectures on the English
humorists. Clough, on the other hand, seems to have gone almost
at once to Cambridge, where a round of dinners and entertainments immediately began to be given in his honor. Longfellow
dined and wined him, Emerson followed with a dinner and an evening at one of Albani's concerts, and afterwards Lowell had the
talented visitor as his guest at Elmwood.[1] He also wrote his friend
Briggs, now editor of *Putnam's Monthly,* to be certain to solicit
Clough's services for that new magazine.

Clough has left a record of one of his days at Lowell's home.
"Yesterday," he declared, "I had a walk with James Lowell to a very
pretty spot, Beaver Brook. Then I dined with him, his wife, and
his father, a fine old gentleman who is stone deaf, but talks to you.
He began by saying that he was born an Englishman, i.e., before
the Revolution [was over]. Then he went on to say, 'I have stood
as near to George III as to you now; I saw Napoleon crowned Em-
peror'; then, 'Old men are apt to be garrulous, especially about themselves; I saw the present Sultan ride through Constantinople on
assuming the throne;' and so on—all in a strong clear voice, and
in perfect sentences, which you saw him making beforehand. And

all one could do was bow and look expressive, for he could only just hear you when his son got up and shouted in his ear." [2]

Lowell made several "plunges" into literature during the next few months, but the result is unimportant to his history. Temporarily away on a trip to New York, he received several letters from Maria and Mabel. "It is a sunny afternoon," his wife declared in late January, 1853, "and I am writing to thee in the parlor with the light of a cheerless sky upon the paper and plenty of wind in the pine branches, although it is not very cold. The gold fishes are balancing themselves as usual, Spangle looking very small in the background and Black Fin enormous in the distance like Hogarth's picture of Perspectives. They *do* eat crumbs most greedily, a fact which I keep from Mabel, for the bowl would soon be converted into a huge bread pudding if she had any idea of it." [3]

Four days later came a note from his only daughter. "I am much obliged to you for telling me that you would bring me something from New York," she said. The servant, Bridget, had put her wax doll, christened Lily, beside the entry stove and melted off her eyebrow. "Mamma has made a new one but one eye is bigger than the other." There was more news about her dog, Spice. He had written Lowell a letter, "or Grandpapa wrote for him"; Mabel could not decide. In this note, Spice had declared that he did not like to be dragged around by his paw. "I think Grandpapa is a great rogue," she added.

Lowell was away again in early April, and again his wife's letters to him contained that same wistful detailing of familiar incidents to which he had by this date become reconciled. "I was glad when I saw through the closed blinds the long bright lines of light that promised thee a pleasant day. I am better and less nervous than I was yesterday, so thee needst not have any fears on my account. Lois came yesterday afternoon and took tea and spent the evening with me, so that I had no time for sad or lonely thoughts. Mabel is out under my window building a house for Spice. The house consists of a tea chest into which poor Spice is crushed as mysteriously as the geni into his box, and then a heavy board is laid upon it.

As she cannot, however, resist peeping in, to see how he is enjoying himself, he takes the chance to spring out and then off they rush together over the garden till'he is caught and brought back again." There was no worry about the future in these brief letters, no reflection any more of a troubled spirit. Instead, her husband found in them only a record of the day's innocent diversions, unless it be that, in their overtones, he sensed what really was lurking there— the echo of a final surrender to the arrogances of an inscrutable world.

To her, in turn, he sent home a diary which recounted the first big-game hunt of his life. He called this work "A Moosehead Journal," and its material was based upon a trip to Maine, made during the summer of 1853 with his nephew Charles. It was addressed to his friend W. W. Story (as "Edelmann Storg"), and Lowell concluded it by confessing that he well knew there was very little about Moosehead Lake in it, not even the Latin name for Moose. He had not intended, he said, to talk about this animal in the first place. He meant, rather, to write simply a journal, "and, moreover, *my* journal, with a little nature, a little human nature, and a great deal of I in it, which last ingredient I take to be the true spirit of this species of writing."

True enough, one would certainly add, if the "I" in question had very much of either interest or importance to communicate. The barrenness of the work is painfully evident to anyone who has read, by contrast, a book like Thoreau's *Week on the Concord and Merrimac Rivers*: Lowell describes the scenery in Maine, and moralizes on man's indifference to nature. He moralizes, next, upon old houses—they have character, he says; he has never seen one which he thought old enough to be torn down. After this follows more moralizing on the mad hurry of our lives. Then there is more description of scenery, an account of his journey by stage to the lake, and an account of Uncle Zeb, a representative New England backwoods character. Lowell's interest in the dialect of this man and in the personalities of his guides alone redeem his pages from complete monotony. The taciturn woodsmen won him unreservedly.

He had never, he wrote, seen more essential courtesy than was manifest in them. "They have all the virtues of the sailor, without that unsteady roll in the gait with which the ocean proclaims itself quite as much in the moral as in the physical habit of a man. They appeared to me to have hewn out a short northwest passage through wintry woods to those spice-lands of character which we dwellers in cities must reach, if at all, by weary voyages in the monotonous track of the trades." This was perhaps his most interesting observation during the trip. He fished a little, and on one occasion his party actually sighted a moose. But the mist from the water had so dampened their cartridges that they failed to explode; there was only the *click, click* of the rifles, as one after another missed fire. To Lowell, these frustrations did not greatly matter. He had gone in the birch (or canoe) with his friends, true enough, but he had declined to carry a gun.[4]

When Maria received the manuscript of this record of his vacation (he sent it to her before forwarding a copy to Story), her fatal illness was already advanced too far for any written word to retard. On his return, he resumed his efforts to revive her; he sent verses she had written to Briggs, and the friendly editor published them. But the decline went on, unfought on her part, and in large measure, it appears, unregretted. "I have copied a poem of Maria's," Lowell wrote on October 6, "which it would be a great pleasure to me to see in the next number. The delight which it gives me to see them printed and liked is a great pleasure to her. And it gives her something to think about—a sort of tie to this world, as it were. I cannot bear to write it, but she is very dangerously ill—growing weaker and weaker. . . . It is only within the last week that I have realized the danger. She has been so often ill and rallied from it that I supposed she would soon begin to get better. But there seems no force left now." [5] He never framed a more accurate sentence. Three weeks after he wrote it she was dead.

Where could one turn now—to what solaces of a long incredible dogma? He faced death as a modern man; there was only the unthinkable reality of his loss, only the stunned awareness that, come what may, this constant companion of the past nine years had been taken from him, forever. Of their four children, only one remained —Mabel, a child of six. It was almost a month before he could write Briggs again. "I do abhor sentimentality from the bottom of my soul," he said then, "and cannot wear my grief upon my sleeve, but yet I look forward with agony to the time when she may become a memory instead of a real presence." He could no longer see her, even in his mind; could no longer even sense her presence at the door, greeting him when he came home at evening. It was all unreal, appeared as if it had never been. "I keep myself employed most of the time—in something mechanical as much as possible—and in walking."

Nor was the state of things at Elmwood calculated to make his suffering more endurable. There was the unhappy memory of his mother, blending itself now with more poignant and more immediate recollections. Then, among those who survived, there was his father. The old man was, at this date, not only stone deaf but at times highly, even alarmingly, excitable. And there was his sister Rebecca. Her eccentricity, always pronounced, had grown worse. For days she would roam the house tirelessly, or sit alone in her room, never speaking a word. Lowell himself would rush out occasionally to parties, would reveal at them an almost hysterical gayety that astonished even his friends, only to return home and despise himself. And at night, late, as he lay in his bed and strained his eyes through the palpable darkness, a vision of Maria would form itself before him, silently shining amid a crescent of angels.[6]

The half-year that followed was a fitful one, naturally. He continued to write for *Putnam's* and *Graham's*. He meditated an edition of Shakespeare and a biography of Swift. Certainly he must do *something,* at any rate, for his income from the property his wife had left him amounted to a bare $600 annually. At length he settled down and edited Marvell, for the series of *British Poets.* For the same series he did his essay on Keats, one of the most trivial commentaries he ever wrote. His best work during this period was unquestionably his nostalgic re-creation of the village of his childhood: "Cambridge Thirty Years Ago."[7] Briggs published it in *Putnam's* during the spring of 1854.

As the season warmed toward summer, Lowell's indignation began to warm with it, touched off by his old hatred of the Fugitive Slave Law. A Negro, Anthony Burns, had been captured by the authorities in Boston and returned to his owner, a Virginia merchant. Such abject compliance made Lowell despise his state. Its people, he said, "seem to take a positive pleasure in doing anything for a man whom they think an aristocrat; and while the Virginia newspapers are descanting on the meritoriousness of shooting Yankee schoolmasters, they are inviting a Virginia slaveholder to dinner. By St. Paul! if things go on and the old Puritan spirit once more get up again (if it be not dead), we may send them schoolmasters such as Oliver sent to Ireland."[8] Although he had already admitted his boredom with "controversy" several years before, the fact had in no sense altered his faith in the justice of the cause which he had once served, militantly, for more than half a decade.

Late in June he left Elmwood for a vacation on the coast. He visited the Charles Eliot Nortons at a Newport then still capable of a simple way of life. From there he went on to Beverley ("the bay of Naples translated into New England dialect"), where his sister-in-law, Mrs. Charles Lowell, had taken a place for the season. The interval was relaxing for him. He rowed and fished and talked with the natives, baked his skin in the steady sun, and dined upon that food which nourished them all at the village—the Lotus. It was a cunning dish, he went on, apt to take various shapes. Sometimes it was fish, or flesh; again it would appear as fowl or eggs. Yet it was always, it seemed to him, Lotus really, inducing not forgetfulness, but Memory that was no longer recollection, because it was passive and able to film his mind at least partly from the shattering realities of the previous year.[9] Yet at times the film proved wholly frail. "It is very beautiful here," he declared to Edmund Quincy, "but the beauty makes me sad when I am alone, thinking how one beautiful soul would have delighted in it all. It is just in the sandiest spots that the springs of sorrow seem to rise, and what witch hazel is there that can point to the associations that set them flowing? The other day I saw two girls in red shawls coming through a lane and found the tears on my cheeks." [10]

When he returned to Elmwood, in October, he began plans for the private publication of Maria's poems. He also wrote E. A. Duyckinck about her, hoping that this editor would see fit to include some specimen of her work in his forthcoming *Cyclopaedia of American Literature*. "All that was written of Lady Digby," Lowell told him, "all that Taylor said of the Countess of Carbery, and Donne of Elizabeth Drury—belongs as well to her, she was so beautiful and good." [11] In other letters he encouraged W. J. Stillman, who had begun a new literary magazine, *The Crayon*. Stillman had recently visited him at Elmwood, making him "fifteen years younger" while he stayed. Lowell was working desperately, all this while, on a series of lectures that were to prove momentous to his future.

This series he had been asked by a relative to deliver at the Lowell Institute in Boston. His general theme was the nature of poetry and the work of the Major English exponents of this art. Having taken payment for the entire course in advance, he was left with no alternative but that of planning all twelve of the lectures as coherently as the time would allow. He delivered the first one January 9, 1855, before a crowded house ("the lectures are *gratis,*" he explained to Stillman)—a house so crowded, in fact, that he was forced to repeat it the following afternoon to those who could not find standing room the night before. Even Longfellow was enthusiastic: "Mr. Richard Grant White, of New York, author of Shakespeare's Scholar, came to tea. He drove in with us to hear Lowell's first lecture; an admirable performance, and a crowded audience." [12] Afterwards they returned to Norton's for supper with the lecturer.

Longfellow's reaction was typical. Charles Sumner wrote from the Senate Chamber that Lowell's remarks on Milton had lifted him "for a whole day. It was the utterance of genius in honor of genius." [13] And from near-by Connecticut the "Sweet Singer of

Hartford," Lydia Huntley Sigourney, soon expressed herself in rhapsody to the now established critic-poet. "The echo of your voice," she wrote him, "has traveled beyond the old Bay State. I must thank you for its droppings of harmony, which have cheered my fireside on the banks of the Connecticut." An attentive friend, she went on, had sent Lowell's remarks to her each week, as they were duly reported by the *Advertiser*. She had read them all with "intense delight." Would he not give them this splendid literature in a volume, that they may be no longer tantalized by the "garblings of the periodical press? And before your departure for Europe, if you should be in this region, will you not favor me with the sight of your countenance and the sound of your voice?" [14] Out of her "admiration of genius" she made this request. Forty volumes to her credit attested the flattering distinction it implied!

The reference to Europe was important, and accurate. On January 31, 1855, Longfellow had written in his Journal, jubilantly, "Lowell is to be my successor. Dr. Walker talked with me about it this morning, and the matter is as good as settled." [15] He was thinking, when he wrote, of the Smith Professorship of Modern Languages, at Harvard. Longfellow had held the position since 1836, when he had succeeded George Ticknor, one of the early products of German scholarship in America. Lowell's annual salary would be $1,200. It was a salary, he declared, which would make him independent. And, moreover, unlike Longfellow, he would have to deliver only two courses of lectures each year. He accepted the offer with the reservation that he be allowed another year abroad to prepare himself to assume its responsibilities competently.

But before he went, he answered the demands of his public by setting forth upon a lecture tour. The experience was a sad one, though profitable. He described the routine of it in a letter from Madison, Wisconsin, in April: "To be received at a bad inn by a solemn committee, in a room with a stove that smokes but not exhilarates, to have three cold fish-tails laid in your hand to shake, to be carried to a cold lecture room, to read a cold lecture to a cold audience, to be carried back to your smoke-side, paid and the three fish-tails again—well, it's not delightful exactly. On the whole I was so desperate that, after a week of it, I wrote out hither to be let off—but they would not, and so here I am. I shall go home with six hundred dollars in my pockets, and one of those insects so common in Italy and Egypt in my ear. Sometimes, though, one has very pleasant times, and one gets *tremendous* puffs in the local papers." [16] From Canandaigua, New York, he had already expressed himself, in more specific terms, about the accompaniments of one of his evenings upon the platform. "After the lecture," he wrote his daughter Mabel, "I was invited to Mrs. (I forget her name), where I met Mr. Filmore who used to be President of the United States, and who is one of the stupidest-looking men I ever saw—a *very* foolish person as far as looks go." [17] The growing American ideal of culture, available in tickets that sold for $2.00 a year, was one which did not attract him at all. A lecture tour, he felt, was exclusively a business transaction. If it meant anything more lofty to the lecturer, his record of the fact apparently has not survived.

When he departed for Europe his second time, after a series of farewell dinners, he again booked passage on a sailing vessel. On this occasion it was the *St. Nicholas,* and he went alone, leaving Mabel in Cambridge under the care of his sister-in-law, Mrs. Estes Howe,[18] and a governess, Miss Frances Dunlap.

His earliest letters from abroad were dated from London, the second week of August. Before reaching there he had spent three weeks in Paris, looking at pictures and meeting important people. Chief among them were the Brownings. Mr. Browning explained to him certain mysteries of the art of painting. Mrs. Browning inspired him, as she inspired so many other romantic Americans. "She is always associated in my mind," he declared, "with Beatrice and with the better part of my life." He had also been reading Tennyson's "Maud," and his reaction to it, as to the lady who wrote such amorous, yet chaste sonnets, was likewise one of complete capitulation. He thought the poem "wonderfully fine—the antiphonal voice of *In Memoriam.* I tried to read it aloud, but broke down in the middle in a subdued passion of tears." [19]

The next day he wrote his daughter, describing a present he had bought for her. "Tell Aunt Lois and Uncle Estes and Miss Dunlap that I did not forget them and would have sent them something too, only that I wish you to feel that you are always the first person with me—so they must wait for their presents till some other time. I send you also dear Mamma's watch which you may wear whenever Miss Dunlap thinks you are large enough. There is a gold chain belonging to it. Mary knows where it is. I wish you to understand that everything that was Mamma's is yours now and that Papa only keeps them for you. But you must be very good to be worthy to wear them." [20]

He saw the sights in England, looked at more pictures, more cathedrals, and dined with his friend Thackeray, who read to him from *The Newcombes*. "Give my love to Longfellow," he said to Norton. "Tell him that to know him is to be somebody over here. As the author of various esteemed works I am nothing in particular; but as his neighbor—it is as good as knowing a lord. England is full of his admirers." He went to Germany and began to study the language seriously. It was a struggle, but he persevered. "The confounded genders!" he exclaimed. "If I die I shall have engraved on my tombstone that I died of *der, die, das,* not because I caught them but because I couldn't." [21]

During the same month, he paused for a moment to air still further his disapproval of Whitman. Posterity, he wrote, will have none of him. He is too violent. "It is not the volcanoes after all that give a lasting and serene delight, but those quiet old giants without a drop of fireblood in their veins that lie there basking their unwarmable old sides in the sun no more everlasting than they —patent unshiftable ballast that keep earth and human thought trimmed and true on an even keel. Ah, the cold blooded old masters, how little they care for you and me! Homer, Plato, Dante, Shakespeare, Cervantes, Goethe—are they not everlasting boundary-stones that mark the limits of a noble reserve and self-restraint, and seem to say, 'Outside of us is Chaos—go there if you like—*we* know better—it is a dreary realm where moan the ghosts of dead-born chil-

dren, and where the ghost of mad old Lear is king'?" [22]   He had
wandered a long way from Whitman, but his point was nonetheless
completely plain: he did not approve of the author of *Leaves of
Grass,* nor could he wholly approve of any experimenter in the arts.
His traditionalism (later termed his "humanism") was becoming unmistakably evident.   But the distinction between this variety of humanism and an approximation of flat imitativeness is yet to be adequately defined by his defenders.

The memory of Maria lingered with him in his exile.   "Do you
know what day it is?" he wrote Mrs. Howe on November 4, from
Dresden.   "It is the fifteenth anniversary of the happiest day of my
life—the day of my betrothal with the noblest woman I have ever
known.   Dear Lois, it is little to say that such a loss is irreparable—
it becomes every day a greater loss—and a real sorrow is forever at
compound interest.   I look sadly at my wedding ring and it is
empty as a magic circle after the Prospero is dead who traced it—
the obedient spirits come no more.   My greatest comfort over here
is that I know I am doing what she would have liked, and I thank
God that I can say with a clear front that thus far I have been faithful in deed and thought to so fine a memory." [23]

His study of German was diligent and continuing.   He worked
at it all day, abstaining from alcohol, until at length, in January,
1856, he was able to declare that he could read it almost as easily as
French.   He was getting through 150 pages at a stretch.   He had
grown sadder, graver, more mature, he said, as month succeeded
month and as his life flowed on in lonely and bleak isolation.   For
back of his routine was the cherished memory which it would be a
desecration to forget.   "I hope you will remember," he said to Mabel, "that Mama watches over you—and that you always see her picture the last thing at night and the first in the morning.   If you live
a great many years, you will never see anything more beautiful to
look at than her face—though the picture does not look a thousandth
part as beautiful as she did when she looked at you." [24]

He spent six weeks in Italy, while the spring farther north was
still unpredictably bitter.   He continued to apply himself "like a

dog" to his German. He went back to Dresden when this interval
was over. Then, as summer neared, he heard a story from America
that aroused a savage resentment in him. Charles Sumner, whom
he greatly admired, and who had spoken violently in Congress on
the "crime against Kansas," had been beaten to insensibility upon
the Senate floor by the gentleman from South Carolina, Preston
Brooks. When he learned this news, Lowell's passion for Old
World culture deserted him. "There never was anything so brutal,"
he exclaimed in a letter to Dr. Howe. "How long are such things
to be borne? . . . As I read these things so far away, it seems as if
I were reading the history of a republic in the last wretched convul-
sion before absolute dissolution." [25] Four weeks later, in July, 1856,
he sailed for home. He had mastered German, and he knew French
and Italian much better than he had known them when he came.
He was going, moreover, to teach at length amid the cloistered serenities of Harvard. But his dander was up nonetheless, and it
was up with a virulence which no academic routine would ever
prove able, entirely, to put down. Though the university was laying its dead hand upon him, as one distinguished critic has implied,[26] that hand was soon to prove entirely strengthless against the
surging vigor of his resentment toward the South. This evil region,
he soon discovered, was sullenly persisting in its old iniquities. His
hatred of it (by a strange compensation) was to grow apace, and
ruthlessly, as his reverence for Maria's sainted memory dissolved.

XI

*"She has only one fault that I know of—she is not rich.
But this I believe I can pardon."*

Lowell to Mrs. Estes Howe, August 13, 1857.
New Letters, 93

WHEN he returned to Cambridge, in July, 1856, Lowell did not
go back to Elmwood to live. He went, instead, to where
Mabel had been staying during his absence, to the home of Dr. Howe
on "Professor's Row." This residence was much nearer the college,
and free from those associations of a grief that was still too poignant
and too distressing to be allayed.

James Walker was president of Harvard when Lowell began his
work in the fall. Walker was sixty-two years old, and had succeeded to his office, three years before, after almost a quarter of a
century as minister of the Second, or "Harvard," Church, in Charlestown. An enthusiastic Unitarian, and wise in judgment, he was
nevertheless amiably inefficient as an administrator. Yet though
small—the faculty numbered only fourteen[1]—the college was at
least beginning in a vague fashion to resemble the institution we
know today. A system of scholarships had been introduced, the
library had grown to almost seventy thousand volumes, and com-
pulsory evening prayer service had been abolished. This last concession to the students did a great deal to lessen those undergraduate
disorders which had proved so common during the two previous
decades. Three years after Lowell assumed his duties, the President
was able to announce, triumphantly: "A lady may now pass un-
attended, at any hour, through the college grounds, secure from
seeing or hearing anything to alarm or offend her." [2]

Lowell's first assignment as a faculty member was to repeat his
Lowell Institute lectures on poetry. This done, he began his regular
classroom instruction in Dante and German Literature.[3] A good

many records of his manner with students have survived. These accounts, in their implications, suggest that he taught with a fairly settled conviction regarding those matters which should be stressed or slighted in the authors read. For one thing, he realized that his field, the modern languages, had yet to achieve full respectability in the curriculum. He knew that conservative academicians viewed French, Spanish, and Italian as of little worth, except "as a social accomplishment or as a commercial subsidiary." [4] But he looked upon such notions as trivial. There were literary masterpieces in other tongues than the Greek and Roman; there had been written, since the Middle Ages, any number of works that were rich and profound in their interpretation of human life. The spirit of those works, the human values which they reflected, was what he primarily wished his students to understand.

If these human values were to be fully apprehended, the teacher, he felt, should not dwell too long upon the rudiments of grammar and declension; he should not reduce his classroom hours to an endless series of unprofitable drill sessions. Late in life he addressed the Modern Language Association on this question, and he made his attitude quite plain. He thought that the purely linguistic side in the teaching of the languages got more than its fitting share of attention, he said. "I insist only that in our college courses this should be a separate study, and that, good as it is in itself, it should, in the scheme of general instruction, be restrained to its own function as the guide to something better. And that something better is Literature. Let us rescue ourselves from what Milton calls 'these grammatic flats and shallows.' The blossoms of language have certainly as much value as its roots." [5]

Holding this belief, he would naturally grow impatient when during a class hour he found some trifling or dull young man stumbling through an eloquent passage, mutilating its aesthetic value. Lowell would break in upon him, read the lines properly, if impatiently, and call upon a more promising student. Moreover, he revealed a further personal trait which rather hampered than assisted the hopeful candidates for wisdom who sat under him. "His corrections and remarks," one student remembered, "were often lost from the want of clearness and open-mouthed carefulness of articulation. When he spoke in public he always made himself heard; but to a small, almost private class, speaking without effort, his modest stillness and his smothering mustache would make us wish that men's hair had been forbidden to grow forward of the corner of their mouths." [6]

His Dante course appears to have been his best, and though the man who has written most interestingly about it did not come to Harvard until the 1870's, his account of Lowell's classroom personality is entirely consistent with earlier reports. Mr. Barrett Wendell applied for admission to the course with the belief, acquired from experience in several others, "that the only way to study a classic text in any language was to scrutinize every syllable with a care undisturbed by consideration of any more of the context than was grammatically related to it." Whatever literature Wendell had previously enjoyed as such, he had had to get through without the aid of a teacher.

Lowell's departure from this customary procedure proved shocking. He never, says Wendell, "gave us less than a canto to read; and often gave us two or three. He never, from the beginning, bothered us with a particle of linguistic irrelevance. Here before us was a great poem—a lasting expression of what human life had meant to a human being, dead and gone these five centuries. Let us try, as best we might, to see what life had meant to this man; let us see what relation his experience, great and small, bore to ours; and, now and then, let us pause for a moment to notice how wonderfully beautiful his expression of this experience was. Let us read, as sympathetically as we could make ourselves read, the words of one who was as much a man as we; only vastly greater in his knowledge of wisdom and of beauty. That was the spirit of Mr. Lowell's teaching. It opened to some of us a new world. In a month I could read Dante better than I ever learned to read Greek, or Latin, or German." [7]

Eighteen years out of the classroom before his return as a professor,

Lowell in this latter capacity was naturally somewhat unconventional. "His method of teaching," declares Wendell, "was his own. The class was small—not above ten or a dozen; and he generally began by making each student translate a few lines, interrupting now and then with suggestions of the poetic value of passages which were being rendered in a style too exasperatingly prosaic. Now and then some word or some passage would suggest to him a line of thought —sometimes very earnest, sometimes paradoxically comical—that it would never have suggested to anyone else. And he would lean back in his chair and talk away across country till he felt like stopping; or he would thrust his hands into the pockets of his rather shabby sack-coat, and pace the end of the room with his heavy laced boots, and look at nothing in particular, and discourse on things in general. We gave up notebooks in a week. Our business was not to cram lifeless detail, but to absorb as much as we might of the spirit of his exhuberant literary vitality. And through it all he was always a quiz; you never knew what he was going to do or to say next. One whimsical digression I have always remembered, chiefly for the amiable atrocity of the pun. Some mention of wings had been made in the text, whereupon Mr. Lowell observed that he had always had a liking for wings: He had lately observed that some were being added to the ugliest house in Cambridge, and he cherished hope they might fly away with it. . . . You could not always be sure when he was in earnest; but there was never a moment when he let you forget that you were a human being in a human world, and that Dante had been one, too." [8]

Though unorthodox in his classroom manner, he proved quite normal, professionally, in at least one respect—the job of giving and grading examinations was an almost insufferable bore to him. Once, when this evil necessity appeared imminent, Lowell requested his students to translate a long passage from Massimo d'Azeqlio, omitting entirely any passage from Dante, probably out of a fear that the text of his favorite author would be desecrated if used. "Weeks passed, and no news came of our marks. At last one of the class, who was not quite at ease concerning his academic standing, ventured, at the close of a recitation, to ask if Mr. Lowell had assigned him a mark. Mr. Lowell looked at the youth gravely and inquired what he really thought his work deserved. The student rather diffidently said that he hoped it was worth sixty percent. 'You may take it,' said Mr. Lowell; 'and I shan't have the bother of reading your book.' " [9]

Then there were his evenings at Elmwood, where he went to live after 1857. He gave liberally of his time there, to those students who were sufficiently persevering to visit him. They would find him, usually, in his library, carelessly dressed, wearing a loose smoking jacket and slippers. He smoked a pipe himself, though he usually offered his guests a cigar. His pipe fairly started, he would begin to talk "in his own quizzical way, at one time beautifully in earnest, at the next so whimsical that you could not quite make out what he meant." Perhaps he had just been reading something that interested him. If so, he would, likely as not, continue his reading, whether the subject was the Apocrypha or the latest newspaper. "All we had to do," Wendell goes on, "was to sit and listen, which was far better than any other way of spending an evening known to me in those days." He was hard to talk to, for he naturally retained little interest in the trivial chatter of undergraduates. "But when he did listen, and when he talked, too, he did so—no matter how quizzically—with a certain politeness that at the time seemed to me, and in memory remains, a typical example of the signification of the word *urbane;* and all this in a smoking-jacket and slippers, by lamp light, before a flickering wood fire whose ashes were crumbling down into a great bed which had grown from hundreds of such fires before." [10]

And there was nothing faked about all this. An author secure in the esteem of his contemporaries, Lowell had little regard for appearances when dictated merely for their own sake. He met Wendell several years after the latter was graduated. But he scarcely remembered his face, was totally incapable of recollecting his name. This former student before him, he appears to have thought, was only a passing incident in the larger problem he had concerned himself with from the beginning, the problem of teaching the world—through those transient creatures who came to him as an epitome of it—what was truly admirable in modern literature.

But something else, more important to his private life, had been maturing throughout this first year at Harvard, and at last it had become too important to be any longer deferred. It was his growing attachment for Miss Frances Dunlap, Mabel's governess during his years in Europe. Marriage to this lady now seemed to him to be dictated by the strongest and most inevitable compulsions. He simply could not resist them any further. But there were, first, certain explanations to be made to his friends and, in particular, to Mrs. Howe, Maria's sister.

"I have told you several times," he wrote her, "that I had no *intention* of marrying again, and that I should not do so if I could help it. But I cannot help it. My whole disposition and temperament have been convincing me for some time that it would be better for me—indeed, that it was a necessity of my nature, without which I was only half myself."

He went on to speak of his betrothed in plain terms. In Miss Dunlap, he said, he had found a person who had interested him more and more deeply during the past four years. She was a person of remarkable strength, yet she was gentle. She was fond of him, and she would "stand by Mabel" if he should die. "You call me fastidious," he continued, "and perhaps I am—at any rate, things affect me strongly for liking and disliking, and it was of first importance to me to find a woman (other things being equal) with whom my nature always felt itself at ease. I do not give this as a reason for marrying—but for marrying *her* rather than any other woman. My feeling for her, I need not say, is something much intenser than anything I choose to say. I feel myself profoundly attached to her, and during our long and intimate intercourse I have continually found reason to respect and value her more. She has only one fault that I know of—she is not rich. But this I believe I can pardon. She loves Mabel and Mabel is more attached to her than she could be to anyone else. I do not think I could do a wiser thing and I am sure I could not do a better." [11]

It was certainly a fair and straightforward statement, to a relative by marriage who had been obviously nettled upon first learning of his decision. His friend Norton, then abroad, had written him sympathetically. Lowell was profoundly grateful to him. He was careless of Mrs. Grundy's sentiments regarding this matter, he declared, "but I do care immensely for the opinion of the few friends whom I value." He told Norton of a recent visit he had made to Portland, Maine, Miss Dunlap's home—writing still in perfect frankness. He liked the family, "especially her mother, who is a person of great character. They live in a little bit of a house in a little bit of a street, behind the great house (the biggest in town) in which they were brought up, and not one of them seemed conscious that they were not welcoming me to a palace. There were no apologies for want of room, no Dogberry hints at losses, or anything of that kind, but all was simple, ladylike, and hearty. A family of girls who expected to be rich, and have had to support themselves and (I suspect) their mother in part, are not likely to have any nonsense in them. I find Miss Dunlap's education very complete in having had the two great teachers, Wealth and Poverty. One has taught her not to value money, the other to be independent of it." [12]

The marriage took place in September, 1857, and Lowell went with his wife and child to live again at Elmwood with his father and sister. The comments just quoted should reveal a fact that was undoubtedly true—that in going through with his plan, against the demurrers of certain relatives, he had made one of the most courageous decisions of his life. Fraught with tragedy though its later stages were to prove, the step was one which he never once regretted.

Still another interest was developing in Boston during this momentous year, an interest that was to be of no end of service in uniting and further publicizing the better-known authors of his region. The firm of Phillips and Sampson, printers of standard editions of famous writers, had at length been persuaded by their literary adviser, Mr. Francis H. Underwood, to bring out a new magazine. It was to be revolutionary in conception. From the first, it was to have the solid support of the nation's important men of letters—practically all of whom were within an hour's ride from the city—and it was to enjoy an equally solid financial security. It was, moreover, to be a monthly that paid exceedingly well for the material it used, was to be edited by a man of international reputation, was to speak, not for Massachusetts alone, but for "the people of the United States." [13]

Now Mr. Phillips had no nonsense about him, and his business had flourished hitherto for the elementary commercial reason that he was able to pirate the works of cherished authors—Byron, Scott, Dickens, and others—and sell them more cheaply than his competitors. He had recently made his company celebrated by issuing Macaulay's *History* at fifty cents a volume—without, of course, any thought of violating the ethics of his trade so far as to pay the Englishman a penny in royalties. The lofty ideals of Mr. Underwood, therefore, had naturally been slow to make inroads upon him. But once they did, his enthusiasm for the prospect proved great.

He staged a dinner, May 5, 1857,[14] and his pride in the names of those guests who attended it was quite too much to be allowed to go unrecorded. "I must tell you," Mr. Phillips wrote his niece, "about a little dinner party I gave about two weeks ago. It would be proper, perhaps, to state that the origin of it was a desire to confer with my literary friends on a somewhat extensive literary project, the particulars of which I shall reserve until you come. But to the party: my invitations included only R. W. Emerson, H. W. Longfellow, J. R. Lowell, Mr. Motley (the 'Dutch Republic' man), O. W. Holmes, Mr. (J. Elliot) Cabot, and Mr. Underwood, our literary man. Imagine your uncle at the head of such a table, with such guests! The above named were the only ones invited, and they were all present. We sat down at three P.M. and rose at eight." Intellectually, he went on, it was the richest experience of his life. "Leaving myself and 'literary man' out of the group, I think you will agree with me that it would be difficult to duplicate that number of such conceded scholarship in the whole country beside."

He described the seating arrangement. At his right, as guest of honor, was Mr. Emerson. Next in rank, to his left, was Mr. Longfellow. Holmes and Lowell followed Emerson on the one side; Motley and Cabot followed Longfellow on the other. At the foot, beaming, sat Mr. Underwood, the "literary man." They had hoped to have also Mrs. Harriet Beecher Stowe, now famous as the author of *Uncle Tom's Cabin,* for her support was deemed necessary to the success of the magazine. But Mrs. Stowe was in England, though she soon proved wholly sympathetic. Hawthorne was also abroad. Only the independent Mr. Thoreau was uninvited, among the important writers available. But his absence went unregretted, and apparently even unnoticed.

The following month, Mr. Underwood was sent to England to secure the help of certain distinguished authors in that country. Lowell was likewise busy, enlisting the aid of both native and English men of letters. He was able to quote the sum of fifty dollars apiece for poems, and from five to ten dollars a page for articles. Holmes had christened the publication the *Atlantic Monthly,* and Lowell himself had been appointed its editor at a salary of $2,500 a year. It seems to have caught public attention from the beginning. The first number appeared in November, 1857. Lowell was able to assure Ruskin, a potential contributor, before two years were out, that the names of almost forty thousand enthusiastic subscribers had been duly set down in the company's books.[15]

He had his editorial principles, and more than once he was compelled to explain them. "I never let any personal feeling influence me consciously in editing the magazine," he once wrote. He wanted to make it interesting to as many *classes* of people as he could, especially to such as give tone to public opinion in literary matters. If it proved merely entertaining, how would it be any better than that published by "those Scribes and Pharisees the Harpers?"[16] And to a contributor and friend, T. W. Higginson, he had already stated that the only time he allowed his own convictions to obtrude was in cases of "obvious obscurity, bad taste, or bad grammar."[17]

The initial installment of Holmes's "Autocrat" distinguished the first number—Lowell had refused to edit the *Atlantic* unless his old friend contributed—and four poems by Emerson gave it a certain controversial flavor. One of these poems was "Brahma." "What does it mean? was the question readers everywhere asked; and if one had the reputation of seeing a little way into the Concord philosophy, he was liable at any time to be stopped on the street by some perplexed inquirer, who would draw him into the nearest doorway, produce a crumpled newspaper clipping from the recesses of a waistcoat pocket, and, with knitted brows, exclaim, 'Here! You think you understand Emerson; now tell me what all this is about—*If the red slayer think he slays,*' and so forth." [18] Though the intention of these verses may seem entirely obvious today, they were quite plainly far from obvious in 1857, a fact which Lowell doubtless saw but did nothing to remedy, for the simple reason that he sensed their value in getting the *Atlantic* generally talked about.

Like editors the world over, he soon found the routine drudgery of his job irksome. He was urged to take a stand upon unsettled issues, often to take a wholly irrational stand. The "religious press" assailed the articles he published—assailed them vigorously and regularly. Dr. Holmes, for example, was termed a reincarnation of Voltaire and an audacious enemy of the true Christian spirit. Contributors clamored when the editor failed to write them specific criticisms of their rejected offerings. And of course there was the endless task of reading manuscripts. "Today is Sunday," he wrote Norton in 1859, "but the sabbath dawns no sabbath day for me. I have been reading proof and picking out manuscripts all the morning. Do you ever get desperate?" They appalled him by their mass. He would look first at one box, then at another, and—fill his pipe. He proceeded to damn certain authors specifically. One, he said, was utterly without an idea. Another could not express himself in fewer than sixteen pages. Still another seemed to spin out his ideas "as uselessly as those creatures that streak the air with gossamer." On one occasion, he lamented, the manuscripts were knee-deep in his study. There were at least 150 unanswered letters lying around his desk. He was tired of the responsibility his work imposed. He needed a "lieutenant" if he was to keep on at all, and to do, in addition, the writing of his own which, more and more insistently, he was impatient to turn out.[19]

But he was learning a good deal. For one thing, he was learning the infallible pattern which, it seemed to him, nearly all love stories inevitably assumed. He believed he could dictate five of them at once. Rehearsing the ragged formula, he proceeded to sketch an example: " 'Julie gazed into the eyes of her lover, which sought in vain to escape her enquiring look, while the tears trembled on her long dark lashes but fell not (that 'fell not' is new, I think). "And is it indeed so?" she said slowly, after a pause in which her heart leaped like an imprisoned bird.'—'Meanwhile, the elder of the two, a stern-featured man of some forty winters, played with the hilt of his dagger, half drawing and then sheathing again the Damascus blade thin as the eloquence of Everett and elastic as the conscience of Cass. "Didst mark the old man tremble?" "Cospetto! my uncle, a noted leech, was wont to say that iron was a good tonic for unsteady nerves," and still he trifled with the ominous looking weapon, etc. etc.' " Lowell declared that he felt like taking a contract to write all such stories himself, at so much a dozen.[20]

Perhaps the most severe lecturing he received as editor of the *Atlantic* was one that came from Thoreau, in June, 1858. Lowell had previously asked Emerson to solicit a contribution from this gentleman, and his friend had been successful. But a detail connected with one of the articles Mr. Thoreau submitted became, very soon, too important to be overlooked, too fraught with principle, indeed, to be tolerated even for a moment. Thoreau had written, in an essay published in the *Atlantic* in May, a sentence which, to quote literally, read: "It is immortal as I am, and perchance will go to as high a heaven, there to tower above me still." This sentence, Thoreau discovered, had been omitted entirely in the printed version of his piece. "I hardly need to say," he wrote Lowell, "that this is a liberty which I will not permit to be taken with my *ms.* The editor has, in this case, no more right to omit a sentiment than to insert one, or put words into my mouth. I do not ask anybody to adopt my opinions, but I do expect that when they ask for them in print, they will print them, or obtain my consent for their alteration, or omission. I should not read many books if I thought they had been thus expurgated."

He did not mean, he subtly implied, to charge Lowell himself with the omission. "But there must be a responsible editor somewhere, and you to whom I entrusted my *ms.* are the only party whom I know in this matter." He requested that the editor indicate, in further installments of his article, that the sentence in question had been left out.

But he was not finished, by any means. "I am not writing to be associated in any way," he insisted, "with parties who will confess themselves so bigoted & timid as this implies. I could excuse a man who was afraid of an uplifted fist, but if one habitually manifests fear at the utterance of a sincere thought, I must think that his life is a kind of nightmare continued into broad daylight. It is hard to conceive of one so completely *derivative.* Is this the avowed character of the *Atlantic Monthly?* I should like an early reply." [21] Lowell never answered this letter. If he replied to the author of it at all, it was in terms of a cynically unfair review of his collected works, published three years after the Concord rebel was dead.

There were also literary prima donnas to contend with. Even Holmes assumed the rôle on one occasion. Lowell wrote J. T. Fields to see him at once "and assure him how essential he is to the Atlantic. He is worth all the rest of us together & has been nettled a little by not being paid so much as he thought right for his 'Asylum for Decayed Punsters.' Nettled, perhaps, is not the right word—but he has conceived a notion that he could carry his wares to a better market. I assured him that he was altogether mistaken. . . . Now you know what ought to be done & I am sure you will do it. An essay from him is as good as a Chapter [of *The Professor's Story*]. He needs only a word said by you to set all right." [22]

Lowell, in short, proved a vigorous and alert editor. He won for the *Atlantic* the enthusiastic support of authors who would probably, except for his assiduous cultivation of them, have given very little notice to the magazine or to the high cause it purported to serve. In addition to all the important and near-important New Englanders (Emerson, Holmes, Longfellow, Hawthorne, Whittier, Thoreau, Motley, W. H. Prescott, Mrs. Stowe, T. W. Higginson, C. E. Norton, and the rest), Bryant, R. H. Stoddard, Bayard Taylor, and Fitz James O'Brien contributed essays and poems from New York; W. D. Howells and J. J. Piatt from Ohio; G. W. Bagby and J. P. Kennedy from Virginia;[23] and Paul Hamilton Hayne mailed in a few delicate verses from the "unliterary" and "contemptible" wastes of Charleston, South Carolina.[24] Moreover, from abroad came offerings from the French critic Sainte-Beuve, and from such English writers as Harriet Martineau and A. H. Clough. Carlyle, Ruskin, Tennyson, Arnold, and Browning apparently could not be interested by Lowell, though one of this group, Ruskin, is definitely known to have been invited to send in almost anything he had available. As for the editor himself, he used sixty-eight pieces of his own during the four years he was in control of the magazine.

In 1861, thoroughly fagged with the task, he resigned it in favor of J. T. Fields. The industrious Mr. Phillips, of Phillips and Sampson, had died unexpectedly, and his business had gone into a receivership. That phase of it which affected the *Atlantic* was taken over by the firm of Ticknor and Fields. Fields was a man of considerable literary distinction, and he thus rather naturally replaced Lowell as editor of the now thriving publication. Lowell surrendered his duties without a trace of animus. "I wish to say in black and white," he wrote his successor, "that I am perfectly satisfied with the arrangement you have made. You will be surprised before long to find how easily you get on without me & wonder that you ever thought me a necessity. It is amazing how quickly the waters close over one. He carries down with him the memory of his splash and struggles & fancies it still going on when the last bubble even has burst long ago. Good by. Nature is equable.

I have lost the Atlantic but my cow has calved, as if nothing had happened." [25]

It was a fine-spirited statement—for the fact that the magazine *was* thriving financially, and being widely read, was primarily the result of the labors of its first editor.

XII

"We believe that the strongest battalions are always on the side of God. The southern army will be fighting for Jefferson Davis, or at most for the liberty of self-misgovernment, while we go forth for the defense of principles which alone make government august and civil liberties possible."

Lowell, *Works*, VI, 109

BY the time Lowell surrendered his editorship, the long-menacing internal cataclysm had come. The area of civil debate in Washington had been forsaken for the final theater of war. Eleven states had renounced their allegiance to that nation for which the *Atlantic* had chosen to speak, had seceded from it out of the conviction that justice was unavailable to them while they remained members of it. The fields of Virginia were rich with the blood of those who, from North or South, had thought and acted, fatally, to vindicate or to cancel out the arguments that compromise and conferences had failed utterly to undermine. These savage divergences had revived in Lowell an old, and by this time unshakable, conviction: the conviction that Right was at grips with Wrong and Evil, the faith that Truth was being challenged by the minions of Sin. And inevitably, as always, Truth had draped itself, he believed, in the raiment of the Cause of the North, while the stubborn South slept blindly, out of ancient habit, with the dark principle of its ultimate undoing.

Soon after he began his work with the magazine, it became evident to anybody who could read that the *Atlantic* was not going to remain silent on political issues. Moreover, the voice of the spokesman who defended Righteousness in its pages was to be that of the editor himself. Once more a Cause was blazing across his horizon, one which he could follow with a holy and abiding

zeal. It took its first form negatively, in terms of a violent denuncia-
tion of the American Tract Society. That once idealistic body had in
recent years become rich and powerful, and was dispensing, by
1858, an annual revenue of almost half a million dollars. This
growth, he felt, had robbed it of its former courage; it had become
conservative and cowardly; in other words, it had ceased to publish
antislavery pamphlets.

How can such things be in this world? "Throughout the South
it is criminal to teach a slave to read," though if it were possible its
servile population could read no book more incendiary than the
Bible. Instead of facing the central issue of American life—the
negro problem—this body is turning out essays on intemperance
and upon the impropriety of sleeping in church. Yet it is impossible, as its own members recently acknowledged, to draw a
Mason and Dixon's line in the world of ethics, to divide Duty by
a parallel of latitude. The only line which Christ knew is that
which parts the sheep from the goats. By deferring to what are
pleasantly called the "objections" of the South toward a militant
policy, "the society virtually exclude the black man, if born to the
southward of a certain arbitrary line, from the operation of God's
providence."

Such dilatoriness made him sick. "We Americans are very fond
of this glue of compromise," he went on. "Like so many quack
cements, it is advertised to make the mended parts of the vessels
stronger than those which have never been broken, but, like them,
it will not stand hot water—and as the question of slavery is sure
to plunge all who approach it, even with the best intentions, into that
fatal element, the patched-up brotherhood, which but yesterday was
warranted to be better than new, falls once more into a bit of in-
coherent fragments." Gone are the days when, to Lowell, war
was "murder." Christ is present to him this time in full and
gleaming armor. "Peace," he said, "is an excellent thing, but principle and pluck are better . . . the peace which Christ promised to
his followers was not of this world; the good gift he brought them
was not peace, but a sword." Not a weapon of territorial conquest,

this sword was the flaming blade of conscience. "Christianity," we should remember, "has never been concession, never peace; it is continual aggression; one province of wrong conquered, its pioneers are already in the heart of another." Christian girls in the South are being sold into Christian harems. The evil is now national in its implications and can be no longer tolerated. Let compromise cease! The Harvard scholar had thus early set forth his sober analysis of the conflict that was soon to erupt in the diction of violence and death.[1]

He turned, soon afterwards, from an organization to an individual—Mr. Rufus Choate, of Massachusetts, who still hoped to avert civil war in this country and who had become convinced that his hopes were unrealizable unless a compromise between the sections could be effected. Lowell did not spare him.[2] The gentleman was a "melodious" orator, to be sure, and he was a learned man, a scholar and a critic. He was also a criminal lawyer who had enjoyed remarkable success in his profession. "All this we concede." But Mr. Choate had now left his moorings, had come out as "the public prosecutor of the Republican Party, a party overwhelmingly triumphant in the free states."

Mr. Choate's primary offense had been that, during a Fourth of July oration, in 1858, he had publicly damned the antislavery movement. He had spoken of a shallow and canting fanaticism which renounced the ideal of compromise in American politics. "There is a distempered and ambitious morality which says civil prudence is no virtue," he had declared. "There is a philanthropy, so it calls itself—pedantry, arrogance, folly, cruelty, impiousness, I call it—fit enough for a pulpit, totally unfit for a people—fit enough for a preacher, totally unfit for a statesman." It was Choate's tribute to Lowell and to his Cause, a cause which he had served for almost twenty years.

Lowell's only resort was to the petty weapon of a slurring evasion. The sarcasms which Mr. Choate vented against the Anti-Slavery sentiment were so old as to be positively respectable, he wrote. "We wish we could say that their vivacity increased with their years."

Of course, he added, Sectionalism was not forgotten in his speech. "Mr. Choate honestly confesses that sectional jealousies are coeval with the country itself, but it is only as fomented by Anti-slavery-extension that he finds them dreadful." The article quibbled with further statements, but it did so cheaply and to little purpose. Lowell was wise in omitting it altogether from any edition of his published works.

The editor was equally contemptuous of Caleb Cushing,[3] the "General C." of the first *Biglow Papers.* One of the most brilliant jurists of his age, and the first Attorney-General to refrain from private practice during his term of office, Cushing had nevertheless written, in 1853, the letter which came to be known as "Cushing's Ukase." He had addressed this letter to the *Boston Post,* and in it he voiced President Pierce's desire "that the dangerous element of abolitionism, under whatever guise or form it may present itself, shall be crushed out." [4] This statement was enough to alienate Lowell completely.

Cushing was like Disraeli, he said, in a survey of his career. He was plucky, handsome, and dangerous in debate; yet unconvincing for the primary reason that he was totally lacking in principle. He possessed one faculty to a preëminent degree: "the faculty of inspiring a universal want of confidence." What did this aspiring candidate for the presidency stand for? Lowell asked, attributing to him an ambition which was by no means controlling. Mr. Cushing, he wrote, answering his own question, "knows very well that the multitude have nothing but a secondary office in the making of Presidents, and addresses to them only his words, while the initiated alone know what meaning to put on them. If, for example, when he says *servant* he means *slave,* when he says *negro-philist* he means *Republican,* and when he says *false philanthropy* he means *the fairest instincts of the human heart,* we have a right to suspect that there is also an esoteric significance in his phrases, *Loyalty to the Union, Nationality,* and *Conservatism."* The editor paused to indict the Democratic Party as a whole, charging that it possessed the remarkable gift of supporting impartially "both sides of every domestic problem which has arisen since it came into political existence." He mustered his illustrations, construing them fluently and to his liking. In all these cases, he then declared, the party had contrived to have the Constitution always on its side by the simple application of Swift's axiom, "Orthodoxy is *my* doxy, Heterodoxy is *thy* doxy." He was aware, he continued, that public men must sometimes swing with the tide. But he required "that they shall not too lightly accept Wrong instead of Right." He relegated Mr. Cushing, as he did all other proponents of compromise at this date, to his always growing category of the damned.

Two years elapsed before the *Atlantic*'s editor ventured again into the political field with an important essay, but his indignation had increased as it stirred within him—unsatisfied because unexpressed. Election day, 1860, was only six weeks off, and meanwhile what was happening to his country? The diagnosis he arrived at was a familiar one, though supplemented now with admissions he had not previously made public. Whatever the effects of slavery upon the states where it existed, he said, there could be no doubt that its moral influence upon the North had been disastrous. Why was this deplorable acknowledgment true? Because the institution "has compelled our politicians into that first fatal compromise with their moral instincts and hereditary principles" which makes all future surrenders easy. The Vartu of the North was at last, it seemed, being fatally undermined.

Lowell detailed the steps by which southern arrogance had entrenched itself at the expense of his own section. "To eat dirt is bad enough, but to find that we have eaten more than was necessary may chance to give us indigestion. The slaveholding interest has gone on, step by step, forcing concession after concession, till it needs but little to secure it forever in the political supremacy of the country. Yield to its latest demand—let it mould the evil destiny of the Territories—and the thing is done past recall. The Next Presidential Election is to say Yes or No." Perhaps, in the interest of balance, one might at this point recall a statement from F. A. Shannon's authoritative *Economic History of the United States:*

"The idea of an aggressive slaveocracy, demanding control of the union as an alternative to secession, was merely an abolitionist chimera."

Stripped to its essentials, the issue involved was merely, Lowell continued, one of "whether the Occidental or the Oriental theory of society is to mould our future." It was all focused in terms of the impending election, Lincoln representing the principles of light and progress, his opponents standing like biblical goats, on the other hand, for all that was dark and unholy. Let us look at these latter creatures, steadily, he said:

There is Mr. John Bell, of Tennessee, representing the Constitutional Union Party,[5] there is Mr. Breckenridge of Kentucky, choice of the radical Democrats, and there is Stephen A. Douglas, who is supported by the moderates of that party. These men are all alike in advertising themselves as defenders of the Constitution. "Meanwhile the only point in which voters are interested is, what do they mean by the Constitution? Mr. Breckenridge means the superiority of certain exceptional species of property over all others; nay, over man himself. Mr. Douglas, with a different formula for expressing it, means practically the same thing. Both of them represent not merely the narrow principles of a section, but the still narrower and more selfish ones of a caste." The same attitude is true of Mr. Bell, heir of "the stock in trade of two defunct parties, the Whig and No-Nothing."

On the other side, in shining contrast, stood Abraham Lincoln, guardian of the faith. His election will not endanger the Union. The Republican party is merely bent upon the extirpation of the dogmas which support slavery, for they are dogmas which, if allowed to flourish, will serve in time "to justify the enslavement of every white man unable to protect himself." Lincoln is naturally a conservative. Choosing him "will do more than anything else to appease the excitement of the country." The editor was cheerful about the decision his countrymen would make in November. "We have entire faith," he declared, "in the benignant influence of Truth."[6] It is somewhat surprising that Lowell reprinted this essay, so unreliable a prophet it proved him to be. Three months after the "conservative" was formally elected (he received only 1,857,610 of the 4,645,380 popular votes cast),[7] delegates from seven seceding states of the South were meeting in Montgomery to form the Confederacy.

It was March, 1861, before Lincoln was able to take over the government from the man who, to Lowell, epitomized the ultimate in incompetence—President Buchanan. How he despised this un-militant gentleman, who refused to raise a finger in protest while his country was crumbling to pieces before his eyes! "To do nothing," Buchanan seems to think, "is the perfection of policy." The editor proceeded, in his article, "E Pluribus Unum,"[8] to mass his grievances against the South with undisguised indignation. We laid out God knows how many millions in conquering and forti-fying Florida, and now she proposes to call herself free. And there is Louisiana, bought and paid for out of the national treasury, yet claiming the right to cork up the mouth of the Mississippi River and make her soil even French, if need be, "whenever the whim may take her." We are not a congeries of medieval Italian repub-lics. We are not a German confederation! And still Mr. Buchanan "admits" the Right of a state to secede. To Lowell this was more than Reason or Justice could endure. "Public sentiment unmistak-ably demands that, in the case of Anarchy *vs* America, the cause of the defendant shall not be suffered to go by default."

Take the case of South Carolina, he continued. The people of that state were utterly imprudent to declare themselves free of the Union. They are now left dependent upon a single crop, cotton, and a disease to it could reduce them all to beggary within a single year. How are they going to afford a standing army? he demanded to know. Heavy direct taxation will prove inevitable, and when these levies begin to fall due, the poorer classes of "secessia" will soon discover by what evil counsels they have been duped. It was simply stupid economics to secede.

Only think for a moment, he eloquently declared, of the rising glory of America, certain to come at no very remote date, unless thwarted by a few miserable obstructionists. It is idle and worse than idle to talk about Central Republics like the Confederacy, republics that can never be realized. "We want neither Central Republics nor Northern Republics, but our own Republic and that of our fathers, destined one day to gather the whole continent under a flag that shall be the most august in the world. Having once known what it was to be members of a grand and peaceful constellation, we shall not believe, without further proof, that the laws of our gravitation are to be abolished, and we flung forth into chaos, a hurlyburly of jostling and splintering stars, whenever Robert Toombs or Robert Rhett, or any other Bob of the secession kite, may give a flirt of self importance."

The sorry prospect of such frustration was, indeed, intolerable for him to contemplate. Were it not for slavery we would doubtless, insofar as our own continent was concerned, have already realized that ancient dream of philosophers and speculative philanthropists—"a single empire embracing the whole world." This dream, for North America, was more than a dream; it was our manifest destiny. "One language, one law, one citizenship over thousands of miles, and a government on the whole so good that we seem to have forgotten what government means." To allow one or two or half a dozen of the southern states to break away from the union "in a freak of anger or unjust suspicion, or, still worse, from mistaken notions of sectional advantage, would be to fail in our duty to ourselves and to our country." Gone, gone past any possibility of recall, was Hosea's willingness for the two sections to set to work and part—they taking one way, we taking "t'other." [10] How might Mexico, Canada, Alaska, and divergent Central America be brought to heel and taught one language unless the nucleus of the Union could be kept together?

Yet the secession movement moved on to its culmination, despite every argument, it seemed, that prudence and idealism were able to urge against it. "The Pickens-and-Stealins Rebellion"—published in the *Atlantic* in June, 1861 [11]—set forth Lowell's earliest views on the war itself. He was delighted that a sentiment so nearly unanimous had responded to Lincoln's call for seventy-five thousand men. He was bitter that Virginia and the other border slave states "had assumed the right to stand neutral between the government and rebellion, to contract a kind of morganatic marriage with Treason." He was bitter also about the English, for being so blind as not to see that the Democratic Party had, in the last election, "divorced itself from the moral sense of the Free States." And he was bitterest of all about Jefferson Davis, whom he dubbed "the Burr of southern conspiracy." The South's constitution was sham, its commissions were sham, its secret agents were rascals, it had stolen money and military supplies from the nation. "A rebellion inaugurated with theft and which has effected its entry into national fortresses, not over broken walls but by breaches of trust, should take Jonathan Wild for its patron saint, with the run of Mr. Buchanan's Cabinet for a choice of sponsors." Lowell never wrote more vigorously in prose than at this date.

At least, he declared, let there be no further question regarding the principle which is at stake. "We believe that the strongest battalions are always on the side of God. The Southern army will be fighting for Jefferson Davis, or at most for the liberty of self-misgovernment, while we go forth for the defense of principles which alone make government august and civil society possible." "Jefferson Davis and Company, dealers in all kinds of repudiation and anarchy," he wrote again, have obliterated every notion of law and precedent, but now that the issue is fairly joined, "a ten years' war would be cheap" if it gave us a country we could be proud of.

Shortly after Lowell published this essay he left the *Atlantic*, as we have seen. Yet he left it upon the friendliest terms, and before the year 1861 was out had begun to aid his successor, Mr. Fields, by sending in the first number of his second series of *Biglow Papers*. These comments in verse upon certain phases of the conflict will be treated elsewhere in this volume. But verse could not wholly contain him. After two years of mounting excitement and apprehension regarding the progress of the war, he was asked to take over another once elegant but now languishing publication, the *North American Review*. Founded in 1815, "by a number of cultivated gentlemen in Boston," [12] it had prospered for many a varying season, but had of late, under the guidance of the Rev. Dr. Andrew P. Peabody, fallen into alarming neglect. Lowell declared to J. L. Motley that it was no longer lively and that it "had no particular opinions on any particular subject." [13] Of course, this was, he felt, an unpardonable condition in wartime. When its publishers, Crosby and Nichols, asked him to take over the editorship, therefore, he consented, though only on the condition that Charles Eliot Norton, of Cambridge, be named as his associate.

Practically the entire second series of *Biglow Papers* had appeared in the *Atlantic* before Lowell turned again to the medium of the political essay, but when he did get back to it his early vigor appeared as great as ever. He began by discussing "The President's Policy," [14] and his opening sentence was an indictment of the South—particularly of South Carolina, for "hurrying ten other prosperous southern commonwealths into crime" out of the simple motive of satisfying an "impatient vanity." He wrote on, for eight full pages, explaining how the North had been ennobled by the conflict and damning the English for sympathizing with the enemy. The Republicans finally won out in 1860, he said, because their war aims mingled ethics with politics, because they drew their arguments "not so much from experience as from general principles of right and wrong."

Lincoln's initial handicaps were great, he continued. Never did a President enter upon office with less means at his command for inspiring confidence in the people. Only half of the Union had acknowledged him as chief executive (twenty-two free states to eleven Confederate states was the exact ratio); even in the North there was a large and dangerous minority. And what contemptible criticisms he has been compelled to submit to! "That Mr. Lincoln is not handsome nor elegant we learn from certain English tourists who would consider similar revelations in regard to Queen Victoria as thoroughly American in their want of *bienseance*." He has also been reproached for his "Americanism" by other British critics; but with all deference, Lowell added, "we cannot say that we like him any the worse for it."

He praised Lincoln's policies, his conduct of the war, and the homeliness of his genius. As President he was faced with the choice of Bassanio in *The Merchant of Venice.* "Which of the three caskets held the prize that was to redeem the fortunes of the country? There was the golden one whose showy spaciousness might have tempted a vain man; the silver of compromise, which might have decided the choice of merely an acute one." Yet the sad-eyed gentleman passed both these by. Perhaps he dallied a bit too long with his decision, "but when he made it, it was worthy of his cautious but sure footed understanding." And how reasonable his public utterances have been since that choice was finally settled, with what familiar dignity has he discussed his problems with his people! He is utterly unconscious of self, is indeed "our representative man."

One of the most acute essays of Lowell's career appeared in his analysis of "General McClellan's Report," [15] an analysis so penetrating and so resourceful in tone that one is led to deplore the fact that he gave up political discussion, in large measure, after peace between the two sections was concluded. That he never wrote with sober judiciousness in this field is a truth which by this time should have become plain. But at least he said *something* important, and he said it interestingly and effectively.

A general, he began in all innocence, is a very important person; he is a national symbol. If he win a battle, we all rejoice with him; if he lose one, the people he represents reflect his grief in every eye, feel his shame in every cheek. Heroes, of course, cannot be made to order; yet if the right sort of leader should appear in a time of crisis, the popular enthusiasm would go far toward making him in fact what he almost always is in their fancy. And no commander in history, Lowell continues, "ever had more of this paid-up capital of fortune, this fame in advance, this success before succeeding, than General McClellan." That dear old domestic bird, the Public, was sure that, in him, she had brooded-out an eagle-chick at last.

Yet consider the results of all our hopes! His Peninsula Campaign was a disastrous failure. McClellan met the enemy and he enjoyed greater numbers, but, instead of conquering him, he succeeded only in getting away! Now he has written an octavo volume in the stupid hope of justifying his incompetence. This last gesture will deceive nobody; it comes altogether too late. For "there is no argument for the soldier but success, no wisdom for the man but to acknowledge defeat and be silent under it."

The way this general has been played up by our journalists in the past was astonishing, if sickening, to consider, Lowell felt. "No *prima donna* was ever more thoroughly exploited by her Hebrew *impresario*. The papers swarmed with anecdotes, incidents, sayings. Nothing was too unimportant, and the new commander-in-chief pulled his teeth by special dispatch to the Associated Press. We had him warm for supper in *the very latest* with three exclamation marks, and cold for breakfast in *last evening's telegraphic news* with none. Nothing but a patent pill was ever so suddenly famous."

The trouble with McClellan is simple. "He appears to have thought it within the sphere of his duty to take charge of the statesmanship of the President no less than of the movements of the army." And all this time he was so unresourceful in his own field as to be unable to move without one hundred and fifty-thousand pairs of legs. Now, in 1864, he is sponsoring himself as a candidate for the Presidency, against Lincoln. His Report, in fact, is a political manifesto. But he is not the person for the place. "The man who is fit for the office of President in these times should be one who knows how to advance, an art which General McClellan has never learned."

Two more essays by Lowell were to make their appearance in the *North American,* before the victory of northern arms became assured. In the first, "The Rebellion: Its Causes and Consequences," [16] he reviewed two recent books on the war, one by E. A. Pollard, a southerner, the other by Horace Greeley. This article is extremely discursive; it foreshadows the endless ineffectualities of the literary criticism of his "humanistic" period. More than a dozen pages are given over to the evident contention that, in stating occurrences and attributing motives, "history is not to be depended on in any absolute sense." Then comes the usual moral pronouncement: "Surely the Lord God Omnipotent reigneth." True, He does not always immediately interfere in our affairs. But He makes Good infinitely lovely to the soul of man, while the beauty of Evil is but a brief cheat.[17]

In disposing of Mr. Pollard—whom Lowell gets round to noticing after twenty-two pages of windy rumination—he sets forth a highly remarkable view of government. Pollard had argued that the primary reason the South withdrew from the Union was its desire to escape from the tyranny of a "numerical majority." Lowell's reply is that "the majority always governs in the long run, because it comes gradually round *to the side of what is just and for the common interest."* [18]

Yet there was one thing he felt compelled to concede about the South, and he generously wrote it out. After all, he realized, the soldiers of the Confederate Armies really believed in their cause. Of course, the struggle was actually "between right and privilege, between law and license," but they simply did not realize this fact. They were still possessed of the quaint notion that their rights and their inheritance as a free people were at stake. Such ardent convictions (even though grossly misguided) made the North hopeful about them. "The high qualities they have undoubtedly shown in the course of the war, their tenacity, patience, and discipline, show that, *under better influences, they may become worthy* [19] to take their part in advancing the true destinies of America."

"McClellan or Lincoln?" [20] his other essay, appeared in October, 1864, neatly timed for the presidential election of the following month. It is direct and vigorous in its point of view. Lowell had something important to say, a particular issue to focus his convictions upon, and he settled down to his subject at once. "The spectacle of an opposition waiting patiently during several months for its principles to turn up would be amusing in times less critical than these." This was his opening sentence about the Democratic Party, which had nominated General McClellan, and it set the tone that was to be maintained to the end.

The trouble with this party was simple. It had favored a compromise with the Confederate States; it wanted the carnage of the past three years stopped. "But," declared Lowell, indulgently, "there are things that are not subjects of compromise. The honor, the conscience, the very soul of a nation cannot be compromised without ceasing to exist." The ethical issues were still, as in the 1840's, the ones which primarily mattered to him.

What is a Nation, a *true* Nation? he asked. What makes the integrity of one worth preserving at any price? He replied to his question in the light of his now altogether familiar formula. "If a nation were only a contrivance to protect men in gathering gear, if territory meant only so many acres for the raising of crops, if power were of worth only as a police to prevent or punish crimes against person and property, then peace for the mere sake of peace were the one desirable thing for a people whose only history should be written in a cash book. But if a nation be a living unity, leaning on the past of tradition, and reaching toward the future by continued aspiration and achievement—if territory be of value for the raising of men formed to high aims and inspired to noble deeds by that common impulse which, springing from a national ideal, gradually takes shape in the national character—if power be but a gross and earthly bulk till it be ensouled with thought and purpose, and of worth only as the guardian and promoter of truth and justice among men—then there are misfortunes worse than war and blessings greater than peace."

It was his old eloquence, and it was urged, as always, with an old and pious compulsion. Whether the nation had *ever* comprised a unity, its different sections applauding one another's proposals in the realm of federal law, or endorsing with genial reciprocity the views of one another with respect to candidates for office—such simple and factual questions never once seem to have existed for him. He was writing in the light of his perennial idealism. Only a student aware of the later stages of Puritanism—when the genuine personal conviction of sin had disappeared, and only the verbalism of its morality remained—can comprehend fairly the Lowell of his middle years. Religion, to his mind, had become a form instead of a reality, a form clung to mainly out of deference to his father's example. But he had freed himself from its ritualistic compulsions. His emancipation left him with little more than its ethical terms, which, to be sure, he amply exploited. God, meanwhile, was reduced to a figure of speech, to a useful symbol of a vanished Awfulness. His name still proved to be of great service, as a rallying cry for Lowell's less unshackled countrymen. But it seems only reasonable to add that that name was to the author now, an instrument (probably a subconscious one) of propaganda, and that it was being exploited in the hope of obtaining the illusion of divine indorsement in a Cause whose issue was piracy.

But one may prefer to face this comment in more specific terms. The underlying tyranny whose continuance was at stake in the struggle, the forthcoming political and economic domination which Calhoun and scores of other southerners had protested against and sought peaceably to avert, appeared to Lowell to be a meaningless evasion. He never once gave it his considered attention, never once surmised that on the heels of the victory of which he was so confident would come a systematic exploiting of the defeated South which had certainly been planned out beforehand by a powerful and finally dominant faction in Congress. The leaders of this faction, shrewdly aware of the advantages of political control—once the North could completely obtain it—were not concerned in the least with the "Jefferson Davis against God" version of the struggle. What they wanted was *power,* and they meant to obtain it and to use it for their purposes, regardless of how completely the economic balance of the nation might be destroyed.

As every schoolboy knows, this destruction did take place, as scheduled, and its effects are evident everywhere in the South today. It is no mere accident that the library of Harvard University, so modest in its resources before the war, is at present greater in its resources than those of all the southern universities combined. Nor is it the result of any deliberate act of that Deity with whom Lowell always appeared intimate that the South and the West have for three-quarters of a century cried out against the financial domination of the country by Wall Street. Their protests have been uttered with sound reason, have implied, as one brilliant critic has phrased it, that the towers of New York "are built upon southern and western backs." [21]

Yet it ought to be plain that no one would wish to censure Lowell merely because of his unionist sympathies. Supporting that faction was natural enough to New England residents of his day. But Lowell was a public figure, the voice of a large segment of his region, and his blindness to the underlying causes of the sectional struggle, his refusal to face the issue at all except in terms of a glib morality, would seem to suggest a fundamental limitation in his nature which every responsible student of his career is bound to notice. He never understood history, in any important way, despite his many references to it. He never comprehended politics, although the most instructive commentary upon the nature of political action ever available to an American had been enacted before his eyes in the published utterances of Webster, Clay, Calhoun, Cushing, Davis, Choate, and a host of other contemporary figures. Moreover, Harvard scholar though he was, he never made any effort worth mentioning to understand the civilization of the South. He proved himself, from his undergraduate days, a dupe of the most irresponsible propaganda his age afforded. He even became, as we have seen, an ardent and continuous manufacturer of it. In somewhat more technical terms, one feels compelled to term him, in simple honesty, the most completely didactic major author in American literature.

XIII

"One must swallow the truth, though it makes one's eyes water."

Lowell to E. L. Godkin, January 1, 1869.
Works, XV, 188

BUT we must retrace our steps, at least slightly. Lowell, as author, was ambidextrous in his militant defense of the cause of the North. The essays, as we have seen, had argued that cause primarily with a mixture of timely and impassioned prose. But he had not lost his talent for verse satire, nor had he in any permanent way stifled his former interest in it. December 9, 1861, he confided to Miss Jane Norton, Charles Eliot's sister, that he had been writing a "Biglow Paper." "I feel as nervous about it," he wrote, "as a young author not yet weaned to public favor. It was clean against my critical judgment, for I don't believe in resuscitations—we hear no good word of the *posthumous* Lazarus. . . . I hope Shady Hill [the Norton home in Cambridge] won't think it dull."[1] It was his casual announcement to one of his friends that the most effective weapon at his command had been reverently reassumed with an abidingly reverent intention.

Eleven letters comprise the second series, and all that were separately published appeared in the *Atlantic.*[2] His characters are the familiar ones, although Parson Wilbur has in the interval remembered a great deal more of his Harvard learning than formerly. Lowell buries the letters proper, in most cases, beneath heavy displays of discursive profundity. But Hosea is still the righteous rustic, whose ignorance of the South and whose bitterness against it have ripened with the years. Birdofredum, rascal as always, is the only one of the three who has changed; yet he remains, as in the former series, Lowell's most entertaining character. His change consists in a whole-souled apostasy. Mr. Sawin has become a southern gentleman. In his first letter to the Parson, he takes up his story where he left it some thirteen years ago:

The Nigger Pomp, you will recall, had just kicked me out. I wandered off, through bayous and criks, my oak leg snapped at by alligators, my live one clawed at by pizon-nettle. But in time, I came to civilization and dropped into a saloon. I had hardly begun to feel like a man again before a feller opposite me lept up, drew his peace-maker, and said, in effect, Dash it, Sir, I'm double-dashed if you aint the one that stole my yaller chattel. Aint you the only stranger around? Warm the tar, Jedge, while we give him a fair trial. Come gentlemen, let's have a drink, and somebody go out and borrow a feather bed. Well, the jury sat and then began to work on me, and quicker'n a flash they had me looking like a turkey chick fit fer a Fejee Thanksgiving. Naturally I felt rather stuck up about it! Afterwards they rode me around the town, free of charge, and showered me with reception eggs, kept especially for just such occasions. The experience taught me what the phrase "southern hospitality" really meant. Finally, they sentenced me to ten years in the jug.

But two years ago, Parson, they caught the real thief. After that they uncorked the jail and let me out. The folks behaved most handsome to me. The Colonel who had accused me was especially courteous. I'll do whats right about it, he said, "I'll give ye settisfaction now by shootin ye at sight." Also when that nigger of mine is caught I'll give him one hell fired lickin for getting the wrong man took up. All that was expected of me was to pay the Widow Shannon for the use of her feather bed. Then they began to drink, at my expense, and to pass resolutions calling me a flawless soldier and a martyr. They even took up a subscription for me and a lot of them endorsed it by making their marks. But that's the fashion down here; they would rather sign a thing than think about what it says.

So now I'm a Confederate, you see. The Union paid me off in gold before we seceded, and gold is a good deal better than Jeff Davis's bonds. I'll tell you why I stayed down here. The niggers do all the work; all we white men have to do is stay on top of them and keep them steady. Then there's the whisky. It's as cheap as flees. When I found this out, I jest decided to freeze right here and marry the Widow Shannon. She needed an overseer anyhow.

Miss Shannon, as I call my wife, is a real lady too. We live here at Turkey-Buzzard Roost and there aint a more accomplished female between our place and Tuscaloosy. She's an F.F.V., has "never had a relative thet done a stroke o' work," and every grown member of her family owes his thousands, at least. Talking about her reminds me of the reason I'm writing to you, Parson. I want you to break the news of my marriage to my other wife up there in New England. Get me disvorced from her. There are a heap of arguments to justify it: I've been in Prison, my state is secedin, I've got the southern brand of Religion, and besides I've been cornfiscated now and all New Englanders are aliens to me.

The Widow kind of threatened me into marrying her, I'll admit. Reason was, she wanted somebody cultivated around, an ornament to society down here. You know of course that, if you want to belong to the social hierarchy in the South, all you've got to know is just a little more than the average darky. Schooling is one thing they can't seem to stand; they think that knowin' much might spoil a boy as a Secesher. There's a lot more I want to write you about, Parson, but I have to stop now to do some mission work; I've got to let a leetle law into Cynthy's hide. Yourn to death.[3]

Lowell's next Biglow Paper, "Mason and Slidell," reflects a poorly concealed fear. These two gentlemen, southern commissioners to European states, had been taken off the British mailship *Trent* by Captain Wilkes of the Union vessel, *San Jacinto*. The English people and cabinet were indignant. A hot protest was filed with Lincoln, contending that their flag had been violated at sea. Lincoln prudently released the prisoners, knowing that a war with one government was more easily managed than open conflict with two. But his action evoked much criticism in a North, thousands of whose citizens were already bitter about the sympathy the

Confederate cause had obtained in England. It was Lowell's intention to mollify this bitterness.

Parson Wilbur, as usual, introduces Hosea's poem, with thirteen pages of discursive preamble, the burden of which is that the true test of manliness is the ability to say, "I was wrong," when the facts command it. This the North had mustered the courage to do. He then proceeds to quarrel with the English for failing to apprehend the great principle which was at stake in the Civil War. The statesmen of that very isolated island have exhibited themselves as remarkably ignorant on this point, have termed the Yankees mere tradesmen, a people possessed of "no better image of God than that stamped upon the current coin." But let us be cautious in retaliating, the Parson concluded. And let us not presume to criticize our Commander-in-Chief. We do not know his plans. We should therefore patiently trust his high purposes.

Hosea's poem itself then follows. It is in the form of a dialogue he overheard between Bunker Hill Monument and Concord Bridge. The first part contains a good many strictures against the people of the mother country. They have become mighty arrogant since they whipped "Nap the Fust," have lately been shaking their fists at everybody. But let us come to the point. The North was in error in the Mason-Slidell case. Let's admit this freely. We had no right to search a foreign ship. Yet before long those people over there will realize that we have come of age. The Monument is the moderator throughout. But the Bridge is worried about the cost of the war. Lowell does not completely succeed in contrasting his two characters, though between them they discuss amusingly almost every important issue which the war had brought into focus.

The Bridge then proceeds to make this much irrefutably clear: The war must be waged in earnest. God is on the side of the North. Then, in verses of briefer meter, Jonathan (or New England) addresses John Bull in the homely terms of one farmer to another. It is a severe and outspoken work: We gave those rascals Mason and Slidell back to you, John, because Abraham thought it was right. Yet there's one thing about this conflict which apparently you don't understand. It is that the motto of the South is, "Poor folks down," while the Northern principle remains, "All men up." Now John, to which principle do you subscribe? We know that God's price is high. But nothing except what He sells wears long, and in some future day you will learn that truth, as we are learning it now.[4]

The Parson heard from Birdofredum again very soon (the first six numbers of the Second Series appeared in rapid sequence between January and July, 1862), and once more, in No. III, it required the "conscience of New England" a good deal of space to explain itself. Eight pages elapsed before the letter proper was quoted. In it Sawin was defending the view that the lineage of southerners was generally superior to that of the residents of the North. At least, opined Wilbur, the early adventurers to Massachusetts paid their passages. "No felons were ever shipped thither." Look at colonial Virginia, on the other hand. As everyone knows, a great part of those who were deported to that section "were the sweepings of the London streets and the London stews." Assume for the moment that many of the names these ragamuffins went by *were* truly illustrious in English history. Isn't it well known that servants were often called by their master's names, just as slaves are today? In support of this view the poet summoned that most trustworthy of historical testimonials, the drama of the Restoration—a body of literature no Wilbur would ever have read, except furtively! Look at the manner in which this so-called gentry has acted: "The first work of the founders of Virginia . . . was conspiracy and rebellion." In sober terms let him ask what has this cuticular aristocracy of the South added to the refinements of civilization "except the carrying of bowie-knives and the chewing of tobacco?"

Sawin's verses next recited the story of his conversion. The trouble with the New England variety of religion, he declared, was that one's professions counted for nothing without Works. Down South it was different. The Widow had told him that their marriage could never be, without he got religion. "How shall I git it ma'am?" he asked. Her answer was pointed: "Attend the nex' camp-meetin."

Well, Sawin followed her advice. He went to a preaching and he heard some remarkable things spoken there. The seed of Ham was given them in charge, the pulpit-thumper shouted. All things, the Bible said, was intended for man's use. And didn't the Greek and Hebrew words that mean a *man* mean *white?* Anyhow, had it been the South's fault that Yankee skippers kept on totin niggers over here and selling them? These slaves had to be kept ignorant. Where would their souls go to, Sawin wondered, if they got to studying about Free knowledge and Fourierism and Spiritualism and other satanic doctrines that kept filtering down from the North? This meeting warn't like one of the Parson's:

> Ther' wuz a tent clost by thet hed a kag o' sunthin in it,
> Where you could go, if you wuz dry, an' damp ye in a minute.

Sawin drank and drank, and the preacher bellowed and bellowed, and the conviction of sin growed and growed within him. It was only natural, when nine-tenths of the parish took to tumbling round and hollering, that he should turn to and follow them. When the Widow saw this she was pleased, beyond doubt. That's what she called acting like a reasonable being, she said. So they finally made it up and concluded to hitch hosses.

Birdofredum's letter slows down in its later pages; what appears there has been said before, more effectively. Its burden is this: Every southern family thinks itself first-rate. No white man works down there, unless he works at beating negroes. William Gilmore Simms is considered a greater literary figure than anybody now writing in the North. Southern money is worthless. Practically all southerners are hot-headed and belligerent by nature, and they all think of themselves as Colonels, and of northerners as the mere rank and file of society. Their papers suppress the truth, print only propaganda. The section is really impoverished. Its leaders despise the democratic ideal of "I'm ez good ez you be." [5]

Lowell's fourth letter is one of the dullest of the series, a weak repetition of arguments already familiar. Wilbur favors emancipation, of course, but suggests that it be effected neither hastily nor vindictively. It might be better to make it "a reform instead of a revolution." Biglow's poem, which follows discreetly, is a humorous comment upon recent northern reverses. It emphasizes another argument in support of Lincoln's treatment of Mason and Slidell. One of these men was a cheap descendant of the Virginia aristocracy; the other began as plain New York trash. But if the government had hanged them, as they doubtless deserved, the two critters would now be martyrs![6]

The gist of letter No. V may likewise be stated briefly. Its method is that of irony. In it Hosea is reporting the speech of the Honorable Preserved Doe, a conservative. Davis, implied the speaker, would be where Lincoln was, if only the People had let the Supreme Court and ex-President Buchanan have their way. It was true that the South wasn't licked yet, but at least, they had pricked the southern windbag. This being so, let the war be stopped and some readjustments worked out. They should not be too severe about slavery, either. What was left of it ought to be saved, for let gentlemen remember that a real abuse was the best thing in the world for a politician to have at hand. He may always win votes by attacking it. But he had talked too long already and was dry. He excused himself in order "to set down and give thet 'ere bottle a skrimmage."[7]

Contribution VI contained a "pastoral" by the Parson himself. It described in vivid terms the coming of a New England spring:

> First come the blackbirds clatt'rin' in tall trees,
> And settling things in windy Congresses,—
> Queer politicians, though, for I'll be skinned
> Ef all on 'em don't head aginst the wind.

He lists other evidences of that always astonishing season. He recites his own love of solitude, his belief in the present, his impatience with those who linger in the past. Meditating these things, he falls asleep upon the steps of his church, and dreams that a remote ancestor comes to him with questions about the War. There follows a debate between the Parson and the early Puritan, a disciple of the smite-'em-hip-and-thigh school. Wilbur freely admitted that the evils of slavery were great. But they must not be too precipitous, he added; they must make their gains permanent. The trouble with his visitant was that he had acted too violently in his own day. He and Cromwell and the Lord had chopped off the head of Charles I, but eleven years later his son was back on the throne, and all the evils his parent personified returned with him. Slavery was the Parson's Charles I, but remember it now had eight million necks. The hardest problem of all was not to win for the black man his rights, but to emancipate the white man.

> It's a long job, but we shall worry thru it;
> Ef baynets fail, the spellin'-book must du it.[8]

The next three letters indicate a sad decline in Lowell's zest for his work. Number Seven he called the "Latest Views of Mr. Biglow." The dying Wilbur informed Biglow that the true object of the war was "the maintenance of the idea of government." The North was doing a great deal more than merely suppressing "an enormous riot." It must, therefore, carry on, unfalteringly. Yet, though the seminal principle of Law cannot properly be made the subject of compromise at all," we must not blind ourselves to the fact that a certain give and take in society is inevitable. *In medio ,utissimus."*

Biglow thought somewhat more drastically on this point. He appended a poem, the burden of which was that the North should persevere in its objectives. Conciliation means being kicked. We have *men* enough, what we need is a *man* (a Lincoln, that is, not a McClellan) to lead us. We must not vacillate. We must be of one mind, as the South is. We must believe as hard in freedom "ez Jeff doos in slavery." If we do this we shall emerge a country with a soul, the Earth's greatest nation.[9]

"Kettelopotomachia" was the Eighth paper. It purported to be spirit rappings from the Parson who, though dead, is still apparently far from sanctified. This work deserves attention. It is in macaronic verse, and its combinations of Latin, dog Latin, puns, and colloquialisms make it extremely difficult reading, but it is doubtful whether more vulgar comments were ever set down about the State of Virginia. One should remember that it was dated as of February, 1866. The war was over. Lowell's note declares the occasion for the poem to have been a free fight between Mr. H. R. Pollard, of the *Richmond Examiner,* and Messrs. Coleman and N. P. Tyler, of the *Enquirer,* concerning the public printing. It occurred in the Rotunda of the state capitol, and though six shots were fired, "no damage resulted, except to a marble statue of Washington."

John Smith founded the Colony, he declared, but King James settled it with broken rascals, blackguards, soldiers out of Falstaff's legion, and with wenches whom they were able to seduce into marriage. Not all natives of the state are of this type, he admitted, but many of its citizens are false to their oaths, stab people with bowie knives, beat negroes, and tar and feather Yankees. Pollard, for instance, is a poor white, Tyler the offspring of a miserable president, and all three are cowards, busy night and day with milking Uncle Sam and their native state (the little cow), though both are dry already.

These men want permission to publish the *Statutes of Virginia,* though the inability to read there is more common than anywhere else. They stand ready to print the laws or to break them. Pollard "liquors up," inserts a huge quid of nicotine between his jaws, flourishes an enormous knife, and says the job shall be his. His opponents, also drinking, chewing, and spitting tremendously, refuse to give in. Tyler shouts the following defiance: "Although I see you double, should you be 20 I will say you lie and will thrash the whole bunch of you. . . . I am a son of a dog if I dont. Pollard prepares to stab him, but now seeing double himself, falls on the floor. Tyler is already there. Coleman stares at them, spits thrice around their bodies in a kind of funeral rite and, hiccoughing, collapses across both. Later, still unconscious, they are dragged to the Calyboose.[10] This paper was not published by the *Atlantic*.

When Hosea wrote next to the editor of the *Atlantic,* the end of the War was imminent. He turned to reminiscence, now, about the good old times, when the talk of the farmers was more pithy than today, and when the dear young lads, now dead on a score of battlefields, played innocently upon his knee. What monster's hand had wrought this desperate change? He shouted his answer, for the world to hear. It was that dripping red hand of yours, Jeff Davis! Yet let us have Peace. And let us greet it, when it comes, not as mourners but with pride, triumphantly. We know, now, that Freedom is no gift that tarries long in the hands of cowards.[11]

Almost a year passed before Hosea addressed the *Atlantic* editor again, and this time proved his last, for he had fully served his purpose. He had been of great use in uniting northern sentiment, had made vocal the point of view of the majority in his section with a rare insight and fidelity. Lincoln was dead now, a martyr. In his place in the White House sat Andrew Johnson, who wished to fulfill the policy of appeasement of his predecessor and who was being denounced by hundreds of editors for his moderation. Hosea joined in the general abuse, intensified it—strengthened by all the force of his rhetoric the impossibility of a reasonable adjustment of Northern and Southern interests:

The South must first be reconstructed. It cannot be trusted as a section until the fact of its political impotence is assured. Make Americans of the Confederates, ran the argument. Teach them now to love their country as in the past they loved their sin. If you leave them Southern, you will keep them as a sore, ready always to fester as formerly. What if they do resent our demands for concrete pledges of acquiescence? They are as mad now as they will ever be. Make them live with the negroes equally as we took in the Paddies from Ireland.[12] These Paddies came to us ignorant and poor. Now they are the bones and sinews of the land. Take the southerner's gun "away from him for good." Render him, in other words, politically and economically helpless. Before we listen to him another time, make him cry "Mother, I have sinned." Let us pay no attention to President Johnson, in his efforts to win a general endorsement of his program. Did he discover the country? Does he pay our taxes? "Was't he that shou'dered all them million guns?" He still believes, absurdly, that secession never took the Rebel states out of the Union. We should travel no more on that old pettyfogging track, for our artillery wheels have cut a road straight through it. Remember, the oath of the South is worthless. Until its citizens are fully converted to our point of view, "let 'em wear a muzzle." Let us try no "squirtguns on the burnin' Pit." Why did we die, after all, unless it was to settle forever that men were men, and not slaves? [13]

Lowell had said his say; there is no one who can pretend to doubt it. He had taken his stand with the extreme Republicans, whom in so many ways he had been half-consciously assisting since the war began. In essays for the *North American,* moreover, he was developing with emphasis the same argument of intolerance and coercion. "The first condition of permanent peace," he wrote, the month it was declared,[14] "is to render those who were the great slave-holders when the war began, and who will be the great landholders after it is over, powerless for mischief." Then he grew magnanimous. Confiscation of Rebel property, he continued, was unthrifty housekeeping, for it would make the section less available for revenue. He turned to the Negroes, to the "freedmen." Would it be enough to make them landholders merely? he asked. "Must we not make them voters also," that they might have the power of self-protection? [Negroes were allowed to vote, at this date, in only six of the twenty-two unionist states.] "The only way to teach them how to use political power is to give it to them." The natural superiority of the white race would be sufficient "to prevent any serious mischief from the new order of things." Some men had spoken of colonization, of "setting the blacks apart in some territory by themselves." But there were insuperable objections to this plan: If carried out, would it not put them beyond the reach of the gracious influences of our "higher civilization?" And "as to any prejudice which should prevent the two races from living together, it would soon yield to interest and necessity." One reads these complacent words today with a cold and quiet amazement. Yet, when analyzed, the point of view they embody becomes as commonplace as that of yesterday's newspaper. It is the point of view of the Communists of our own era, of those bright and utterly emancipated reformers who have never been able to comprehend the meaning of tradition in a society that has once respected it.

Summer found Lowell reaffirming his views. The South had hoped to possess the government by a sudden coup d'état. If that failed, it expected a peaceful secession that would result from paralyzing the commerce and manufactures of the free states. He traced the sad story of this disappointed ambition, with copious asides damning the English for supporting the enemy. Consider the atrocities of the War! "In Missouri the Rebels took scalps as trophies," made "personal ornaments of the bones of our unburied dead." Later in the struggle they literally starved union prisoners, he added, implying that a perfectly integrated railroad system existed, with which farm products could be whisked, unmolested, from any southern farm to any southern point of internment.

What did it all add up to? Simply this: The conflict was not to be in any sense concluded "by merely crying *quits* and shaking hands. The slaveholding states chose to make themselves a foreign people to us, and they must take the consequences." The question for a wise government, in such a case, he went on, was not, "Have we the right to interfere? but much rather, Have we the right to let them alone? If we are entitled, as conquerors—and it is only as such that we are so entitled—to stipulate for the abolition of slavery, what is there to prevent our exacting further conditions no less essential to our safety and the prosperity of the South?" [15]

Yet what, Lowell went on, could one do with President Johnson, who still seemed bent, against all rational dictates, upon carrying out what he termed the Martyr's appeasement policies? He had even taken the question to the country. Well, to begin with, one could damn him. One could revile him as a drunkard, could charge him with poor taste, could blame him for appealing to a mob instead of to the Congress, where the issue ought rationally to be determined. In this last gesture he has debased his country from a republic to a mass meeting. He has assumed a sectional ground, not a national one, and has ignored the wishes of New England, though New England was a deciding factor in his election to office. The President should cease his heresy and proclaim to the South that the United States "are resolved, by God's grace, to Americanize you, and America means education, equality before the law, and every upward avenue of life made as free to one man as another." It was the old idealism of a quarter of a century before, the old faith in Vartu and benevolence, the old ignorance of actual conditions, and the old blindness to those tangible villainies, that, even as Lowell wrote, were being enacted in practically every southern state, after a pattern which he himself had defined and sponsored.

XIV

"Yes there is one thing they [the English] always take for granted, namely, that an American must see the superiority of England. They have as little tact as their totem *the bull."*

Lowell to C. E. Norton, November 11, 1888.
Works, XV, 220

LOWELL'S hatred of England during the war was greater than at any other time of his life. It was a hatred that prevailed over his very strong attachments to certain natives of the island whom he had come to know intimately—men like Thomas Hughes and the lamented Arthur Hugh Clough. Of course, the outspoken eagerness of many prominent Englishmen to see the Union dissolved should be set down as a primary reason for his attitude. Another would seem to be reflected in certain hitherto unnoticed correspondence which he carried on at this time with his friend John Lothrop Motley, who was serving as American consul at Vienna.[1] If Lowell ever needed any encouragement to despise England, he could certainly have found it in the statements of his absent friend.

"What's good's all English, all that isn't aint," began one of Motley's series of comments. He had recently received a copy of "Mason and Slidell," and that line in it he found himself quoting "whenever I perform my daily task of reading the *Times*." It should be inscribed, he went on, "over the portal of the great international exposition just opening in London.

" 'O Lord we thank thee that *we* are not like other men, republicans and sinners' is the bottom of the thought of every honest John Bull.

"But there is, after all, a difference. In our resentment against the cynical attitude of the English aristocracy towards us, and in our disgust at the toads and vipers which their humble servants of the press spit upon us in their daily talk (the natural effect, I suppose of a surfeit of toad-eating) we should remember two things." One, Motley explained, was that though the dominant classes hated America with a magnificent hatred, "they have abstained hitherto from giving the slaveholders anything more than their 'moral support.'" And that would not be enough to satisfy the South.

In the next place, these things should be considered: "England —as represented by her dominant class—has succeeded in offending both parties to our Civil War, not because (as in her self laudation she imagines) her course has been strictly neutral and just, but because, while abstaining from action, she has, by tongue and pen, reviled and calumniated the North with a persistent venom almost incredible—and because, while flattering and applauding and encouraging the slaveholders, she has not moved a finger to help them and has hitherto refused them recognition." Yet all this was perhaps the inevitable result of reasons that any historian could see. For "England is governed by an aristocracy, and its instinct is to rejoice that democracy is come to grief and to assume that democracy is a bubble that has broke." How insular was the thinking of this class, Motley felt, completely blind as it was to the truth that *no* form of government except the democratic can *ever* exist in America! "And in Europe," on the other hand, "there is no such thing as a people—least of all perhaps in England. Thus it is that the spontaneous uprising of everybody, the mechanics, the merchants, the slaveholders, the day laborers, the poets, the professors, the capitalists, the students, the people—in short, the sum total of a population where castes don't exist—is utterly incomprehensible to Europeans. . . . The phenomenon fades away in the fog of old world ignorance and prejudice."

These views proved vastly interesting to Lowell. Whether they were the source of several of his own opinions at this time does not seem important; at any rate, the question is largely beyond determination. But this much is plain: When Lowell and Norton, in January, 1864, issued their first number of the sagging *North American Review,* Motley was the man whom Lowell hoped very soon to engage as a regular contributor. "Our pay isn't much," he explained, "but you shall have five dollars a page, and the object is in a sense patriotic. . . . You shall have *carte blanche* as to subject." He ventured a few suggestions. How about the Schleswig-Holstein affair, or Recent German Literature, or the National Resources of Austria? Lowell went on to add his opinions about the state of the country: If Lincoln is re-elected, the War will soon be over. The mercantile classes are longing for peace, but the people are more firm that ever. All the snobs, too, are Secesh. But "we have the promise of God's word and God's nature on our side." [2]

Motley, begging off, pleaded his personal case well, though he furnished in his letter more significant comment than is contained in most articles of six times its length. "The very first time I ever write for any periodical—quarterly, monthly, weekly, or daily—" he said, "it shall be for the *N.A.R.*" But long ago he defined a program of writing for himself, one which would take him a century and a half to fulfill. "In the last year and a half I have only written one of the five volumes which anyhow I must accomplish before being laid up in ordinary." This troublous circumstance was what made him so niggardly about his time. And of course there was Secretary of State Seward's new and absurd practice of publishing each year the dispatches that were sent out and received by his department. It was a policy that had annoyed and distracted him no end. It obliged him to write "the most circumspect and idiotic trash."

Lowell had asked for a commentary upon Schleswig-Holstein and upon Europe generally. Motley supplied one that was entirely informal, though more solid than anything any other available contributor appeared able to conceive. "The moral which the few great powers are reading to us all," he said, "especially to America, is to be strong. It is less sublime than that of our dear Longfellow but awfully practical. 'Let us *not* suffer *but* be strong.' These are hard times for small people. Poor little Denmark has just committed [suicide] with a drug which a few years ago we were all trying to get for ourselves, English sympathy, not knowing that the bottle should be marked Poison. Well, fortunately we didn't get it and have long since, I trust, ceased to hanker for it, having learned that English hatred which was freely administered instead is a far more wholesome beverage. We have been growing stronger since the Trent affair, and I think that 'Mason and Slidell, a Yankee Idyl' had a good deal to do with curing us from our wishy-washy sentimentalities. May your shadow never be less! Certainly, Denmark would not have been cut completely in two had she not trusted to England."

Regarding the South, Motley and Lowell were in entire agreement. "I don't say how long they can keep up the mutiny," wrote the former, "yet I live every day in hopes that the gang will turn against the ringleaders. This, I think, will certainly be the case if Lincoln is reëlected, for then the mutineers must see that they are in for four more years of the same work and this is more than they can stand." But if McClellan, "the young Napoleon," came in, he added, "I agree with you that the mutiny will get fresh breath and strength."

Lowell meanwhile was writing in a similar vein to Norton. He was not a fool about England, and Norton in his tolerance for the people of that country, was entirely wrong, he declared. "You think better of them than they deserve, and I like them full as well as you do. But because there are a few noble fellows there like Goldwin Smith, whom one instinctively loves, it doesn't blind me to the fact that they are not England and never will be—that England is an idea, that America is another, that they are innately hostile, and that they will fight us one of these days. God forbid! you say. Amen! say I. But we are fighting the South at this moment on no other grounds, and there are some fine fellows in the South too. England just now is a monstrous sham. . . . I think a war with England would be the greatest calamity but one—the being afraid of it. . . . Goldwin Smith tells us she has changed since 1815. But has there been any great war since? Especially any great naval war? The root of our bitterness is not that she used to do so and so, but that we know she would do it again. The wolf was wrong in eating the lamb because its grandmother had muddied the stream, but it would be a silly lamb that expected to be friends with any animal whose grandmother was a wolf." [3]

Yet England was but one of a great many issues that absorbed Lowell's energies during these restless years. He was no Harvard Brahmin, retired into his ivory cloister and puttering about—as one critic has stated—in the dull "Sahara of medieval scholarship." [4] He was scarcely a Brahmin in any sense at all, except for his tastes and his affection for certain men who were. He was busy with literary friends, cautioning them and encouraging them by turns. He was advising others about all sorts of matters—the architecture of the college, the trees that should be planted in the Yard, and ways in which the library holdings could be increased. And there were numerous letters to many loved ones to write, in an always futile effort to picture in less desperate terms those losses which war had already made final.

On the subject of the buildings at Harvard he proved unusually interesting. He directed his criticisms to a member of the Corporation who had solicited them, Judge E. R. Hoar, of Concord. "I know that nearly all our college buildings are hideous," he said, and they were more unsightly as they were later in date. He was about to ask the Judge to look at the new president's house, for instance; but no, that would be asking too much. Could anything uglier be contrived? Was there a doom upon them that they must always get just what they didn't want? "You wanted a large house, you have a small one; a dignified house, you have a porter's lodge; a substantial house, you have one more than half of cardboard—all snips and jags and outs and ins." Then there was College House. The Corporation had put up one ugly row with a flat Mongol face and then decided, apparently, to continue the offense indefinitely. "Good taste is cheaper in the end than bad. If anybody ever leaves you any more money to build with after seeing what you made of Mr. Brooks's legacy, he must be a man of great firmness of purpose." [5]

But what could be done about it? Hoar had asked. Lowell

ventured several suggestions. "Can you not build something old fashioned, which will *seem* old?" Could he not use gables and solid chimneys, to avoid the *factory*-look of the present style? Could not the front windows of the dormitories be made an ornament instead of a deformity? "Let them have hoods to give a little shadow; let them be wide and low rather than high and narrow. . . . Don't be afraid of having bay windows. . . . Be willing to give something for beauty as well as use." The effect of mass should be considered. Even ugly buildings gained a certain dignity from that. Lowell suggested a quadrangle. But above everything he wanted no gingerbread work. "Simplicity is the first element of dignity. . . . Advertise for plans. . . . I would . . . stimulate the architects to show a little invention." What Lowell primarily desired was "something that an association can love to cling around. . . . Give us broad steps whose worn edges, in future years, will recall the many young feet that have long been dust." [6] The noble approach to the present Widener Library is an effect Lowell would probably have approved, unless it should strike him as a violation of the "intimacy" of the Yard.

And then the other problems, so many other problems! Charles G. Leland was editing *The Daily Fare* during the second week of the Philadelphia Fair of 1864. "Would you have any objection," he asked, "to let me publish your name among the contributors? It would be a tower of strength to attract the good—and scare away thieves. The moral effect would be enormous." [7] Again, there was Mr. William Dean Howells, who needed both encouragement and a warning. His article on "Recent Italian Comedy" was in print. Lowell wanted another on Modern Italian Literature. Howells had enough in himself to do honor to American letters; he should keep on cultivating himself. But "you must sweat the Heine out of you as men do mercury. You are as good as Heine—remember that." [8]

And there was Mrs. Francis G. Shaw. Her son Robert had organized a company of Negro troops during the war and had been killed while leading them in the attack on Fort Wagner. "Not a day has passed," Lowell wrote her a month afterwards, "that I have not thought tenderly of you and yours; but I could not make up my mind to write you, and the longer I put it off, the harder it grew. I have tried several times but broken down. . . . There is nothing for such a blow as that but to bow the head and bear it. We can think of many things that in some measure make up for such a loss, but we can think of nothing that will give us back what we have lost. . . . I would rather have my name known and blest, as his will be, through all the hovels of an outcast race, than blaring from all the trumpets of repute." [9]   The meaning of the war whose high purposes he had sanctified was coming home to him at last, in human terms.

There was his own nephew, Charles Russell Lowell, who had enlivened the vacation Lowell recorded in his "Moosehead Journal." The reports of him testify uniformly of his courage and unselfishness; they were traits which won for him, at twenty-nine, the rank of Brigadier General in the Union Army.   In the spring of 1863 he had become engaged to Robert Shaw's sister, Josephine.   In October of the following year, he was killed in action at Cedar Creek.   He was Lowell's favorite among all his relatives.   Motley, in a note of condolence, spoke of him in the most exalted terms.   "He seems to me," the historian declared, "exactly one of those beautiful and heroic shapes that are to stand forth in our history as long as it endures—one of the very highest types of our civilization—scholar, gentleman, soldier.   His splendid services and his noble death will excite the imagination and move the tears of Americans yet unborn. . . . It must be a relief even to the hearts broken by his death to dwell upon the brief but glorious record of his life." [10]   Motley's tribute was typical, was indeed representative, of millions of others that had come, in various ways, to millions of other relatives, in thousands of other homes, North and South.

Meanwhile, what could one say of these dead, how could one collectively do them justice?   What utterance could be made, in a form beyond transience, which would record the sudden frustration of their lives and one's gratitude for the sacrifice their love of freedom had demanded? The occasion that opened to Lowell was auspicious. It was July, 1865, and Harvard was commemorating its fallen. Lowell was to deliver the ode [11] that would bespeak for these brave men a fit and final acknowledgment, was to recite those words which, insofar as words are able, might be cherished in justification of all they had given.

He was rapt in the fervor of conception. He lost sleep, lost his appetite, became lean and haggard and desperate, waiting for the inspiration which seemed utterly reluctant to come. Phrases haunted him in his dreams, distracted him because of their unwillingness to rhyme.[12] And his mind was tortured and wrathful still over a chance slur he had read a year before in an English newspaper, a remark which declared "that nothing was to be hoped of an army officered by tailor's apprentices and butcher boys." When he first saw this statement his nephew had just been killed. Yet this was all that his loss seemed to signify to the ignorant and indifferent cynics of London. How could his mind crystallize the long pageant of indignities it had suffered, and state as well the ideals which had strengthened it, in the cool patterns of poets centuries dead?

Yet his mind did crystallize itself at last, flooding his senses with the luxury of tumultuous conception. The result was a proud poem, strong and sustained, certainly the best of his purely serious works. He began with an apology. Does not one do the dead wrong, he asked, to bring so feeble an offering to men who have already written their story in blood? And yet they died for *Veritas,* for that Truth which the insignia of Harvard has proclaimed now for more than two full centuries. Many before them have sought it among dusty books. But these, our lost brothers, fought for it, and found it at length, unshakably, in death.

He paused to meditate on the brevity and the unpredictability of human life. To many, it seems a mere jest of Fate's contriving— nothing is certain, all is chaos and tinsel. Yet we do not wholly despair. Something the cynic is unable to fathom keeps us hopeful of our birthright to heaven. It is a light across the sea, which points the soul beyond any hope of peace or ultimate surrender. And what sustains this unproved solace? Is it not the example of such men as we are gathered today to remember, in this strict and formal ritual? They are men who fronted a lie in arms, who refused to yield before it, are a type of the old heroic breed.

And Lincoln, our martyr-chief, is a symbol of them all. When Nature came to make him, she threw aside her Old-World moulds. Choosing sweet clay from the heart of the unexhausted West, she created him a shepherd of mankind, modest, free of European influences, and heroic—"the first American." Lowell passed on to sound a dirge for the virtuous, unreturning Harvard dead. In the brave ranks before him his eyes could dwell only upon the gaps. And yet no ban of endless night exiled the lost sons from those who survived them. The paths of virtue "end not in the grave." In imagination he could see them all, mustered in a gleaming row, with brows forever young, transfigured, beyond the accident of change. Perhaps they all did seem to die forever, to lie forceless in the dark. But no, the testament of the soul is otherwise. These men have certified to the world the existence of a fresh and imperial race. Who now can sneer and say again that we trace our line to plebeians? A new nation is born of the struggle; it is its pith and marrow that we celebrate. Let us, in its honor, bow down and praise.[13]

XV

"We have not yet acknowledged him [the Negro] as our brother . . . and yet it must be done ere America can penetrate the Southern States."
Lowell, *Works*, VI, 381

WHEN peace and reconstruction, in 1865, began to spread their ill-matched wings over the nation, the plump, short, and beard-shrouded man of letters was thoroughly alive and busy. His fingers were firmly at rest on the late enemy's pulse, his view about the patient's condition definite and professional. That patient (the South) needed a strong dose of reindoctrination and constant watching lest its old ailment recur. The article which embodied Lowell's views on this problem was one of the most vigorous he ever wrote, and like many of his other political utterances it makes those he later offered as literary criticism seem empty or flabby by comparison.

It was a study with which he took leave of political issues—except for a few brief references to them in his letters—for more than two full and unpredictable years. The course of action being followed toward the South thus appears to have met with his general approval, to have left him therefore with little more that needed saying. He called his essay the "Seward-Johnson Reaction." [1] It was published in the *North American* for October, 1866.

Members of the President's cabinet and delegates from every state, north and south, had traveled to Philadelphia, in August, to attend a convention. It was to be a simple love-fest, a gathering in which the animosities of so many months would be resolved, publicly, into oblivion. On its opening day, August 14, bands played "The Star Spangled Banner" and "Dixie," and Federal and Confederate officers alike buried their former belligerence in the certain promise of coming amenities. But two recent riots in the South still rankled bitterly in the hearts of the radicals. In Memphis, less than three months before, forty-six Negroes had been killed in a two-day conflict with whites; and in New Orleans, only three weeks back, another two hundred had lost their lives by violence. This last incident Thad Stevens had described as the direct result of "Universal Andy Johnsonism," and, supported by Charles Sumner, Ben Wade, and others, he insisted that the President be held personally responsible for it.[2]

The resolutions drawn up by these amiable delegates were altogether temperate and conciliatory. "Slavery is abolished and forever prohibited," one of them read, "and there is neither desire or purpose on the part of the Southern states that it should ever be reëstablished upon the soil or within the jurisdiction of the United States." Further declarations asserted that freedmen "in *all*[3] the States of the Union should receive, in common with all their inhabitants, equal protection in every right of person and property." As to the proposed constitutional amendment—the fourteenth—it was said that every commonwealth deserved the privilege of voting upon it, not merely those of the victorious North. Finally, the delegates recorded their support of the chief executive. Such, remarks one authority, was the Philadelphia convention, a presage of peace, an omen of a southwide approval of President Johnson's policies toward the defeated section.[4]

But Lowell, in these moderate phrases, sensed only treason and cowardice; he was bent upon the fulfillment of a far more desperate program. And when, shortly afterwards, Johnson himself openly indicted the Congress from which southern representatives were excluded, charging it with usurping fundamental principles of government and with seeking to establish a despotism, he found himself incapable of any further restraint. This snake must be scotched, this vile tendency in the government crushed out, as the ominous belief in slavery and rebellion had already been crushed out before it:

Lowell turned first to notice the leader in that convention—Mr. Seward, the Secretary of State! He was a man whom one could not contemplate without sorrow, for there was a time when his services to the country were honorable and distinguished. But now one saw him in the decline of his abilities, in the dry rot of his mind, subdued by his servility to an irrational leader. Timid by nature, the late war had unbraced him, had made of him a mere temporizer. The reason was not hard to discover: Seward had always looked upon parties as the mere ladders of ambitious men.

He then proceeded to abuse the President, berating him as vulgar, as a lord of misrule, an abbot of unreason. He passed on to a criticism of Johnson's theory of government. Mr. Johnson, he said, claimed that he has not betrayed the trust to which he was elected, mainly because the Union party had always affirmed that the rebellious states could not secede and therefore that they were still in the Union. Such an argument was sophistry. The simple fact was that for four years they were outside the nation and at war with it. And there was that other claim of the moderates that the object of the war was to restore the Union and the Constitution as they existed before 1860. This could never be! Again, the President had spoken of the evils of a centralized authority, like Congress, and had been making his "swing around the Circuit," carrying his protest to the people. Such action meant, to Lowell, that he was carrying it to the greatest despot of all, for "the true many-headed tyrant is the Mob, that part of the deliberative body of a nation which Mr. Johnson, with his Southern notions of popular government, has been vainly seeking, that he might pay court to it, from the seaboard to St. Louis, but which hardly exists, we are thankful to say, as a constituent body, in any part of the Northern States outside the City of New York." Lowell's phraseology was adroit. When the People failed to agree with his own opinions, it implied, they were no longer the People but the Mob.

Johnson, he went on, was unwilling to confer the ballot upon the Negroes at once. Yet, if the North failed in this, would it not be depriving the freedmen of their only adequate means of self-defense? Lowell brushed aside as irrelevant the fact—already cited—that the privilege of voting was denied Negroes in certain states of the North. "It is not with these states that we are making terms," he said. What must be realized as of fundamental importance was that "a people so boyish and conceited as the southerners," who had learned nothing from the war except to hate the men who subdued them, would interpret indecision on the part of the Union as cowardice. "Is it not time that these men were transplanted at least into the nineteenth century, and, if they cannot be suddenly Americanized, made to understand something of the country which was too good for them, even though at the cost of a rude shock to their childish self conceit?" [5]

But how is all this to be done? he asked. The answer he gave his own question was final. "We shall gain all we want if we make the South really prosperous; for with prosperity will come roads, schools, churches, printing-presses, industry, thrift, intelligence, and security of life and property. Hitherto the prosperity of the South has been fictitious; it has been a prosperity of the Middle Ages, keeping the many poor that a few might show their wealth in the barbarism of showy equipages and numerous servants, and spend in foreign cities the wealth that should have built up civilization and made way for refinement at home. There were no public libraries, no colleges worthy of the name; there was no art, no science—still worse, no literature but Simms: there was no desire for them. We do not say it in reproach; we are simply stating a fact." [6]

To E. L. Godkin, among others, Lowell in these articles on the defeated section had proved himself an irresponsible sentimentalist. In April, 1865, three months before he began to publish his own weekly magazine, the *Nation,* Godkin had sent a paper to the *North American* to which the magazine's friendly editors had taken a good many exceptions. Replying to them, the young contributor made several decidedly pointed statements about Lowell. "It seems to me," he wrote, "that in advocating negro suffrage because this is a democracy and negroes are men, he adopts that very French method which he condemns. The Anglo-Saxon method which he commends is not bound by logic, nor does it feel obliged to push any political principle to its extreme consequences. Therefore, for it, it is not enough to prove the negro's sex, age, and humanity, in order to establish his right to the franchise or the expediency of giving it to him. He has to rebuke the presumption of his unfitness for it, raised by his origin—his ancestors having all been either African savages, or as nearly beasts of the field as can be made; by his extreme ignorance—having been kept in darkness by law; by his defective sense of social obligations—never having enjoyed any rights, not even the commonest. It would, therefore, not confer the franchise on him without being satisfied as to the effect his exercise of it would have on the material and moral condition of the society in which he lives, or, in other words, on his own highest interests." [7]

Godkin was obviously insisting upon a minimum intelligence test, before the ballot should be given to anybody. He hated logic in politics, he said. The Negro ought to be compelled to read on election morning not the Bible, nor the Constitution (which could be memorized), but a passage from a daily newspaper. Moreover, for at least ten years after his emancipation, he should be required "to prove himself to be earning a livelihood by regular labor, or supporting a family in the same way (of course the last involves the first), as a test of that moral fitness against which his having been bred in slavery raises a presumption." Almost four years elapsed, and many villainies with them, before Lowell began timidly to acknowledge the wisdom of this view.

When he made his acknowledgment, moreover, he did so in an article which he never saw fit to reprint. The title he gave it was "A Look Before and After," [8] and though he did little pining for what was not, he deplored rather generously what actually was. That the moral instincts of his people had been kindled to a white heat by the war he freely acknowledged, but he added that a state of white heat is difficult and perhaps dangerous to preserve. Moreover, a victory, even the most glorious, is valueless unless one, after attaining it, could answer the question, What are you going to do about it? Having made this statement, he paused to consider the radical Republican Party, that party which for three years had been enjoying the untrammeled privileges of complete authority in the government. This group had derived its whole power from its "superior ethical position." Now, however, it was obsessed with the temptations of the spoils system; it was drunk with undisciplined authority. Pressing problems were facing the country, problems which cried out for intelligent and unselfish treatment.

Lowell went on to describe those problems in a way that, though heavy and prolix, revealed clearly that his insistence upon morality in national affairs was by no means a disguise for more sordid objectives. There should be a civil service, he said, and Mr. Jenckes's bill to provide one deserved enthusiastic support. Such a reform, he went on, was desperately needed, for the simple reason that the change in names by which recent events had come to be known "shows that our moral standard is lower. A swindle is called an operation, a rogue a financier, the unscrupulousness in politics which would once have received the brand of knavery is admired as smartness, and the sense of shame is lost in the multitude of those who share it. Congress itself is fast becoming a broker's board for operators on the Treasury." [9]

And again there was the question of finance and taxation, he wrote, troubling the country with an acute insistence. "Nations, like armies, must go upon their bellies." Why were not congressmen revealing their alertness to this truth? Let them, still further, be mindful of this cardinal principle, a principle, incidentally, which he himself had never chosen to recall before: "Whatever the relation of the rebellious States to the Union, the people of those States became our countrymen again the moment the war was over." Yet look at the requirements of voting which we are demanding at this moment in Virginia! They were such as would systematically exclude the coöperation of the very class of men whose support should be sought by every honorable means. The essay closed with an enthusiastic endorsement of General Grant as President.

The state of his country, in other words, was, at this date, not at all as he had wished it to be. He had spoken of brotherhood and virtue, had believed that the desire to realize these exalted concepts was the force which had guided his section to war and victory. Now the evidence of actual achievement was before him, posed in that naked truth which he had always professed to reverence. Lowell had simply been duped again, had proved himself that same naïve advocate of unrealizable righteousness to whom Briggs had been compelled to read a lecture a full quarter of a century before. His thought during this tumultuous twenty-five years had patterned itself with a curious consistency, as the present record of his frustration bears witness. Yet before his startled and incredulous eyes the world he knew had fallen away into the tyranny of reconstruction; and it was now evident that he had himself been powerfully instrumental in leading it there, under the misguided belief that its destination was heaven.

Certain scholars have made elaborate efforts to synthesize Lowell's political and aesthetic thought, to reduce it to a set of ideas which, they feel, gave centrality to his writing. One must respect their findings and their patience, although without forgetting that he wrote a very great deal and that a careful selection of statements from his letters, his prose, and his poetry can be made to add up to almost anything. Mr. Warren Jenkins appears to have been more judicious than most in his study of "Lowell's Criteria of Political Values." [10] A ponderous essay, bristling with evidence, it still leaves a good many side issues unnoticed. But one is not inclined to quarrel seriously with the conclusions its author has actually reached.

Mr. Jenkins points out that from youth to old age Lowell believed society to be in a continual state of evolution, that the doctrines of Christ would be supreme finally, high moral principles alone prevailing. He favored universal suffrage, moreover, because "an appeal to the reason of the people has never been known to fail in the long run." Lowell was, indeed, frequently given to statements of this sort: "The people I believe to be perfectly sound and honest," or "I have great faith in the good sense of our people." He probably had, indeed—except when the people became what we have seen him term them once for listening to President Johnson: "the mob." And in later years, when he found the Irish flooding his streets and crowding into political power in New England, his former confidence turned cloudy and all but deserted him. Should we really give the ballot, he wondered, to men who are unable to identify even a statue of Washington?[11]

The study confirms another important fact which has been frequently emphasized in the present volume: Lowell's political thought was founded upon morality. It was from this point of view that he judged the pageant of his country's unfolding history. One should not forget, however, that absolute ethical values prevailed in his world little more than they do in our own, and that precisely what *was* moral and right Lowell himself reserved the privilege of declaring. It is one of the oldest of human frailties and indulgences, and as a tendency it appears, unfortunately, to be a good deal more intimately allied with selfishness and rationalization than with the canons of disinterested virtue.

XVI

*"England is the only country where things get a thorough
discussion and by the best men."*
Lowell to Thomas Hughes, July 18, 1870.
Works, XV, 260

"I GIVE on an average twelve hours a day to study." It is Lowell confessing his devotion to the contents of his library, a place that was fast becoming, for him, living room, writing room, editorial room, and reading room in one. Leslie Stephen spent an interval at Elmwood in the summer of 1868 and later described the manner of life there. "All around us," he declared, "were the crowded book-shelves, whose appearance showed them to be the companions of the true literary workman, not of the mere dilettante or fancy biographer. Their ragged bindings and thumbed pages scored with pencil marks implied that they were a student's tools, not mere ornamental playthings. He would sit among his books, pipe in mouth, a book in hand, hour after hour; and I was soon intimate enough to sit by him and enjoy intervals of silence as well as periods of discussion and always delightful talk." [1]

Into this sanctuary, by almost every mail, came all sorts of literary requests and inquiries, as they had been coming for years. There had been pitiful letters from Mrs. Clemm, Poe's mother-in-law: An English publisher is bringing out an edition of the dead poet's works. She will receive nothing in royalties until all expenses of manufacture are paid, but she may sell some copies herself and keep the profits. "Mr. Longfellow (at my request) has taken five copies and paid me for them: If you will so far oblige me, let me know how many I shall send you, and if it will be perfectly convenient to yourself to advance me about ten dollars. You little know how desolate it is to be alone in this world. I have no *home,* no dear *Eddie now."* She thought of the unfortunate interview between

Poe and Lowell, when Lowell had appeared dull to Poe and Poe had certainly been arrogant to Lowell. "How much I wish I could see you, how quickly I could remove your wrong impression of my darling Eddie! The day you saw him in New York *he was not himself.* Do you not remember that I never left the room?" [2]

Then there was Sophia, the widow of Nathaniel Hawthorne. Mrs. Hawthorne was editing her late husband's notebooks, and she had talked to Longfellow about her work. "He said," she wrote Lowell, "as others have, that there must be a biography running through, upon which these pearls may be strung. I have been told that I must do this. I hoped that the constant revelations of himself in the notes would be sufficient, with no more. I have feared to bungle a very delicate, ethereal fabric by putting my hand to it. I knew that Mr. Hawthorne had often expressed horror at the idea that his life would be written, and I am conscious that I have not the skill to do it, though I am aware that I alone am acquainted with many manifestations of himself. Mr. Longfellow said that if I could not do it, he knew of but one person in the world who could, and that was Mr. Lowell. He said no one had a nicer appreciation and love, and no one so great an artistic faculty and critical insight. That if you would consent, it must be perfectly satisfactory to his nearest friends and the public.

"Dear Mr. Lowell, will you erect this immortal monument to the memory of Mr. Hawthorne? I am sure that he would be willing to be put into your hands. Mr. Longfellow wisely observed that this must be done while we were living and ready to aid in facts and dates. For that if it were done hereafter, there would be fatal mistakes—but if you did it now, all future notices must be referred to your authentic and classic authority, and so his life would be safe, as if in amber, for posterity. It is very important, doubtless, that it be accomplished immediately, for every reason— I do not myself feel a very strong assurance of mortal life. It seems as if I had to make a constant effort not to fall asleep as he did. I am obliged to clutch my children very tightly to preserve my feet from falling; but I hope God will give me strength to live as long as they need me, and till I have contributed my mite to building this monument to my husband's name."

"If you consent," she added, "as I devoutly hope you will, you will also help Julian in his career—: for if these journals be published now, with a biography by you, there is no doubt that when Julian graduates, there will be means to educate him for his profession, and he will owe to his father and to you a position in the world. As you are interested in Julian and know him, I speak of this. He deserves to have every legitimate facility, for he is most gifted and noble—I venture to say to so kind a friend, for I think you will not judge that I doat [*sic*]. Silent as Julian is, he has a gift with his pen (inherited, no doubt—) which is remarkable."[3]

The sequel to this fervent request is still not wholly clear. Scudder's opinion is that Lowell was enthusiastic, having learned "that there were seventeen volumes of notes, besides the letters which could be collected." "After consideration, however," he continues, "Mrs. Hawthorne feared to take the risks involved in having the precious manuscripts go out of her hands, and the plan was abandoned."[4] More plausible is the view of Dr. Randall Stewart, who edited the *American Notebooks* from the original manuscripts, that Sophia's extensive revisions of her husbands notes—made in the hope of having him appear more respectable to the world—would have proved embarrassingly evident had Lowell been allowed to see the original material.[5] Yet the idea that he might do the biography seems to have persisted for the next two decades. Edmund C. Stedman rejoiced when Lowell resigned as Minister to Great Britain chiefly for the reason that he would now be free to "complete" it.[6] But Lowell was able to complete nothing extensive after that desperate and shattering year.

There was even an entreaty that he do a work of fiction, now that peace had revived the publishing business. Mr. W. C. Church wrote him inquiring about a rumor he had heard a few weeks before. Lowell, the rumor ran, was writing a novel. "There is not the least truth in the story," Lowell informed his correspondent. "I suppose I must have mentioned to some indiscreet person the fact that so long as 1853 I had planned a story of moral life (so to speak) in New England, had sketched the characters and even written the first Chapter. But something happened during that year which broke forever the continuity of my life and left all my literary schemes at loose ends. I am just now trying to knit some of them together again—but I altogether doubt my ability to write a good story, least of all one calculated to be popular, which is what *you* want. I begin to feel that I belong too much to the last generation." [7]

His judgment was entirely sound. The manuscript of that chapter survives, and its dullness and general disorder are beyond controversy. It is a rambling document of some 2,500 words, given over to a satiric description of an isolated New England village. The narrator, in the first person, discourses upon such topics as the discordant singing in the barroom and the grotesque achitecture of the Baptist meetinghouse and the nearby variety store. Several native characters are indicated by name, but none is described. There is no action in the fragment, not even the beginnings of an action, and it is developed in the most ponderous prose he ever wrote. Except for an occasional moral interpolation, one would find it difficult to imagine Lowell as its author. Yet the work is in a sense characteristic of the New England renaissance. Emerson, Thoreau, Holmes, and, for the most part, Longfellow, were able to write relatively little that might be termed a sustained achievement. The same is true of Lowell. Hawthorne alone, among the most revered of this group, seemed capable of the necessary detachment and persistence. Yet for Lowell to attribute his inability to continue the work to Maria's death is to do his own critical talents scant justice. A more charitable confession to Mr. Church would have been to declare that the technique of the novel was a subject he had never seriously studied, and that when he found himself faced with the practical problem of writing one his basic ignorance of method overwhelmed him. [8]

But what a job the *North American Review* had become, now, in the late summer of 1868, with his associate abroad for an indefinite stay and the whole responsibility of getting it out left to him! It is true that Norton had named Mr. E. W. Gurney to take his place as editor, but when September came round, Mr. Gurney proved to be not only ill but about to be married. "I had not a line of copy," Lowell wrote J. T. Fields three weeks later, "nor knew where to get one." A hurried note to a friend brought in two articles—one on Herbert Spencer, "t'other on Leibnitz. I put the former in type, but did not dare to follow with the latter, for I thought it would be too much even for the readers of the N.A. By and by, I raked together one or two more—not what I *would* have but what I *could*." He had edited the fall number without help, but much against his wishes. He had read all the proof and done many other necessary duties which he had "agreed not to do" when he made his arrangement with the printers. He wanted his name withdrawn from the cover. "I never desired to be its editor and I put my resignation in your hands." [9] Later, for financial reasons, he relented—kept on with the drudgery his work entailed, in fact, until 1872. But it seems safe to add that the *North American* never claimed his attention or his interest as did the *Atlantic*. He was aging, and he now lacked a controlling mission.

To other men, even to strangers, he was writing on the subject of "literary morals." What, precisely, is plagiarism? one correspondent had asked. Lowell's reply was detailed. All learning, this gentleman should remember, is necessarily secondhand. What he would like to emphasize is the difference between appropriating a man's scholarship and assimilating it. "In the one case it lies a mere load of indigestible rubbish upon the brain; in the other it is dissolved and worked over into a new substance, giving sustenance and impulse to one's native thought." The distinction, he added, should thus be clear. "I may read by a man's lamp, but if I tap his gas pipe, I ought to attach a gasometer that shall record precisely how much I borrow." [10]

The social, political, and academic views which Lowell was propounding at this period were among the most definite he ever expressed. He was coming out, now, in the realm of questions much broader and more indicative than ever the slavery question had been. There was the eight-hour law, for example, a measure upon which his stand was unequivocal from the date he first heard of it. "Pray give Henry Wilson a broadside," he wrote to E. L. Godkin in 1869, "for dipping his flag to that piratical craft of the eight-hour men. I don't blame him for sympathizing with his former fellow-craftsmen (though he took to unproductive industry at the first chance), but I have a thorough contempt for a man who pretends to believe that eight is equal to ten." [11] He was still apparently unable to see an economic question in other than moral and abstract terms.

Two months later he wrote his daughter at length, defining and even dramatizing his views on this issue. A cadaverous gentlemen had called, he said, requesting that he subscribe $100 to the Labor Reform League—"an arrangement which is to give us back those admirable guilds of the Middle Ages and abolish Political Economy from the face of the earth." "You know," he continued, "that that tough old aristocrat the Marquis of Thompson Lot [a humorous pseudonym for himself] is capable at times of great frankness of speech, and this astonished missionary got the full benefit of it." The following is the dialogue, as Lowell reported it:

Lowell (replying to the request that he subscribe): Not a stiver, though I would gladly subscribe to put 'em down. What they want is to make this world comfortable to the lazy and the botchers of work, which it never was and never will be till you get rid of God and His laws. This is the five and twentieth Millenium and Fool's Paradise that has been promised in my time. You want to contrive by law that brains and no brains shall always be on an equality. How are you going to keep 'em so? You talk about Capital, but you mean Property—the very basis of all civilization. . . .

Cadaverous Missionary: The-the-I don't know what the reason is, but I never had such a difficulty in expressing myself in my life.

Lowell: That's because you're not used to freedom of speech. Here you've got Wendell Phillips and William B. Greene down for a hundred dollars each. How did they earn it? Did they ever do a day's work in their lives?

Cadaverous Missionary: Well, I don't know as they ever did.

Lowell (riled by the *as*): You're a great sufferer from indigestion?

Cadaverous Missionary: Well, yes, I suffer considerable from dyspepsy.

Lowell: May I ask if you are at work in any productive form of industry?

Cadaverous Missionary: I can't say that I am just at present. My health has been so feeble.

Lowell: Suppose you tried working on a farm?

Cadaverous Missionary: I did in the fore part of my life, but it was too hard, I wasn't rugged enough. But you'll admit that they ought to shorten the hours of work in factories where they don't git a mite of fresh air all day long?

Lowell: Did you ever see an American that liked fresh air? I never did. Why, I can hardly get a window open in a car without being mobbed. Are the girls that work in factories less healthy than the farmers' wives?

Cadaverous Missionary: Well, it's because the farmers' wives are overworked.

Lowell: What? In villages where there are cheese factories? Nonsense! It's because they are too lazy or too ignorant to make decent bread, or to tolerate ventilation, that they look so cadaverous. I suppose the present arrangement will last my time. If not why I'm all ready to mount your guillotine.

Lowell was almost done with his unfortunate guest, but before he dismissed him he let fall a characteristic observation: Certainly he believed in two classes of men, the leaders and those who are led. The trouble with him, he added, was that he thought he could "make the world over so that what the Lord made for the bottom shall *stay* at the top—" [12] Once more Lowell would seem to have been unable to think of the labor problem in economic or political terms. God, apparently, had ordained the workingman's status, and the Marquis, for one, did not mean to temper with His holy purposes. He was beginning at last to think and talk like a Brahmin.

Then there was England. Lowell had worried about his country's relations with that island for a good many more years than he cared to remember. During the war itself, as has been indicated, his indignation became bitterly outspoken. The matter was complicated by the fact that he knew and admired so many of its natives personally. How could he keep untarnished his affection for these men, without violating another affection more intimate and deserving?

He approached the problem with an essay, and he supplemented it in letters to these friends with elaborate explanations and qualifying phrases. The article he termed, "On a Certain Condescension in Foreigners."[13] He wrote it, he informed Godkin, "mainly with the hope of bringing about a better understanding. My heart aches with apprehension as I sit here in my solitude and brood over the present aspect of things between the two countries. We are crowding England into a fight which would be a horrible calamity for both—but worse for us than for them. It would end in our bankruptcy and perhaps in disunion."[14]

What, in this instance, had his indignation wrung from him publicly out of his long awareness of England's arrogance? The answer is that it had wrung nothing very courageous, very little that was not weakened by apology. He began his essay with an account of a walk through the streets of his native village. The beauty of its natural scenes was enriched for him by recollections from the literature of the mother country. Enraptured by the sunset clouds, he became so fond as to think that even Collins might have composed his "Ode to Evening" there, or another great poet have written his lines on "Solitude." All his traditions, unfledged though they were, seemed sanctified in this refulgent moment. Lexington was none the worse for him for not being in Greece, nor Gettysburg because its name was not Marathon.

His reverie is broken in upon by a stranger, a German, who almost immediately asks for $5.00. Lowell demurs, and the foreigner proceeds forthwith to berate America. The country has no arts, science, literature, culture, or any native hope of supplying them. Again, Americans are a people wholly given to money-getting. Lowell leaves the critic in haste, to avoid knocking him down. Afterwards, with many displays of erudition, he begins to talk about America. We should not condemn everyone who proves unable to see us with enchanted eyes. Our fate has been to succeed the Dutch as the butt of the cultured world's jests. Basically, we are disliked by Europe for a very simple reason: we are attempting the democratic experiment. Certainly we have our faults. For one thing, we have got to learn that statesmanship is the most complicated of the arts. This means that those men who represent us should be fully qualified and responsible.

He pauses then to consider another charge. It is said that we are vulgar. "This is one of those horribly vague accusations, the victim of which has no defense. An umbrella is of no avail against a Scotch mist. It envelops you, it penetrates at every pore, it wets you through without seeming to wet you at all." [15] Just wherein are we vulgar? We are cleaner than the English, both morally and physically. Then Lowell suggests the answer to his own question. When we speak, we do not stammer, as the English learned to do from their spineless courtiers. And we do not pronounce the dipthong *ou* as they, and we say *either* and not *eyther,* "following therein the fashion of our ancestors who unhappily could bring over no English better than Shakespeare's."

With this comment he began to hedge and to flatter: A second-rate Englishman is hateful to gods and men, yet that this planet has never produced a more splendid creature than a first-rate one, witness Shakespeare and the heroes of the Indian Mutiny. He thought of his own friends in England, and his heart warmed into compliment. "Among genuine things, I know nothing more genuine than the better men whose limbs were made in England. So manly-tender, so brave, so true, so warranted to wear, they make us proud to feel that blood is thicker than water."

He proceeded to list a few random offensive statements of visiting Englishmen: One had announced his sympathy for the Confederates—"They are the gentlemen of the country, you know." Another had said we were "meager"; still another, that we talked through our noses; and a fourth, whom certain Americans had cordially entertained, had later come out in print with the stupid comment that we welcomed foreign visitors in the hope of relieving the tedium of our own dead-level existence. What shall we do about such obvious ill manners? Shall we shut the doors of our hospitality to Europeans? "Not I, for one, if I should so have forfeited the friendship of L. S. [Leslie Stephen], most lovable of men. He somehow seems to find us human, at least, and so did Clough, whose poetry will one of these days, perhaps, be found to have been the best utterance in verse of this generation. And T. H. [Hughes], the mere grasp of whose manly hand carries with it the pledge of frankness and friendship of an abiding simplicity of nature as affecting as it is rare!" [16]

He turned to the positive virtues of his country. It is much more than a mere place to eat, sleep, and trade in, he insisted. "There was never colony save this that went forth, not to seek gold, but God." [17] Our people for more than two centuries have been sturdily conquering the wilderness about them. Consider, moreover, the idealism which informed the North during the recent war. The North fought for an abstraction, for the idea of nationalism. This valiant act matured us. "Our discussion of important questions in statesmanship, in political economy, in aesthetics, is taking a broader scope and a higher tone." Let our visitors realize that we are not merely curious creatures, but belong to the family of man. We have done an immense amount of silent work here; our country is no mere object of external interest but "part of our very marrow." He thought of Oliver Wendell Holmes, and a tribute seemed eminently appropriate. "I know of one person who is singular enough to think Cambridge the very best spot on the habitable globe. 'Doubtless God *could* have made a better, but doubtless He never did.'" Then he became bolder. England has a conviction "that whatever good there is in us is wholly English, when the truth is that we are worth nothing except so far as we have disinfected ourselves of Anglicism." We must be treated naturally, as human beings. "Dear old long-estranged mother-in-law," he said finally, "it is a great many years since we parted. . . . Put on your spectacles, dear Madam. Yes, we *have* grown, and changed likewise. You would not let us darken your doors, if you could help it. We know that perfectly well. But pray, when we look to be treated as men, don't shake that rattle in our faces, nor talk baby talk to us any longer."

It remains an urbane and still readable essay. The knowledge of English literature and manners it displays is both rich and appropriate, since his emphasis is far less upon "foreigners" generally than upon British travelers in his own country. Yet it reflects at the same time a vacillation in Lowell which one can scarcely admire. He loved his own country and he loved his English friends, and the conflict of this divided allegiance greatly vitiated the strength of his argument. Certain impressions, it seems, had reached him (the essay is nowhere documented) to the effect that the average intelligent citizen of the mother country was hostile to America, and the rumor distressed him no end. How could he lay it to rest, he wondered, without offense to anybody? The answer he arrived at would appear to imply: through criticizing and praising the English by turns. One recalls Lowell's own statement: "If the tone of the uncultivated American has too often the arrogance of the barbarian is not that of the cultivated as often vulgarly apologetic?" [18] He certainly protested "too much" in this vindication, if the nation he described in the Commemoration Ode was worth defending at all.

And he continued to protest and explain in letters to his friends abroad. Such statements as the following are an example: It is the temper of the English press that we object to. There is a curious misapprehension about us among your people, as if we had been a penal colony. Consider what Longfellow overheard two English ladies say in Rome during a discussion of the manners of American girls: "Well, you know, what can be expected of people who are all descended from laboring men or convicts?" He felt that all we want is to be treated in a manly way. "If only some man in your government could find occasion to say that England had mistaken her own true interest in the sympathy she showed for the South during the Civil War!" [19]   The idea of being thought ill of by the English was becoming decidedly unpleasant to him.

Meanwhile, how tedious his work at Harvard had grown! His complaints about it seem almost chronic in the confessions dated after the war. In 1866 the college had given him a tutor as assistant, but had reduced his salary to $1,500. "I begin my annual dissatisfaction of lecturing next Wednesday. I cannot get used to it. All my nightmares are of lecturing." [20]   This was in 1867. Two years later, there was a course of twenty lectures to get ready for and to groan over.[21]   And as the winter of the same session threatened, he wrote to Godkin, despairingly, "with four lectures a week, I am as busy as I can bear just now." [22]   One week later a colleague was taken ill, "and I had to take his classes in French and German—losing five weeks thereby. . . . Twenty lectures scared me, and now my next is the sixteenth and I am not half through." He had resorted to the now sanctified expedient of reading to his classes "with extempore commentary." That he was thoroughly bored and restless was unmistakable.

Despite this fact, it is equally unmistakable that he was genuinely interested in the Harvard library. Its limitations, he wrote Samuel Eliot, one of the Overseers, were almost everywhere distressingly obvious. He proceeded to amplify, with only minor reservations. "Thanks to Professor Child the department of Romance and Ballad Literature is remarkably full. But in Modern Literature (especially contemporaneous) we are still very deficient." There was Goethe for example: "A short time since I had (and I suppose it is still true) a better collection of Goethiana on my own shelves than could be found in the Library." His cousin Charles Norton was far richer in editions of Dante, and in books relating to him, than was the University. In recent *belles lettres* there was nothing like completeness, and the same was true of literary journals.

The library was likewise weak in original editions, he went on. There was no folio Shakespeare, and there was none of the elder dramatists, not even of so late a playwright as Dryden. "It seems to me that of all leading authors there should be a complete series of editions—Wordsworth, for instance, and Coleridge make great changes in their earlier poems." If Harvard could not obtain original manuscripts at present, let it at least have copies made of them. Let the librarian examine a standard library catalog and fill in the deficiencies, or let him pick up some copy of a scholarly review and consider how many of the articles in it could have been written with the help of his shelves alone.[23] The letter expressed one of Lowell's most profound and continuing interests.

His income reduced by his new arrangement at the college, Lowell was forced to look in other directions for financial aid. At the invitation of President Andrew D. White, of Cornell, he gave a series of lectures there in the spring of 1869.[24] But this venture was by no means sufficient to sustain him against the urgent responsibilities of his home. He turned to a last expedient, that of disposing of a part of his land,[25] and by 1870 he was resolved to let it go "whenever I can sell it for enough to live on modestly." The next year he was able to tell Leslie Stephen the good news. He had surrendered the estate, all but Elmwood and two acres, for a sum that would afford him $5000 a year, with $1400 for his daughter, who was soon to be married. "The city," he explained, "has crept up on me, curbstones are feeling after and swooping upon the green edges of the roads, and the calf I used to carry is grown to a bull. I have gone over to the enemy and become a capitalist." [26]

For this sacrifice of ancestral acres, what offset, what compensation? The answer was one that warmed his heart as he considered it. He would at last be free from teaching. Six years before he had admitted to Norton, "I am not the stuff that professors are made of. . . . My professorship is wearing me out." Now, as he reflected on the mild but insidious tedium of his academic career, his opinion had suffered no change, unless it had deepened. "I am grown learned (after a fashion) and dull. The lead has entered into my soul. But I have great faith in putting the sea between me and the stocks I have been sitting in so long." [27] He had been teaching for seventeen years, and he was thoroughly sick of it. Only a trip abroad, it seemed, could purge his mind of that dismal experience.

XVII

*"I have already read over one volume of my prose and am
astonished to find how clever I used to be."*
Lowell to Misses Lawrence, January 30, 1888.
Works, XVI, 199

BEFORE he set sail, in July, 1872, Lowell had published in
fairly rapid sequence three books which, supplementing his
earlier ones, established him among the genteel as America's leading man of letters. One volume was poetry, the other two were
literary essays. Twenty years had passed since his verses had been
printed in anything resembling a collected edition. *Under the
Willows,* published late in 1868, was meant to fill this chasm, although, as he confessed in an introductory note, his most lively and
humorous poems were omitted from it, "as out of keeping." [1]

The result of these omissions is a certain dignity not wholly free
from the dullness which frequently consorts with this admirable
quality. Fifty poems comprise the offering, and all but five of them
were written before the war. This fact is understandable enough
when one considers how completely the issues of that struggle
diverted his expression into other and more urgent channels. There
was little purpose in courting the muse idly, in other words, when
she might be harnessed to the cause of Justice and Virtue.

His subjects and themes are mainly intimate ones, recording his
hopes, his ideals, and occasionally his personal tragedies. Several
others retell with little embellishment or novelty certain Old World
legends with which almost everybody is familiar. Nothing in the
'volume is very pretentious, except the Commemoration Ode already noticed. He writes, for instance, about Aladdin, the Nomads,
the Voyage to Vinland, and the Singing Leaves. There are tributes
to friends, such as Longfellow, Jane Norton, and John Bartlett.
There are several ballads and several descriptive poems. And, as

one might expect, there are also a number of little moral meditations, along with compliments to June, to birds, to dead authors, and to Beauty.

Regarding the nature of these verses, no one, of course, would wish to be censorious. He never considered the volume as one upon which his reputation would in any important way depend. The most reasonable comment concerning them would be to say that they are incidental, are little more than by-products of another achievement which he regarded, rightly, as much more significant and influential. They belong to his idle hours and his relaxed moods, to those rare intervals in which he was able to put out of his mind the problems of his too-harrassed world.

The result is a verse that is frequently inverted and flat, heavy with matter-of-factness.[2] All too often, also, he obtrudes his sermons directly and abstractly, with a certain unction that is scarcely commendable. He tells his readers, for instance, that wherever ten men are gathered, humanity itself is present in epitome. He talks again, in Wordsworthian accent, of the spiritual influences which purify his soul, chastened as he is now, through sorrow, to apprehend them. He tells the story of a man who is made a king by proving faithful to a trust. He reprints a poem first published almost twenty years before, about a daughter buried beneath the deepening snow. There is a meditation upon the sacred nature of Duty; another on a Presence which could never be apprehended except through glimpses, like Shelley's vision of Intellectual Beauty; and still another piece which, in strangely jocular rhythms, portrays the emptiness of his house after Maria's death.[3]

Echoes of Wordsworth and Tennyson in the volume are too obvious to escape notice.[4] Lowell reflects a settled tendency, moreover, to resort to ecstatic verses about nature when any more compelling subject proves inaccessible.[5] Doubtless he loved nature as well as anybody, yet the point is irrelevant here. What is more nearly unmistakable is the equally obvious fact that *Under the Willows* is a dull and unimportant book, and that it reflects to a suspicious degree the feeling of its author that the tradition in which he had excelled

—the tradition of native American humor—was somehow discreditable if not actually vulgar.

Among My Books appeared in February, 1870. It is a collection of six long essays. Four of them treat men of letters—Shakespeare, Dryden, Lessing, and Rousseau. The others, far more valuable, are concerned with the subjects of "Witchcraft" and life in "New England Two Centuries Ago." Lowell is invariably more interesting when handling a native theme than when he attempts to deal with a foreign one.

These literary essays represent the nadir of his effectiveness as an author. The vigor of his abolitionist prose and verse, though usually misplaced, was at least unmistakably evident. Here it has been dispelled, has run out into a discursiveness and incoherence so great that only his reputation with America's reading public, one suspects, could have induced his publisher to print them in book form. Probably the simplest way to illustrate his critical manner would be to analyze a typical specimen, such as his "Shakespeare Once More." [6]

It is a 105 page performance, and it appeared first in the *North American Review* in 1868, while Lowell, of course, was one of the editors. It begins with a characteristically glittering half-truth: "It may be doubted whether any language be rich enough to maintain more than one truly great poet." He points out that Shakespeare's age was the Renaissance and that the English language was just beginning to assume its modern form. It was a fresh language, one in which poetic beauty had at last become possible. Nineteen pages are spent in developing this obvious idea, pages cluttered with literary allusions, relevant and irrelevant, all handled gracefully. The contents of his fine library were being paraded in perfect order.

He next discusses the editors of Shakespeare, but limits himself mainly to the First Folio. It cannot be fully trusted, he declares. Certain errors in it are too gross to escape detection; its value rests in the fact that for eighteen of the plays it is the only authority we have. Lowell pauses then to indicate the healthy influence Shakespeare has exercised upon the race, by withdrawing men's minds "from baser attractions" to reflect on his unrivaled themes. There is an interesting statement here of Shakespeare's insight into character: "The more we have familiarized ourselves with the operations of our own consciousness, the more do we find, in reading him, that he has been beforehand with us, and that, while we have been vainly endeavoring to find the door of his being, he has searched every nook and cranny of our own." [7] This comment introduces a conjecture —trivial, historically—that the dramatist's failure to edit his works can be attributed only to his premature death; "that he should not have intended it is inconceivable." Then comes another digression upon the qualifications of a good editor.

Lowell is now ready to talk about the art of criticism. What attributes should a good critic possess? he asks. The answer is that he must be free from any personal bias, must acknowledge the existence of certain principles "as fixed beyond question." The reader who expects him to proceed to examine Shakespeare from this point of view will be disappointed. He digresses to speak of Lamb, who apparently followed no critical dicta, yet who made some interesting discoveries in Elizabethan literature. He defends balance and unity as prerequisites for a work of art. He discusses Style and Imagination and praises the literature of the Greeks. This last topic reminds him of the tedious manner in which Greek is taught in the colleges. The great authors, truly, he says, have been degraded to mere "drillers in grammar, and made the ruthless pedagogues of root and inflection, instead of companions for whose society the mind must put on her highest mood."

One should realize that strength is consistent with repose, he continues, that grace is but a more refined form of power, and that a thought is no less profound because it is so limpidly expressed that we may take in its meaning at a glance. John Donne forgot this last truth and has been exiled, in consequence, "to the limbo of the formless and the fragmentary." Wordsworth, too, is found wanting on this score. "His longer poems are Egyptian sand wastes, with here and there an oasis of exquisite greenery, a grand image, Sphinx-like, half buried in drifting commonplaces."

He turns again to chronology, the point he had emphasized in the opening pages of the essay. Shakespeare was fortunate in coming after Spenser, who "invented" the art of writing well. He has left no progeny for the simple reason that it is only poets of the "second class," the mannered ones, who find imitators. Despite Lowell's previous indorsement of the Greek dramatists as affording a critical basis for judging literature, he tells us next that Shakespeare should not be measured "by a Sophoclean scale." He proceeds to compare him with Milton. The latter had imagination "in its secondary office." It was immanent, not in his "very consciousness," as with the master, but "in his memory." Echoing a comment of Charles Lamb, he proceeds to indicate Shakespeare's use of crowded metaphors: In him, moreover, thought and language (or imagery) are one. He is especially great in description. Lowell begins to illustrate his points by quotations from the plays. He has arrived at page 42 of the essay.

What Lowell has to say from this point out may be summarized very briefly: Shakespeare acquired his great knowledge through conversation and profound thought. His plays are compared with those of the Greek playrights, in a digression of ten additional pages. *The Tempest* is discussed as an allegory, and Shakespeare's classical, unsympathetic critics are ridiculed. Then he advances a "formal" evaluation of *Hamlet,* which is preceded by a statement of certain basic aesthetic principles. A work of art, he declares, should be "in keeping." This means, first, that the reality of costume and of history ought to be rendered faithfully; again, that the variety in the work should be harmonized into a unified impression. In explaining the first of these items he is extremely vague, and it is impossible to determine whether, to Lowell, the truth of history and costume may or may not be violated; or is it important, since Shakespeare constantly violated both.

He is now in the midst of his formal criticism. He records his impressions of scenes. He illustrates the nature of the hero's mind with analogies from Dante. He discusses Hamlet's feigned madness. He confesses that the work was not written primarily to inculcate a moral. The conclusion arrived at after some twenty pages is that Hamlet was not incapable of resolve, but that somehow "the bond between the motive power and the operative faculties is relaxed and loose." Thinking had become to him more interesting than action. It is Coleridge's theory precisely, stated without acknowledgment and with great diffusion. Lowell found no flaws in the play. He simply recorded the suggestions that stemmed from his reading, both in the text and the commentaries. The result is an essay both structureless and confusing, yet typical of his manner when his subject was a phase of literature.

His study of Dryden is a further illustration of this manner. There is the same rambling bookish introduction, the same preliminary toying with his subject. Then follow the obvious generalizations: Dryden was the first of the moderns. His age was skeptical, and he wrote what the age demanded. He was thoroughly manly. His taste was not an instinct; it had to be slowly cultivated. His diction lacked refinement, never entirely escaping a certain colloquial familiarity. As a dramatist, especially in comedy, his most settled trait was his "nastiness." Lowell concludes this part of his commentary with a strange critical observation, in view of Dryden's popular success as a playwright; the only explanation for it is that the dramatist made it himself, in different words. He "had no aptitude whatever for the stage, and in writing for it he was attempting to make a trade of his genius—an arrangement from which the genius always withdraws in disgust." His critical prefaces are accorded considerable merit: On the subject of translations, he has written better than anybody. Moreover, he had, to an extraordinary degree, the gift of the right word. He was not a great poet, but he was certainly a strong thinker, a tonic to those who are inclined to looseness in writing. To present these views, with proper embellishments, Lowell required 109 duodecimo pages.[8]

It is much the same story with "Rousseau and the Sentimentalists," though he does manage to dispose of his subject in half the length of the Dryden study. The thesis here is that the sentimentalist does not practice what he proclaims. This was Rousseau's fault, a fault which Lowell amplifies and illustrates for more than thirty pages. Then, quite contradictorily, he reverses his position and declares that Rousseau was "sincere." His faults are explainable in the light of the French temperament, which should not be judged by the blunt standards of the English. There was a "sickly taint" in the whole school of sentiment. Its proponents failed to look upon nature "as a strengthener and consoler, a wholesome tonic for a mind ill at ease with itself." They regarded it, instead, as a feminine echo of their own moods. But Rousseau was intellectually fearless. His excesses are far from equalling those of the writers in his tradition who followed him.[9]

"Lessing" is written in Lowell's most shiftless manner; it is merely—except for the usual discursive twenty-page introduction—a summary, with frequent comment, of the life of this important author. In his preliminary statement, he deplores the heaviness of German scholarship but commends its "admirable thoroughness." Then follow the biographical details, with genuine admiration for Lessing's manliness and restraint under personal losses. His poetry is dismissed unfavorably, especially his epigrams, which are "shockingly coarse." But nowhere in his seventy-eight pages does Lowell say anything discriminating or evaluative about Lessing's critical theories or his importance in the literary tradition of his country.[10]

In "Witchcraft," [11] Lowell turned to a subject that had long proved of continuing interest to him, as the list of fourteen volumes appended to the study obviously proves. It is, as always, prolix and unorganized, but it illustrates to an eminent degree his talent for selecting the nice anecdote, the amusing quotation, out of ponderous and generally unreadable books. The student of the present age will find it significant for a further reason. For the thesis of the essay, buried though it remains beneath a welter of haphazard commentary, is the thesis which informs Professor George Lyman Kittredge's monumental volume on *Witchcraft in Old and New England*. Both men show that, in Lowell's words, "the great persecutions for this imaginary crime have always taken place in lonely places, among the poor, the ignorant, and, above all, the ill fed." Both insist that the most distressing examples of the witch mania in this country—the Salem trials and executions—were "exceptionally humane" when compared with many others that occurred in the Old World, that the New England magistrates were neither "besotted or unfair" in dealing with the evidence submitted them, and that the natural reaction "from the Salem mania of 1692 put an end to belief in devilish compacts and demoniac possessions sooner in New England than elsewhere."[12]

"New England Two Centuries Ago" is another subject with which Lowell found himself very much at home. It reflects the experience and the reading of almost half a century. Once more he is ostensibly writing a review, but his knowledge overflows the limits defined by his authors into the rich realm of the anecdotal and irrelevant. It is the nearest approach to a personal essay in the volume.

"Faith in God, faith in man, faith in work"—with this somewhat glorified trilogy (the second item he strongly qualifies later) Lowell summarizes the teaching of the founders of his section. He points out, shortly afterwards, a fact of which Independence Day orators are still largely forgetful, but which recent scholarship has firmly established:[13] The Puritans of Boston Bay, he declares, were in no sense believers in democracy. "They had no faith in the Divine institution of a system which gives Teague, because he can dig, as much influence as Ralph, because he can think, nor in personal at the expense of general freedom."[14] They were "large minded and far seeing men. . . . They knew that liberty in the hands of feeble minded and unreasoning persons . . . means nothing more than the supremacy of their particular form of imbecility; means nothing less, therefore, than downright chaos."

He went on with his announced task, that of gleaning what was "morally picturesque or characteristic" in the volumes he was discussing. He sketched the lives of leading figures, quoted from letters and diaries, praised Cromwell, defended the Puritans' indorsement of slavery, and submitted specimens of their unorthodox spelling. His intention was clearly, in many of these cases, that of suggesting various comic contrasts between the seventeenth century and his own age. His method is that of selecting liberal excerpts from his sources, with brief comments of his own. Yet the total impression he manages to establish is one of admiration for his subjects. They were not all men of grand conceptions and superhuman foresight, true—for "an entire ship's company of Columbuses is what the world never saw." But they believed in Faith and Work, "were alive to the highest and most earnest thinking of their time."

"My former volume of Essays has been so kindly received that I am emboldened to make another and more miscellaneous collection. The papers here gathered have been written at intervals during the last fifteen years, and I knew no way so effectual to rid my mind of them and make ready for a new departure, as this of shutting them between two covers where they can haunt me, at least, no longer." [15] With these words Lowell introduced his second prose work within the twelvemonth. He called it *My Study Windows.* It appeared in February, 1871.

The majority of the selections are tributes to great public characters or to authors, living and dead. Several others are severe reviews of writers of whom he disapproved, and two are personal essays. In this latter form his success is uneven. "A Good Word for Winter," to cite an instance, comments on the fact that "the old fellow" has not had justice done him. After developing this view, Lowell proceeds to set forth a series of literary allusions to the bracing season that stands for "no nonsense." Ovid, Cotton, Thomson, Akenside, Cowley, Milton, Virgil, Cowper, Goethe, Wordsworth, Pope, Martial, Emerson, Coleridge, and Thoreau, among others, are cited as men who have written memorably about it. But the result is little more than a series of quotations, loosely strung together. Lowell himself had very little of interest to contribute to this imposing display, except the evidence of his assiduous reading.[16]

"My Garden Acquaintance" represents a more successful venture in informality. He begins it with an account of White's *Natural*

History of Selborne, a book redolent with "the delightfulness of absolute leisure." To this gentleman the revolt of the American colonies was of no importance, though the arrival of the house martin a day earlier or later than last year proved "a piece of news worth sending express to all his correspondents." Lowell went on to praise the kingdom of the animals.

"They never dream of settling it by vote," he said, "that eight hours are equal to ten, or that one creature is as clever as another, and no more." Mr. White's world is one of changeless certainties. Fortunately, Lowell adds, he has spent his own life amid rural surroundings. He recounts his experience with birds—with robins, the catbird, crows, orioles, bobolinks, and flickers. Others he once knew intimately have disappeared—the heron, the whippoorwill, the cliff swallow, the brown thrush. Yet those that remain represent friendships of a lifetime. He has made a Penn treaty with them all. If they refuse to come near enough, "I bring them close with an opera glass—a much better weapon than a gun. I would not, if I could, convert them from their pretty pagan ways." Look at them all, he invites his readers finally. He does not believe there is a single one but does more good than harm, "and of how many featherless bipeds can this be said?" [17]

The tributes in the volume are to Lincoln, Emerson, and Josiah Quincy. Written while the war was in progress, the first betrays the customary extravagance of his thinking at that time. There are the usual fulsome tributes to northern virtue, the usual denunciations of the South, and a defense of the "greater truth" of the doctrines of the abolitionists. The essayist, of course, can find nothing to censure in Lincoln: He is wholly unselfish. He is a symbol of pure manhood. He is our representative American.[18]

Lowell was intimate with Edmund Quincy, and his essay, "A Great Public Character," based upon this friend's life of his father, is naturally sympathetic. "I am glad to have the biography of one who, beginning as a gentleman, kept himself such to the end—who, with no necessity of labor, left behind him an amount of thoroughly done work such as few have accomplished with the mighty help of hunger." The comment sets the tone of the piece, and Lowell's method, in developing it, is to "pick out plums" from the book, with the digressive elegance and triviality which by this time has become a thoroughly settled habit with him. Quincy's limitations as an administrator [19] and his tight-fisted arrogant Federalist convictions are nowhere treated, except in a tone of amused indulgence.[20]

It is much the same story with "Emerson the Lecturer," although with far greater justice in this case. One of Lowell's briefest essays, it remains one of his best. He limited himself to a single phase of his subject, and for once he managed to get to that subject in his first paragraph: "It is a singular fact that Mr. Emerson is the most steadily attractive lecturer in America." What is his secret? "Is it not that he out-Yankees us all? that his range includes us all? that he is equally at home with the potato-disease and original sin, with pegging shoes and the Oversoul?" True enough, one finds it hard to get at his meaning, but then "we do not go to hear what Emerson says so much as to hear Emerson." Lowell recalled first listening to the Concord sage "during the consulate of Van Buren." He mentioned the thrilling vitality of the speaker's words, forgetting that those early lectures (as the class poem makes plain) filled him instead with undergraduate contempt. Yet the essay might well be termed as graceful a compliment as he ever wrote.

The literary studies—seven in number—remain to be noticed, but they can be dealt with briefly. Chaucer, Pope, Carlyle, Swinburne, Thoreau, James Gates Percival, and a collection, the "Library of Old Authors," comprise his subjects—with the exception of the "Condescension in Foreigners" piece already treated. The Chaucer essay gracefully says the usual things about this author. It records the influences, French and Anglo-Saxon especially, which helped to shape his talent. It praises him as one of the three or four great story-tellers of the world. Metrically, "I cannot believe that he ever wrote an imperfect line." He was great at description, though not distinguished as a dramatic writer. He is never forceful, but always smooth. His satire is kindly. He is a most sacred happy spirit, "in spite of some external stains." [21]

--◦◦❦{ 219 }❧◦◦--

Pope's stains are much more pronounced. His was an age "of intellect without faith," and it was impossible that anything truly great—that is, great on the moral and emotional as well as the intellectual side—should be produced by such a generation. For the truth is that Pope and his contemporaries derived from the French tradition, and "the mistake of the whole school of French criticism, it seems to me, lay in its tendency to confound what was common with what was vulgar." Pope was not a great thinker, and the philosophy of the *Essay on Man* is disgusting. Moreover, his nature poetry is artificial. But he could express a thought tersely wherever he found it, and "as an accurate intellectual observer and describer of personal weaknesses, Pope stands by himself in English verse." Yet his "stains" rise up another time to haunt Lowell's now settled conscience, and his statement about them would seem to prove that, when faced with a specific issue, he was largely incapable of judging an author in historical terms.[22] "In his epistle on the characters of women, no one who has ever known a noble woman, nay, I should almost say no one who has ever had a mother or sister, will find much to please him." Perhaps these ladies were as bad as bad could be, "but if God made poets for anything, it was to keep alive the traditions of the pure, the holy, and the beautiful." Consider the *Dunciad,* he went on. It is much nastier than it is witty, is filthy even in a filthy age. "One's mind needs to be sprinkled with some disinfecting fluid after reading it." [23]

The Carlyle survey is altogether hostile, except for a few brief acknowledgments at its close. This writer has erred [as did Lowell himself, repeatedly] by confounding moral with aesthetic standards. He is lawless, stylistically—a preacher and a prophet, perhaps, but never an artist. What of his doctrines? His basic one of hostility to the democratic idea Lowell finds intolerable. To him the mass of men are not men at all, but sheep, Lowell declares, though he might have recollected the fact that they were little more than sheep, at best, to his own Federalist idol, Josiah Quincy. Carlyle, he adds, has woefully degenerated as a writer. Since publishing *Sartor Resartus* more than thirty years ago, "he has done little but repeat himself with increasing emphasis and heightened shrillness. He is really "a remarkable example of arrested development . . . continues to be a voice crying in the wilderness but no longer a voice with any earnest conviction behind it." His later work, in the phrase of Goethe, is a "literature of despair." Lowell quarrels with his subject's generous treatment of Frederick the Great, who was actually no more than a "tyrant." Yet Carlyle's pictorial and dramatic abilities are excellent, and "his value as an inspirer and awakener cannot be overestimated." [24]

Lowell had little use for Swinburne, and in his review of the tragedies of this author the reason for his dislike is unmistakable, buried though it may seem to be beneath his usual displays of erudition. The faults of *Chastelard* are those of the very worse school of modern poetry—"the physically intense school, as I should be inclined to call it, of which Mrs. Browning's 'Aurora Leigh' is the worst example, whose muse is a *fast* young woman with the lavish ornament and somewhat overpowering perfume of the *demi-monde,* and which pushes expression to the last gasp of sensuous exhaustion." Yet *Atalanta in Calydon,* he admits, is an exception to this judgment. "It is a true poem, and seldom breaks from the maidenly reserve which should characterize the higher forms of poetry, even in the keenest energy of expression." [25] Lowell never failed to condemn sensuousness when it suggested the sensual, except in the work of Keats. In treating the verses of this poet, he excused it as a tendency which became more "refined" with maturity.

What Lowell wrote about Thoreau, in perhaps the most widely known of these studies, is remarkable to this day. Never did the snobbish urbanity of his later years appear to greater disadvantage. The trait is inherent in the argument of his opening paragraph: What contemporary, if he were then alive, could forget the Transcendental Movement of thirty years ago, that signal for a sudden mental and moral mutiny set astir by Carlyle's essays and joined by representatives of all three of the sexes—men, women, and Lady Mary Wortley Montagues? "Every possible form of intellectual and physical dyspepsia brought forth its gospel. . . . Everybody had a mission (with a capital M) to attend to everybody else's business. No brain but had its private maggot, which must have found pitiably short commons sometimes."

A ticklish problem appears to have presented itself to Lowell at this point. How could he disparage transcendentalism without writing unfavorably of his friend Emerson? His way out of his predicament proved skillful—by praising Emerson as the real founder of the movement in this country, by terming his Phi Beta Kappa address in 1837 the "Yankee version of a lecture by Abelard," and by relegating Thoreau to the status of a pistillate plant "kindled to fruitage by the Emersonian pollen." Thoreau was thus reduced to the status of an imitator of the master, was shunted off into the lunatic fringe along with such contemporaries as Bronson Alcott and Margaret Fuller. It is fitting, Lowell adds, that Emerson should have edited the works of his Concord neighbor, for "they are strawberries from his own garden." Lowell then settles down to his subject. He has just read through Thoreau's six volumes, he declares, and "I shall try to give an adequate report of their impressions upon me both as critic and as mere reader."

The report, which duly follows, is as uncharitable a document as the author ever wrote about an important literary figure. Thoreau, he begins, had so high a conceit of himself that he accepted his own defects and weaknesses of character as virtues and powers peculiar to himself. When he found that he was wanting in the qualities that make for success, he decided that success itself was contemptible. His critical talents, for want of continuity of mind, were decidedly limited and inadequate. He had none of that artistic mastery which controls a great work to the serene balance of completeness [though for that matter, it might be suggested, neither had Emerson or Lowell]. He was not a true observer, since he saw only what he looked for. He prized a lofty way of thinking not because it was good in itself but because he wished few to share it with him. He sought for perversity in his ideas and revived the age of *concetti*. A greater familiarity with common men would have done him good, by showing him how many fine qualities are natural to the race.

He lacked a healthy mind, or he would not have been so fond of prescribing; his whole life, indeed, was a search for the doctor. He had no sense of humor. His attitude toward nature was diseased, for the proper way to enjoy this important influence is, simply, in a mood of complete relaxation. At any rate, nature seems to have had neither a sanitary nor sweetening effect upon Thoreau. He was a man who looked with utter contempt upon the august drama of destiny of which his country was the scene. Finally, his prose is monotonous; he concerns himself far too frequently with trifles.

For all these grievous shortcomings, what offset? Lowell's answer is stingy and feeble. There is no writing comparable to Thoreau's "in kind," he says, though what "in kind" means we are left to conjecture. "He gives us now and then superb outlooks from some jutting crag," yet his Walden experiment "actually presupposed all that complicated civilization which it theoretically abjured. He squatted on another man's land; he borrowed an axe; his boards, his nails, his bricks, his mortar, his books, his lamp, his fish hooks, his plow, his hoe, all turn state's evidence against him." Yet he wrote fine prose, and his whole life was a rebuke of the waste and aimlessness of our American luxury. Though not an originally creative author, he belongs with Donne and Novalis. He was, at least, peculiar.[26]

Accounting for this almost wholly hostile estimate is not easy. It might be mentioned, however—for what it is worth—that Thoreau's pronounced contempt for Cambridge culture was in no sense an attitude toward which Lowell would have been tolerant. Thoreau was an individualist, a man bent upon living his own life, and if this hazardous endeavor rubbed such outwardly complacent friends as Emerson in ways not wholly comforting, why then these gentlemen would have to make the most of it. Again, it will be recalled, Thoreau sent Lowell one of the most insulting letters he ever received, on the subject of the right of the *Atlantic* editor to meddle with certain sentences in an article that had been specifically asked for. This letter was not forgotten. Late in Lowell's life, in 1887, Thoreau's biographer, H. S. Salt, wrote him requesting copies of any correspondence which he might still have in his files.[27]   The request was ignored.   This too vigorous contemporary from neighboring Concord remained to the end not quite respectable, by the standards of the one-time Smith Professor of Modern Languages at Harvard.

The modest reputation which James Gates Percival, of Connecticut, enjoyed in his age, Lowell succeeded in rather thoroughly snuffing out, in the review of that poet's works, first published eleven years after his death.   The specific complaints against this unfortunate author's prolixity and bitterness over his country's neglect of him are not nearly so important as are Lowell's own pronouncements upon the nature of true literary excellence.   In the first place, Mr. Percival remained a provincial, not a national, author [as did Lowell, incidentally, in his most vigorous work].   This reviewer then turned to reflect on the West, and the writer who might soon emerge from that untamed region.   What should such a man aim at in the literary field?   Lowell's answer is "elegance and refinement," rather than "the rude vigor that is supposed to be his birthright."   In other words, he should look homeward, culturally, toward New England and Europe, and the fact that Whitman and Mark Twain failed to heed this warning was a mistake Lowell never learned to forgive.[28]

The review of the "Library of Old Authors" is the last essay of the volume, except for the already noticed "On a Certain Condescension in Foreigners."   It is a savage study, done in the early *Edinburgh Review* manner, but it reveals a careful concern for the texts of the works of the writers included in the series.   With two exceptions, Lowell insisted, these books "are creditable neither to English scholarship nor to English typography."   The introductions are poorly and ignorantly written.   It would be unfair to demand that one of the editors, Mr. Holliwell of the Royal *Irish* Academy, write in understandable English, he declared, adding his disgust with this gentleman for preserving "all the sacred blunders of Elizabethan typesetters" out of an absurd desire to re-issue the first printed text.   Lowell later proceeds to define a simple and convincing theory of editorship. A reprint of an English author, he says, "ought to be intelligible to English readers and, if the editor does not make it so, he wrongs the old poet." The review is almost uniformly scolding in tone, but anyone who has examined the material in question will probably decide that the reviewer's indignation was justified.

What shall one say about this rich exhibit of Lowell's interest in literature, an exhibit which should prove beyond controversy his persistent concern with foreign and native authors? (Taken together, in fact, one may find in his collected works some special study of virtually every important English writer from Chaucer to the Victorian age.) For one thing, by way of reply to the question, it is evident that his reading during the half-dozen years following the war proved both continuous and fruitful. His own estimate that he spent an average of twelve hours each day in his library seems to have been in no sense exaggerated. He was editing the *North American Review,* of course, and he was often faced with the problem of contributions to it, particularly the problem of printing articles by writers of some reputation. Where could he get them, except by frequently relying upon his own widely recognized talent? It was both good business and good sense, he seems to have felt, to compliment the pages of his magazine with his own work.

Mr. Norman Foerster has found in these contributions (and in similar ones which followed them) the evidence of a definite, if never specifically formulated, aesthetic on Lowell's part. His study is of undoubted importance. Lowell, we are told, believed that "literature is the ideal representation of human nature. Each literary work must have first of all a self contained form, possessing such qualities as unity, design, proportion, clearness, power, economy, control, sanity, impersonality. This form is organic. . . .

"Form determines quantitatively the beauty of a given work of art; spiritual imagination, guided by reason, determines it qualitatively. In the 'possible unity' of the greatest degree and the finest kind of beauty, we may conceive of the perfect work of art.

"The function of a work of art is to give delight. Of delight there are two general grades: first, the delight of recreation . . . and secondly, the joyful exercise of the higher faculties of mind and spirit working in harmony and so producing happiness rather than mere pleasure. For the fulfilment of both grades of delight, excellence of form is requisite; but the higher grade demands in addition moral or spiritual excellence—the contagion of a fine personality or the inspiration of an ideal vision of life." [29]

"If it were possible for us," continues Mr. Foerster, "to lay aside our memory of the personality of Lowell and of the weakness of his essays, and to concentrate our minds solely upon the system of ideas outlined above, we should certainly be drawn to the conclusion that we have here the sanest and most comprehensive conception of literature formed in America prior to the twentieth century." Doubtless all this is true. Yet it is equally true, as Mr. Foerster himself implies,[30] that in Lowell's mind the aesthetic just quoted never existed in anything like the unity and clarity with which it is now stated. Mr. Foerster's distillation is brilliant, but, one must add, it is not Lowell; and insofar as it is ascribed to Lowell it fundamentally misrepresents the nature of his mind. For the central facts about that mind were its discursiveness, its self-conscious irrelevance, and inner uncertainty, the compulsion of which was always present to disperse his meditations.[31] Perhaps he had sat too long in the professor's chair, had fallen a victim of its digressive privileges. No one can positively say. Yet the evidence is unmistakable that any basic coherence in his thinking about literature appears to have come to him only at intervals, and by happy though sadly infrequent accidents.

XVIII

"If I am not an American, who ever was?"
Lowell to Joel Benton, January 19, 1876.
Works, XV, 377

AFTER a voyage "as smooth as the style of the late Samuel Rogers," Lowell arrived in Queenstown in early August, 1872. It was his third trip abroad, and he meant to remain two years. Reflection had convinced him with renewed intensity of his unfitness for a professorship. What was the main business of that occupation, anyway? Was it not the ability "to remember names and to be cocksure of dates?" [1] The learning of which he had been so positive, with notes before him, now seemed vaporous and unreal. "Am I the right sort of man to guide ingenuous youth? Not a bit of it!"

Yet he was certainly a person of no ordinary attainments, a fact one distinguished Englishman had just declared publicly. Mr. Charles Kingsley, Canon of the Cathedral of Chester, guided Lowell on a tour of that region. At the end of two days of sightseeing, "Mr. K. made a speech on the excursion and all of a sudden mentioned as its chief incident the presence of etc. etc. 'undoubtedly the greatest satirist since Juvenal and superior to Juvenal in etc. etc.' I could only do as pious Englishmen when they pray, bury my face in my hat." [2]

Following a short stay in England, he went with Mrs. Lowell to Paris. The manners of the French proved altogether to his liking, and in the shops he was soon taking off his hat and *monsieuring* and *madaming* with the best of them. "If you buy a pennyworth of matches," he wrote his daughter, "they are as civil and as ceremonious as at some great commercial transaction. They somehow make you feel *welcome,* while the English seem anxious to be rid of you." [3]

Of course he was reading a great deal, as always. In particular, he had just finished a *real* Arthurian romance, "Fergus"—"a genuine blossom for which no triumph of artifice can compensate"—and had followed it with certain of Tennyson's recently published *Idylls of the King*,[4] devouring them at a gulp by sitting up "like a naughty boy until half past one." The contrast between the real thing and the poet laureate's imitation proved both curious and instructive. "There are very fine childish things in Tennyson's poem, and fine manly things too," he admitted, "but I conceive the theory to be wrong. I have the same feeling (I am not wholly sure of its justice) that I have when I see these modern-medieval pictures. I am defrauded; I do not see reality, but a masquerade. The costumes are all that is genuine, and the people inside them are shams—which, I take it, is the reverse of what ought to be." The similes in Tennyson's work, he went on, seemed dragged in by the hair; they had the flavor of something extracted from notebooks. Yet the man was undoubtedly a great artist, the greatest to appear, indeed, since Thomas Gray.[5]

Among his most eager diversions during the winter was book-buying. The habit was one which would yield him, he felt, a revenue as long as he lived. The cheapness of what are called standard authors was wonderful, he wrote Mrs. Burnett, and he could obtain books bound for two francs and a half in a style that would cost me as much in dollars at home. "I am gradually getting to be a sharp customer and have a discount made on whatever I buy. I never give the asking price."[6] At times, he confessed, his zest for these purchases led him beyond his depth. There were the four quarto volumes of *Le Chevalier au Cigne*, for instance. He paid $33.50 for it, but would "not have thought it dear at a hundred." The same day he announced that he was going out after a copy of the *Poètes Champenois*, which he had luckily stumbled upon for only $180.[7] The result of this habit, at the time of Lowell's death, was an extremely useful library of seven thousand volumes. The majority of his books went where he had intended them to go, and where they would prove most useful—to Harvard. Among other provisions in his will was one which declared a long-cherished intention: "I give to the corporation of Harvard College, the Library thereof . . . any books from my library of which the College Library does not already possess copies, or of which the copies or editions in my library are for any reason whatever preferable to those possessed by the College Library." [8] His love of books was, beyond question, one of the most permanent and admirable characteristics of his nature.

Winter passed most pleasantly. He walked a great deal, read a great deal, came to know the streets of the city like a native, visited the art galleries, and when evening came, taught French to his wife and to their old Cambridge friend, John Holmes. He also came to reflect more sharply upon the French temperament and what it might signify in cultural terms. What did all their trivial courtesies add up to? Certainly, he decided, they were an excellent discipline, "for I have always been of the mind that in a democracy manners are the only effective weapons against the bowie-knife; the only thing that will save us from barbarism." [9]

The inevitable longing of the traveler for his home grew upon him with the beginnings of spring. Thomas Bailey Aldrich, who had rented Elmwood during Lowell's absence, wrote him in April in a way that strengthened this feeling acutely. The experience of receiving a letter from that home, written by someone whose name was not his own, seemed very odd. "I can see my study so plainly as I sit here, but I find it hard to fill my chair with anybody but myself. . . . It is a pleasant old house, isn't it? Doesn't elbow one, as it were. It will make a frightful conservative of you before you know it. It was born a Tory and will die so. Don't get too used to it. I often wish I had not grown into it so." [10]

Back in England he met Ruskin and Carlyle, but was not remarkably impressed. The latter proved "very sweet and gentle," the other "a man of sentiment who seeks refuge from a sense of his own weakness in strong opinions (or at any rate the vehement assertion of them) as men reassure themselves by talking aloud in the dark. I conceived Rousseau the better for having seen him." This was in May. The same letter revealed to his daughter the fact that Oxford was soon to bestow upon him the degree of Doctor of Civil Laws. This honor was duly conferred. "Mr. Brice [*sic*] [11] made a speech in Latin to the Vice Chancellor Dr. Liddell enumerating my many virtues, the Vice Chancellor conferred the degree, I marched up some steps, shook hands with him and seated myself among the other doctors. Then we had to listen to the prize essays in Greek, Latin, and verse, and walked back to lunch in the hall of All Souls." After this routine came a horticultural fête, dinner at Christ Church, and more dining and visiting the next day. It was rather fatiguing, this allowing oneself to be doctored, though everybody seemed kind. But his nostalgia for Elmwood would in no way abate, despite almost every imaginable allurement the Old World was able to muster. Most consoling of all to him, far more consoling than his itinerary, was the fact that he was "still in love at fifty-four." [12]

He went to other lands, lands new to him, to the various cities of the Low Countries. Later he visited Venice, Florence, Rome, and Naples. In one of these places he reached a further interesting conclusion about America. Back home, he decided, there was no real leisure; yet only in a world willing to allow this virtue to flourish could good humor and wit and all the excellencies of art be found in more than an exotic state. "It is not that one needs to be idle, but only to have this southern atmosphere about him. Democracies lie, perhaps, too far North."

His health, meanwhile, was far from what it might have been, and was coloring, for the worse, perhaps, his notions about his unpredictable world. Months before, he had signed himself to a friend as "Llumbago Llowell." Now a new ailment had developed. He called upon a doctor in Rome, and learned that his malady was "suppressed gout." "Suppressed" was an accurate word, he avowed: "It has a fancy of gripping me in the stomach sometimes, holding on like a slow fire for seven hours at a time." [13] The first courtesies of disintegration were at last growing into familiars for him.

He was beginning, as a result, to think of death in a manner more poignant than, in the past, had seemed needful or personally relevant. Certain news from home augmented the tendency. He had

had a notion, he wrote George Putnam, that as one grew older he got used to death, and in some sense it was true, but no habitude. was able to render men less sensible to deaths which make them older and lonelier by widening the gap between their past and present selves. "Our own lives seem to lose their continuity, and those who died long ago seem more wholly dead when some one who was associated with them and linked our memory more indissolubly with them goes out into the endless silence and separation." [14] He was referring to the recent loss of a cousin, Amory Lowell. For many, many months he had hardly seen her; but the thought of her, living, kept fresh in his mind the memory of his uncle John, and of his own father, dust now these thirteen years.

He made his plans to return home with eagerness. There was an old eye ailment to contend with—"a drop of black blood," he called it—which he had inherited from his mother. It would spread itself over the pupil, darkening everything, including his faith. He had spent more money than he anticipated, and the income he relied on from the sale of his land had diminished. It looked as if he would be compelled to resume his teaching again, despite his confession to Norton that not more than once a week did he seem able to do anything effective with his students. "The rest of the time my desk was as good as I." [15] But before he sailed, as if to prepare him for the old routine, Cambridge University conferred upon him the degree of Doctor of Laws. "You don't know," he said, referring to the public orator's Latin speech, "what an odd kind of posthumous feeling it gives one." July 4, 1874, he and Mrs. Lowell were in Elmwood.

He settled down at once to those habits which had become second nature to him—endless reading and criticizing. "Ten hours a day, on an average, I have been at it for the last two months," he wrote in September, "and get so absorbed that I turn grudgingly to anything else." He was going through the publications of the Early English Texts Society. And to a friend, Mrs. Francis J. Lippitt, he was also expounding the topic of fleshliness in poetry. "As for the aphrodisiac or cantharides style of verses, I do not believe that the sexual impulses need any spurring, nor, if they did, that the rowel should be forged of that most precious metal of poesy whereof the shield of Achilles or the Grecian Urn could be hammered. The line between the sensuous and the sensual is that between sentiment and sentimentalism, between passion and brutish impulse, between love and appetite, between Vittoria Colonna and Madame Bovary." He went on to praise one of the most sentimental though popular lyrics in the language, Shelley's "Indian Serenade," in which the most intense emotion imaginable is evoked and paraded without cause.[16] Almost alone, Lowell declared, this poet "has trodden with an unfaltering foot the scimitar-edged bridge which leads from physical sensation to the heaven of song. No, I certainly do *not* believe in the value of any literature that renders the relation between the sexes more ticklish than nature has already made it." Such writing would upset our moral center of gravity, and being morally questionable, he strongly implies, it is also aesthetically questionable. How much of Chaucer, or Shakespeare, or Jonson would have passed this test we are left to conjecture. Certainly Whitman failed it, when it was applied to him. In Lowell's mind it remained a settled principle, one whose result was systematically to exclude large segments of human experience from poetic treatment. Poetry to him, as to many other romantics, was essentially refined and exclusive; its subject matter and technique should both, therefore, be radically supervised. The important poets of the present age are still having to contend against the damaging influence of his point of view in the public mind. It explains in large measure their neglect today.

He was teaching again at Harvard—this time, courses in Old French and Dante. And he was giving highly sensible advice to friends about the way a language ought to be studied: "Let me counsel you to read a little German every day and you will be surprised to find how soon it grows easy to you. Insist on knowing the exact meaning of every sentence, and use your grammar for that only. In this way you will insensibly grow familiar with the grammatical construction. I think a great deal of time is wasted in preliminary studies of grammar. Tumble into deep waters at once if you would learn to swim." [17] It required our professors of modern languages fifty years to appreciate the wisdom of this method. Many of them, indeed, are still blind to its advantages.

An importunate Baltimore admirer was curious about his religious opinions, and asked if he were an Episcopalian. "No," he replied, "though I prefer the service of the Church of England, and attend it from time to time. But I am not much of a church-goer, because I so seldom find any preaching that does not make me impatient and do me more harm than good. I confess to a strong lurch towards Calvinism (in some of its doctrines) that strengthens as I grow older. Perhaps it may be some consolation to you that my mother was born and bred an Episcopalian." [18] The truth is that Lowell had been caught between the two worlds Matthew Arnold spoke of in another connection: he could neither accept nor reject the Christian myth. It was the dilemma of his age, and perhaps, less hopefully, of the present age. The following year he phrased the problem in this way, to his old friend Leslie Stephen: "I don't think a view of the universe from the stocks of any creed a very satisfactory one. But I continue to shut my eyes resolutely in certain speculative directions, and am willing to find solace in certain intimations that seem to me from a region higher than my reason. When they tell me that I can't *know* certain things, I am apt to wonder how *they* can be sure of that, and whether there may not be things which they can't know. I went through my reaction so early and so violently that I have been settling backward toward equilibrium ever since. As I can't be certain, I won't be positive, and wouldn't drop some chapters of the Old Testament, even, for all the science that ever undertook to tell me what it doesn't know." [19] It was his final stand, as far as can be determined. Though his inclination was slightly toward the faith of his father, essentially his father's church had disappeared for him as an institution. There remained only its moral code, which on many occasions he found it convenient to modify and interpret precisely as he pleased. The chaos of individualism had caught up with him and had made him, for better or worse, a modern man.

Meanwhile, he had been writing certain poems whose timeliness and vigor had brought down upon his head the large damnation of many intrenched interests. One of them, "The World's Fair, 1876," was tense with his indignation over what fifteen years of unchecked Republican rule had done for the country. His rhetorical chickens had all come home at last, to roost on the steps of the North's sullied Vartu. Lowell did not relish their appearance at all. In eleven terse couplets he itemized his grievances: The civil service was a farce, the cost of government high, paper money—not gold—was being advocated, juries were corrupt, political bosses controlled the people, plunderers bled them and proclaimed such rascals as Boss Tweed to be martyrs. His lines proclaimed an entirely sincere, if still self-righteous and moral, indignation.[20]

Other verses, under the title, "Tempora Mutantur," elaborated his disgust. "A hundred years ago, if men were knaves, why, people called them so." Plain words served for plain things then, and the prison was the natural destiny of the malefactor. But times have marvelously changed:

> Now that to steal by law is grown an art,
> Whom rogues the sires, their milder sons call smart,
> And "slightly irregular" dilutes the shame
> Of what had once a somewhat blunter name.
> With generous curve we draw the moral line:
> Our swindlers are permitted to resign;
> Their guilt is wrapped in deferential names,
> And twenty sympathize for one that blames.
> Add national disgrace to private crime,
> Confront mankind with brazen front sublime,
> Steal but enough, the world is unsevere—
> Tweed is a statesman, Fisk a financier.[21]

Suppose, the poet continues, that some public servant is actually arrested. The judge who tries the case probably is one who owes his office to the accused man's manipulations. The result is that,

> Whitewashed, he quits the politician's strife
> At ease in mind, with pockets filled for life.

Moreover,

A public meeting, treated at his cost,
Resolves him back more virtue than he lost.

Should he seek that ultimate tribute of his fellows, the tribute of reverence, only one further step is required: he must teach a Sunday School class!

Both poems were vigorous, as were the attacks upon the author which followed their publication. For Lowell was assailing obvious evils in a manner too direct to avoid offending such men as wished those evils to continue. Many editors charged "that he was no true American; that he was in fact a snob; that he had elbowed against dukes and lords so much and so long that he could not any longer tolerate Democracy." Mr. Joel Benton decided to reply to these slanders, attesting their inaccuracy and the poet's good intentions. What he wrote brought forth from Lowell both gratitude and a further explanation of his motives.

"I had just come home from a two year's stay in Europe," he told his defender, "so it was discovered that I had been corrupted by association with foreign aristocracies! I need not say to you that the society I frequented in Europe was what it is at home—that of my wife, my studies, and the best nature and art within my reach. But I confess that I was embittered by my experience. Wherever I went I was put on the defensive. Whatever extracts I saw from American papers told of some new fraud or defalcation, public or private. It was sixteen years since my last visit abroad, and I found a very striking change in the feeling towards America and Americans. An Englishman was everywhere treated with a certain deference: Americans were at best tolerated. The example of America was everywhere urged in France as an argument against republican forms of government. It was fruitless to say that the people were still sound when the Body Politic, which draws its life from them, showed such blotches and sores. I came home, and instead of wrath at such abominations, I found banter. I was profoundly shocked, for I had received my earliest impressions in a community the most virtuous, I believe, that ever existed." Certainly, he went on, I would rather be left to my studies than meddle with politics. I wrote what I did in the plainest way, so that he who ran might read. These fellows who are attacking me have no notion what love of country means. "It is in my very blood and bones. If I am not an American, who ever was?" [22]

Three memorial odes, all of them intended for public recitation, belong to the year 1875-76. Lowell wrote revealingly about the technical problems these pieces evoked for him. How could he avoid monotony? was the question. "The least tedious measure is the rhymed heroic, but this palls unless relieved by passages of wit or even mere fun. A long series of uniform stanzas (I am always speaking of public recitation) with regularly recurring rhymes produces somnolence among the men and a desperate resort to their fans on the part of the women. . . . I know *something* (of course an American can't know much) about Pindar. But *his* odes had the advantage of being chanted. Now my problem was to contrive a measure which should not be tedious by uniformity, which should vary with varying moods, in which the transitions (including those of the voice) should be managed without jar. . . . Harmony, without sacrifice of melody, was what I had mainly in view." [23]

He achieved this harmony to a pronounced degree. The odes read well, and are sustained by a rhetorical eloquence that is perhaps as much as one may expect to communicate to a large and impersonal audience. Lowell's imagery is occasional and vague in these works, abstract and ruminative, and as for his subject matter —particularly in the "Ode Read at Concord" and in "July Fourth, 1876"—he simply had little of importance or interest to say. In the former poem he praises the spirit of freedom which animated the Revolutionists, and prays that their memory will inspire his own age. In the latter he writes of the Goddess America who, born in a seven-year ordeal of thunder and blood, is blessed now with security and peace. The present condition of his country seems vulgar, it is true, but this fact he brushes aside. On her natal day he can think only of love. The poem closes with a lengthy reminis-

LOWELL IN 1875

cence on Columbus, and a prayer that God will not cease to befriend "the land to human nature dear." [24]

Much more important, and revealing, is the third piece, "Under the Old Elm." It was read at Cambridge on the hundredth anniversary of Washington's taking command of the American forces. Beginning with a tribute to the scene, and to the tree itself—"Repeating its green legend every spring, And, with a yearly ring, Recording the fair seasons as they flee"—the poet passes on to announce the expected moral: We fall as leaves; the trunk remains. He turns to the figure of Washington, called up by memory's soundless voice. A century ago he stood here, close-lipped and tall, vaguely famed for an old fight in the woods. His men were scarcely more than a motley rout—an army all of captains, skilled to debate their orders, not to obey them. How the reputation of their leader has changed since first he looked down upon those querulous followers! The poem is primarily, and properly, a tribute to the General's character, but that tribute involved one singularly disturbing crux: Washington was a Virginian, a southerner. How could one reconcile the nobility of his nature with the geographical perversity of his birth?

Lowell could not do it at all, in any of those terms which in the past he had so solidly and effectively defined. Was it possible for anything commendable to flower forth out of Nazareth? He was driven to a recantation, to an apology, and he addressed it, as a New Englander, directly to Virginia as a symbol of the South:

> If ever with distempered voice or pen
> We have misdeemed thee, here we take it back,
> And for the dead of both don common black.[25]

He added these lines, he informed a friend, and the stanza of which they are a part, only in the hope of doing "good." [26]

Doubtless he actually did a great deal of good toward healing those external wounds that had bled, already, far too long. But his well meant gesture was too tardy to prove effective. One may appropriately remember here a comment by Paul Buck: "A culture which in its life was anathema to the North could in its death be honored." [27]

XIX

*"I remember how, fifty years ago today, I, perched in a
great oxheart cherry tree, long ago turned to mold, saw my
father come home with news of Adams's death. I wish I
could feel, as I did then, that we were a chosen people."*

Lowell to Mrs. S. B. Herrick, July 4, 1876.
Works, XV, 394

MY dearest little girl—do not give yourself the least anxiety
about that rumor of my going abroad," as Minister to Russia. "There is nothing in it. The offer has been made me and I have
written the Secretary of State declining it. *This* must be kept *wholly
to yourself at present."* [1] Lowell thus reassured his daughter, in the
autumn of 1874, that he was not greatly tempted by the first diplomatic plum his friends arranged to have served up to him. But the
idea itself proved attractive, and he did not close his mind to it during the next two years. Instead, he began to work actively in both
state and national politics. He had definite ideas about the condition of the country and he also had a considerable body of followers.

Certain of those followers, led by Mr. Edward P. Bliss, appealed to
him directly in April, 1876. They represented themselves as dissatisfied with recent tendencies in the Republican Party, and desired to
call a meeting on the Harvard campus. Would Professor Lowell
consent to preside? [2]

He certainly would! The function, he confessed, was not exactly
in his "line," but he was "willing to do *anything* which may be
thought helpful in a movement of which I heartily approve. I am
not so hopeful, I confess, as I was thirty years ago; yet if there be
any hope, it is in getting independent thinkers to be independent
voters."

Lowell reported this occasion to Leslie Stephen in a way which
scarcely did himself justice. "Last night I appeared in a new ca-

pacity as chairman of a political meeting, where I fear I made an ass of myself." Yet he stated, clearly, in a single sentence further on, a conviction which he was never afterwards to desert. "We have got to work back from a democracy to our original institution as a republic again. Our present system has resulted in our being governed by a secret and irresponsible club called the United States Senate for their own private benefit." [3]

The injustice of Lowell's modest reference to his rôle at this meeting is evident when one considers the results of it. He was named permanent chairman of a committee formed to organize the voters of Cambridge, and in the first election which followed—an election to choose delegates to the coming presidential convention—Lowell and his followers outmaneuvered the government bloc and succeeded in defeating its delegates, who wished Blaine nominated for the presidency. As a result of this success, he and his friend the Rev. James Freeman Clark were themselves sent to the Republican convention in Cincinnati, to choose a proper candidate.

Qualms assailed his conscience when he faced the sour alternatives confronting him there. For whom could he vote and at the same time keep inviolate his own self-respect? Mr. Bristow, of Kentucky, appeared to be the only answer. A member of Grant's cabinet, this gentleman had already established himself as a practical reformer. "I believed," Lowell wrote Mrs. Herrick, "that a Kentucky candidate might at least give the starting point for a party in the South whose line of division should be other than sectional, and by which the natural sympathy between reasonable and honest men at the North and the South should have a fair chance to reassert itself. We failed, but at least succeeded in preventing the nomination of a man [James G. Blaine] whose success in the Convention (he would have been beaten disastrously at the polls) would have been a lesson to American youth that selfish partisanship is a set-off for vulgarity of character and obtuseness of moral sense. I am proud to say that it was New England that defeated the New England Candidate." [4] The result was that Rutherford B. Hayes, "a man of excellent character, friendly to civil service reform, and opposed to severe measures in the South," [5] became the choice of the Republicans against the nominee of the Democrats, Samuel J. Tilden.

In defending that choice publicly, Lowell delivered himself of a characteristic statement. There was at the time a much larger class of voters than usual, he said, "who are resolved to cast their ballots less in reference to party ties than to what in their judgment is the interest of the whole country. The two parties are so evenly balanced that the action of this class is of supreme importance. Among these are doubtless some wrong headed men, some disappointed ones, and some who think that any change, no matter what, may be for the better and cannot be for the worse. But in general these dissatisfied persons are men of more than average thoughtfulness, weight of character, and influence. They feel profoundly that the great weakness of the democratical form of government . . . is a great and growing want of responsibility in officials . . . a great and growing indifference to the claims of character as compared with partisan efficiency or unscrupulousness. We hear, to be sure, of responsibility to the People, but in practice this amounts to very little. Just before election the politicians become tenderly aware of the existence of the People, they recognize their long lost brother, and rush into his arms with more than fraternal fervor." He saw only one remedy for this condition. It was that of making the candidates for office feel their responsibility at the polls, "the only point at which they are sensitive."

He went on to declare his sympathy with the principles of the Republican party, as he understood them. "But it has no sacredness for me when it degenerates into a contrivance for putting unfit men or tainted men into office, and for making them 'Honorable' by courtesy who are not so by character. When a party becomes an organization to serve only its own private ends, when it becomes a mere means of livelihood or distinction on easier terms than God for our good has prescribed, it has become noxious instead of useful. Now, fellow citizens, it cannot be denied that the Republican party has suffered by too long and too easy a tenure of office. We ought to be thankful to its opponents for the investigations which have shown us its weak faults. Let it never be said that we object to any investigation of character. Let it always be said that we object to men who need to be investigated."

He was by no means finished. They must choose men who were above suspicion, he went on. It was said that the party could be reformed from within, but was this statement less true of the Democrats? He remembered the first printed ballot he ever saw. Fifty years ago, it had been, in Baltimore, and upon it was a picture of the American flag and the inscription, "Hurrah for Old Hickory." What those verbal cheers, translated into votes, had meant for his country he would never forget. They meant the beginning of the spoils system, that system "which has led to all the corruption in our administration, and which, if not cured, will lead to the failure of our democratical experiment."

How about honest money? he asked. The question meant that efforts of the debtors of New England in the South and West who were interested, after the Panic of 1873, in obtaining a greenback currency "only slightly below par"[6] were to him definitely dishonest. Then he turned to Mr. Tilden. The latter's election, he declared, would prove a national calamity. "We are not willing to risk any of the results of the nation's victory. One of the most important of those results was the assertion of our indivisible nationality. Mr. Tilden and the party which he directs have always been extreme in their interpretation of the reserved rights of the individual States, going so far even as to include that of rebellion among them. Should such principles prevail, revolution would become constitutional, and we should have another Mexico instead of the country we love. We should be admitting that the war, so costly to our prosperity, so incalculably dear in hopeful lives, was both a blunder and a crime. I for one am not ready for an admission like this."[7]

Indeed he was not—no matter what brief poetic overtures might seem appropriate to the citizens of Virginia. Nor did his usually alert moral sense prompt him to a further protest against the

Republican party when, the morning after election day, it was found that Tilden lacked but one disputed electoral vote to attain the presidency, although Hayes lacked a total of twenty. Nineteen of this number, it will be recalled, were tied up in the proverbially Democratic states of South Carolina, Louisiana, and Florida. All of them, after a procedure which need not be dwelt upon here, were at length cast for Hayes. Lowell, in brief, was to receive his first appointment in politics from an administration which, regardless of its later achievements, attained its power in violation of every principle he had defended in his able speech to the voters of Cambridge.[8]

That appointment came with a traditional reserve and informality. William Dean Howells was the chief instrument in effecting it. "I do not know whether it crossed his mind after the election of Hayes that he might be offered some place abroad, but it certainly crossed the minds of some of his friends, and I could not feel that I was acting for myself alone when I used a family connection with the President, very early in his term, to let him know that I believed Lowell would accept a diplomatic mission. . . . The President said that he had already thought of offering Lowell something, and he gave me the pleasure, a pleasure beyond any other I could imagine, of asking Lowell whether he would accept the mission to Austria. I lost no time in carrying his letter to Elmwood, where I found Lowell over his coffee at dinner. He saw me at the threshold, and called to me through the open door to come in, and I handed him the letter, and sat down at table while he ran it through. When he had read it, he gave a quick 'Ah!' and threw it over the length of the table to Mrs. Lowell. She read it in a smiling and loyal reticence, as if she would not say one word of all she might wish to say in urging his acceptance, though I could see that she was intensely eager for it. The whole situation was of a perfect New England character in its tacit significance; after Lowell had taken his coffee, we turned into his study, without further allusion to the matter."

"A day or two later," Howells continues, "he came to my house to say that he could not accept the Austrian mission, and to ask me to tell the President so for him and make his acknowledgements, which he would also write himself. He remained talking a little while of other things, and when he rose to go he said, with a sigh of vague reluctance, 'I *should* like to see a play of Calderon,' as if it had nothing to do with any wish of his that could still be fulfilled. Upon this hint I acted." [9]

Howells's action proved effective. Lowell had been mentioned not only for Austria but for Berlin, yet he continued in his preference for Spain. Howells talked with Secretary of State Evarts about the problem. The Secretary decided that certain shifts could be made. Then, in late June, the President himself came to Cambridge to receive an honorary degree from Harvard. Lowell was profoundly pleased with him. He was more handsome than his photographs attested. Mrs. Hayes, too, was both simple and well-bred. Lowell was sure that both the chief magistrate and his wife had in them "that excellent new thing we call Americanism, which I suppose is that 'dignity of human nature' which the philosophers of the last century were always seeking and never finding and which, after all, consists, perhaps, in not thinking yourself either better or worse than your neighbor by reason of any artificial distinction. . . . Their dignity was in their very neighborliness, instead of in their distance, as in Europe." [10] He had already accepted the appointment and was now "His Excellency," with all the title implied. If only his father were alive to read those letters after his son's name in the Harvard triennial catalogue! "You remember Johnson's pathetic letter to Chesterfield. How often I think of it as I grow older!" For many years, in truth, he had waited for a post that would bespeak a full and public tribute to his talents. Now that it was offered him, he seemed scarcely to want it. Leaving Elmwood, with its numberless birds—and its cankerworms—had become by no means a simple gesture for a retiring scholar of fifty-seven. [11]

A good while before he sailed—indeed, as far back as December, 1875 [12]—he had published another volume of essays. He called it *Among My Books* (Second Series), and the title proved entirely accurate. For the five studies which comprised it—studies on Dante, Spenser, Wordsworth, Milton, and Keats—were ones which only long hours in his library could have made possible. They are studies, moreover, which define for the volume its distinctive tone and its limitations.

Taken together, they are unimportant as literary criticism[13]—though they tell one a good deal about Lowell. Complaining of the unhappy effect of his professorship, he declared, the year the book appeared: "It damped my gunpowder, as it were, and my mind, when it took fire at all (which wasn't often) drawled off in an unwilling fuse instead of leaping to meet the first spark." Of his work after the Civil War, this judgment is largely true. The essays appear to have been heavy tasks—so heavy, and so inclusive in their demands upon his knowledge, that the problem of organizing them became entirely too difficult to solve. He contented himself largely with reading the several authors and with pointing out long-settled excellences and defects. As W. C. Brownell once suggested, he had the literary scholar's love of words, and a great fondness for books, but he lacked a passion for ideas. He let himself slip into the habits of indolence peculiar to the academic mind. He preferred reading to thinking.[14]

"There are two ways of measuring a poet," Lowell declared in the Spenser essay, "either by an absolute aesthetic standard, or relatively to his position in the literary history of his country and the conditions of his generation." [15] Actually the latter, or historical, judgment was one Lowell rarely applied. His sense of history appears largely trivial, except in the case of Old and New World Puritanism. On this subject he was remarkably well informed.

Certainly there are interesting passages and happily phrased judgments in every study. In "Milton," particularly, he wrote some of the most engaging banter of his life. His subject, or victim, in this case was David Masson, that solemn Scotchman who so filled his biography of the poet with political, literary, and ecclesiastical information as to produce what Lowell termed a rambling history of the seventeenth century, one in which Milton shows himself only as an unexpected apparition "who, like Paul Pry, just pops in and hopes he does not intrude, to tell us what he has been doing in the meanwhile." [16] Masson, in fact, "occupied 1,378 pages in getting Milton to his thirty-fifth year." We should be thankful, Lowell added, that Methuselah's life story "(if written in the same longeval proportion) is irrecoverably lost to us." He was insisting here upon an entirely sound principle of biographical inquiry. Historical background was necessary, he declared, and its use altogether valid, but one should employ only those segments of it which are "really operative on the character of the man we are studying." The irony of Lowell's strictures derives from the fact that he made them with the same irrelevant prolixity for which he condemned the author of Milton's life. They comprise one-third of the essay!

This discursiveness is probably the most obvious characteristic of the collection; it rides him like the Old Man of the Sea. Especially is it evident in the Wordsworth commentary, in which the judgments parallel the more incisive ones that Coleridge arrived at sixty years before, in a manner embarrassingly suggestive of plagiarism. [17] Illustrative quotations abound. One, in "Spenser," extends to fifty-six lines, and another, less than two pages afterwards, runs on for another eighty-three. It is a shoddy method, the method of the classroom, and it is suggestive mainly of Lowell's mental indolence. He had little of importance or freshness to say about his subjects. He could only polish and amplify those critical jewels which others had mined before him.

Yet one cannot resist the conviction that his appointment to Spain was wholly merited, and flattering to his country. No more distinguished American writer, with the exception of Emerson, now mellowly senile, was living and similarly acknowledged by fellow Americans. Lowell had become almost an institution, a figure who for a third of a century had been known and esteemed by thousands. He embodied the learning and dignity—in short, the culture—in which his people had come to believe passionately, and they knew that in him certain of the most esteemed characteristics of their nation would be completely upheld. In urbanity, he was the match of any diplomat alive.

His ship sailed July 14, 1877, from Boston. The usual ceremonies for sending off a public figure were all faithfully observed. The *Parthia* steamed down the harbor followed by a tug to bring back those friends who could not bear to part with him before he reached the outer light. Lowell confessed his opinion of such elaborate courtesies in a letter to Norton: "If the agent of the Cunard line," he said, "had given a month's meditation to devising what would annoy me most, he could have hit on nothing to beat this."

XX

"We are now expecting General Grant with terror."
Lowell to his daughter, November 18, 1877.
New Letters, 230

LOWELL'S journey to Madrid proved leisurely, like his duties
once he was settled there. Thoreau remarked in his best-
known book that nothing new ever happens in foreign parts, and
"as for Spain, for instance, if you know how to throw in Don
Carlos and the Infanta and Don Pedro and Seville and Granada,
from time to time, in the right proportions . . . and serve up a bull-
fight when other entertainments fail, it will be true to the letter, and
give us as good an idea of the exact state or ruin of things in Spain
as the most succinct and lucid reports under this head in the newspapers." [1] Lowell's diplomatic correspondence to the Secretary of
State fully confirms this judgment of his wry contemporary. [2] He
was even driven to serving up the bull-fight, along with assorted
scraps of gossip, scandal, and descriptions of festivals that often read
with the elaborate casualness of personal essays.

He went to the Spanish capital by way of London. Every day,
while there, he would walk to Hyde Park after breakfast, to smoke
his cigar. As he sat in the meadowy air, the past of literature and
his imagination merged with the hum of wheels that never ceased.
It was still Dr. Johnson's London, he felt, and looking westward into
the filmy distance he could see the sheep crawling in the sun, unreal
as a pastoral of the last century, as if they might have walked out
of an eclogue of Gay's. Fancy conceived them watched by berib-
boned shepherdesses and swains. Now and then a scarlet coat would
cross his eye, like a stain of blood on the innocent grass. And always
before him streamed the coaches and the citizens, men and women
whose violent contrasts of costume and whose oddities of face and

figure led him to conclude that Dickens had, after all, not written caricature when he described them in his novels.[3]

Next there was Paris. He stayed in the same hotel at which he had been a guest five years before. Essentially it was the Paris of his memories, and more than ever it struck him as the handsomest city in the world. He was as pleased as ever with the caressing tones of the Frenchwomen and "with the universal courtesy of the men." One lady at a kiosk had asked him about John Holmes, the brother of Oliver Wendell. He loved animals, she said, and that represented, for her, the ultimate test of a gentleman. Lowell reached Madrid August 14, 1877, and every honor of office seemed fairly thrust upon him at once. "We can't go in a cab like ordinary mortals, but must have coachman and footman in livery. . . . There are moments when I feel that I have sold my soul to the Devil." [4]

Perhaps he had, so elaborate seemed the routine in which, reticent scholar though he was, he found it necessary to move. He went to see the King, at La Granja, the summer palace, which lay fifty miles from the capital. Eight mules with red plumes and elaborate trappings formed his team. He arrived at midnight. Fourteen hours later came a pair of royal coaches—for the Minister and his chargé d'affaires, and they started at a footpace for the palace, a hundred yards away. Lowell spoke to His Majesty in English, listened to the King's reply in Spanish. The next day he walked by the King's side, and His Majesty talked to him at length, "even quoting one of my own verses. He had been crammed, of course, beforehand." [5] But this seemed, nonetheless, a wholly commendable achievement for a young man who had not reached his nineteenth birthday. At two o'clock the following morning, His Excellency departed once more for Madrid.

An old ailment, the gout, overtook Lowell almost as soon as he had settled upon a home there. It assailed one foot and then the other. He was laid up for weeks. And then, in January, came "two more of those dreadful attacks in the stomach to which I have been liable for the last few years." They proved so severe that for a time he "really thought something was going to happen that would drive the legation to black wax." Then his feet would swell and the abdominal throbbings would stop. Small wonder that the routine of tedious official receptions seemed almost more than he was able to endure.

Yet he was still the scholarly student of language, still intellectually curious. Knowing the literature of Spain much better than the natives with whom he dealt was not enough. He wanted to master the vernacular, and he set about the task systematically. To this end he engaged, as tutor, Don Herminegildo Giner de los Rios, "a most agreeable man," who came to him every morning for an hour or more.

He described the routine of a typical day in a letter to Grace Norton: "Get up at 8, from 9 sometimes till 11 my Spanish professor, at 11 breakfast, at 12 to the Legation, at 3 home again and a cup of chocolate, then read the paper and write Spanish till a quarter to 7, at 7 dinner, and at 8 drive in an open carriage in the Prado till 10, to bed at 12 to 1. In cooler weather we drive in the afternoon." [6] When there was no gout to suffer with, and no reception to attend, the world seemed pleasant enough.

He was beginning to make up his mind about the people to whom his government had accredited him. There was something oriental in his nature, he said, which sympathized with their "let her slide" temperament. They go through all the forms of business as they do of religion, without any reference to the thing itself, just as they offer you their house and everything in it. They are unenterprising and unchangeable. The latest accounts of them are just like the earliest, and they have a firm faith in Dr. Mañana—he will cure everything. "In short there is a flavor of Old Cambridge about 'em, as O.C. used to be when I was young and the world worth having."

But the hours they kept were too much for him. "They go to a reception *after* the opera, so that half past 11 is early. At a dance they are more punctual, and I have even known them to begin at 10, but they keep it up till 2 or 3. They seem childishly fond of dancing. But there is no such thing as conversation, nor any chance for it.

As for scholarship, there is, I should say, very little of it, in the accurate German sense. I don't think they value it any more than they do time." Like the Romans, they employ inferior races to do their intellectual drudgery. Yet who was he to condemn their leisurely ways? "They get a good deal out of life at a cheap rate, and are not far from wisdom, if the old Greek philosophers who used to be held up to us as an example knew anything about the matter." [7] By some strange alchemy, this land was effecting a sea change in Lowell; his moral prejudices lay practically dormant. Could it be possible, after all, for people to cherish a way of life unlike one's own without thereby branding themselves as wholly degenerate and blind? It was beginning to seem that they could.

The diplomatic problems he was faced with during his stay were unimportant, a fact which explains in part such reports to Secretary William Evarts as No. 65, in which he described the marriage of Alfonso XII to Princess Mercedes. This document exceeds two thousand words. More practically, it should be said that he negotiated an indemnity payment of $500,000 for Americans who claimed that their property had been damaged by insurrectionists in Cuba. He reported General Grant's visit to the Peninsula, and the resentment of the Biscayan provinces over excessive taxes. He recounted, in an eight-page communication, "a bit of scandal" that described a jewel theft by a member of the nobility.[8] He filed with the Spanish Secretary of State a very urbane and flattering protest against an edict of the Treasurer of Cuba exempting German subjects, but not Americans, from the payment of certain arrears of taxes. "I need not recapitulate here," he declared, "the conclusive arguments of Mr. Odee [his chargé d'affaires] nor suggest to a mind so enlightened and so stored with political experience as that of Your Excellency how disproportionately small is the advantage to be derived from such inequalities of impost when compared with the irritation and complaint which they are sure to occasion and with the needless complications which would be likely to ensue. To secure an insignificant fiscal advantage, in its very nature ephemeral, at the risk of lasting political consequences tending to render more difficult of realization the sincere desire of both countries for the most amicable relations with each other, would be a policy in nowise accordant with the liberal views of statesmanship which have hitherto characterized His Catholic Majesty's government toward that of the United States." [9]

Then there was the death of Queen Mercedes to be related, five months after his account of her wedding. It was an event which saddened him personally as did no other public incident during his stay. He even wrote of it in a sonnet, detailing richly the theme of youth and beauty violated by the grave. [10]

Another lengthy report explained a change in the ministry with amplifications sufficient to show convincingly his talents as a good listener and shrewd judge of internal affairs. "I need not say that in Spain more than anywhere else discontent is liable to take a political turn, which means for the most part a violent one. . . . The middle classes have become intelligent, rich, and conscious of their value and of the power which results from it. They would be content, or at any rate quiet, under a constitutional monarchy, where the elections, the press, education, and religious belief were free. . . . Intrigues are going on continually, and as the king of course has the right of dismissing and summoning ministers, these intrigues, as always hitherto in Spain, centre around the Palace. . . . The *empleomania* which is the dryrot of Spain, as it threatens to become of the United States, supplies every leader with a momentarily devoted band of adherents, ready to transfer themselves at any moment to a promising chief, as a cloud of gnats shifts indifferently from the head of one passerby to that of the next. There are always at least three pretenders to the seat of power; the ousted line of the royal family, the conservative and the radical republicans. Don Carlos [Thoreau's symbol!] is at present out of the question because he is out of funds." [11] Lowell's problems in Madrid may not have been cosmic ones, but his awareness of them was penetrating and broad. The reputation of the Spanish embassy as the hardest-working one on the continent did not suffer appreciably during his two and one-half years' interval as its head.

At the same time, its reputation for humor doubtless increased, if one may judge from one of the dispatches to Mr. Evarts. This time the subject was a French citizen, M. Fourcarde, who wished to import refined oil into Madrid under the pretext that it was crude and hence untaxable. "To this end," Lowell wrote, "he established his storehouses in the suburbs, and then hiring all the leanest and least mammalian women that could be found, he made good all their physical defects with tin cases filled with petroleum, thus giving them what Dr. Johnson would have called the pectoral proportions of Juno. . . . For some time these seeming milky mothers passed ·without question into the suspecting city and supplied thousands of households with that cheap enlightenment which cynics say is worse than none." But on a certain fatal day Fourcarde sent in "a damsel whose contours aroused in one of the guardians at the gates the same emotions as those of Maritornes in the bosom of the carrier. With the playful gallantry of a superior he tapped the object of his admiration and—it tinkled. He had struck oil unawares. Love shook his wings and fled; Duty entered frowning; and M. Fourcarde's perambulating wells suddenly went dry." [12]

More personally revealing than his judgments on the Spanish character were several opinions Lowell set forth in letters to friends. One of them had to do with science. He had been translating into Spanish a sketch of Charles Darwin's life, and he wrote Mrs. W. E. Darwin—daughter-in-law of the scientist and Mrs. Norton's sister —about his work. He was not engaged in this little exercise, he said, through any recently acquired affection for Science as such. "I hate it as a savage does writing, because he fears it will hurt him somehow." [13] This was no temporary view. A year later he remarked to F. J. Child: "I think the evolutionists will have to make a fetich of their protoplasm before long. Such a mush seems to me a poor substitute for the Rock of Ages—by which I understand a certain set of higher instincts which mankind have found solid under their feet in all weathers. At any rate, I find a useful moral in the story of Bluebeard. We have the key put into our hands, but there is always one door it is wisest not to unlock."[14]   It was the protest of a sentimentalist, but it was sincere.

Then there was Communism.   Soon after his arrival in Madrid, Lowell had written George Putnam about a reception given by the Prime Minister.   On his way to it he had been all but mobbed by the crowd of natives that filled the streets and refused to make way for his carriage.   He didn't blame them for their stubbornness, he said.   Putnam was at once alert.   Was his brother-in-law turning communist?   Lowell was quick to explain.   He had intended no such sentiment, he insisted, "but, though I am one of those who go in chariots for the nonce, I confess that my sympathies are very much with those who don't.   Communism seems to have migrated to your side of the water just now.   But I confess I feel no great alarm; for if history has taught us any other lesson than that nobody ever profits by its teachings, it is that property is always too much for Communism in the long run.   Even despite the Silver Bill, I continue to think pretty well of my country."[15]   The movement in the United States to permit the free coinage of silver was apparently communistic to him![16]

And the always troubling problem of the soul's immortality— What did Lowell really think of that? Grace Norton was asking. His answer was unmistakable; he believed without question. "Suppose we don't *know*," he wrote. "How much *do* we know after all? There are times when one doubts his own identity, even his own material entity, even the solidity of the very earth on which he walks. One night the last time I was ill, I lost all consciousness of my flesh. I was dispersed through space in some inconceivable fashion and mixed with the Milky Way. It was with great labor that I gathered myself again and brought myself within compatible limits, or so it seemed; and yet the very fact that I had a confused consciousness all the while of the Milky Way as something to be mingled with proved that *I* was there as much an individual as ever."[17]

Perhaps he needed this faith to sustain him during the latter months of his residence in Spain, for those months were filled with an anxiety as great as any he was ever to experience.   Late in June,

1879, Mrs. Lowell became ill of a fever, and the following month it was clear that the trouble was "typhus of the most malignant kind." Queen Mercedes had died of it the year before. "Twice yesterday," he wrote, "the doctors thought all was over. No motion of the heart could be detected—the hands and feet and nose became cold—the dear face had all the look of death—the eyes altogether leaden and fixed. She had been without speech for twelve hours. What speech she had had for several days had been mere delirium."[18] Then, by miracle, she revived. An operation was performed, and during it she spoke coherently, in French to her nurse, in Spanish to her maid, in English to her husband. But her mental disorder soon returned—disorder the like of which he had already witnessed, in his mother and sister, more than his share. He was utterly helpless, his emotions exhausted. "I do not remember what I wrote you," he disclosed to Henry Adams. "I suppose I gave you the dry facts, for I have schooled myself to do so in writing to my daughter, and I have been these two months in the great desert that stretches beyond all sentiment."[19]

Friends were more than helpful. One, Madame de Riano, stayed with the invalid almost constantly for six weeks. Her husband would sit with Lowell at dinner and accompany him afterwards on his evening walk. J. W. Field visited him briefly, and returned a few weeks later with his wife. Then there was Dwight Reed, Lowell's secretary, without whose assistance he "should have gone quite desperate." But he could not express what the loneliness of his night had sometimes been, he added, "when I have heard the clock strike every hour and every quarter till daylight came again to bring the certainty that she was no better."[20]

Winter arrived, and with it the knowledge that his domestic happiness would remain clouded permanently. January 20, 1880, a cipher telegram reached him from Washington. Decoded, it read as follows: "President has nominated you to England. He regards it as essential to the public service that you should accept and make your personal arrangements to repair to London as early as may be. Your friends whom I have conferred with concur in this view." [21]

He was pleased, of course; it was the highest honor in the service. His reply asked for two months' delay, urging the impossibility of moving his wife any sooner. The delay was granted. But when March came, the date on which she would be well enough to travel still seemed immeasurably remote. He left for England alone to present his credentials to the Queen; as he explained to his sister-in-law, Mrs. Charles Russell Lowell, he made the journey against his will. "I went," he said, "only because the Doctor assured me that Fanny was recovering from her last relapse and that it would be better for *her*. But while I was gone she grew worse. Even the doctor, who had never lost hope before, despaired of her, and I got a telegram in London which gave me the blackest twenty-four hours of my life. . . . *Now* her sweetness is that of a child—my face has smoothed out a whole railway-map of wrinkles and I am twenty years younger." [22] This was written in April, the month he was finally able to bring her to London.

But the sweetness of a child is not always, unfortunately, the sweetness of unschooled innocence. In Mrs. Lowell's case it was the awful sweetness of a mind being destroyed by a desperate disease. She would never be really well again. He was to bury her wasted body in England.

XXI

*"One of the worst diseases we have to cure in the Irish who
come over here is their belief that the laws are
their natural enemies."*

Lowell to Thomas Hughes, July 18, 1870.
Works, XV, 259

ENGLAND proved much more heavily fraught with excitement
and official business than did Spain; there was no time at all
for such relative trivia as descriptive essays or court gossip. His
salary was now $17,500 a year, $5,000 more than he received in
Madrid, but he earned it—more than earned it. In fact, he would
have found it grossly insufficient had not Mrs. Lowell's continuing
illness excused him from those reciprocities of entertainment his
office normally called for. He was invited out more times than he
could count, saw the inside of more English country houses, to quote
one friend, than any American who ever lived.[1] But he also came
to know a great deal about Her Majesty's government. He was
forced to deal with it constantly, and always delicately.

By long odds, Lowell's most persistent problem was the one
involving certain activities of naturalized Americans in Ireland. It
was a single, dramatic episode in a very old and bitter story. A
major phase of it centered in the struggle for the soil itself, a
struggle between Irish peasants and their English landlords, who
were largely absentee. To this latter class, as one authority has
stated,[2] "ownership was valued chiefly for the income it brought—
the rent collected from the peasant holders. Where the tenant
was unable to meet his obligation the landlord, exercising a legal
right, evicted him. The occupier, however, had different notions
of his relation to the land. He valued it for two reasons; first, it
was his birthright, and secondly, it was the only means of keeping
the wolf from the door. Land as a birthright had more than a

sentimental significance; it meant the right, hallowed by custom, of using land in perpetuity. Thus, though the tenant paid the owner 'rent,' the occupier paid the conqueror 'tribute.' Eviction in English eyes was a due process; to the Irish peasant it was outlawry." It was a conflict, essentially, between two concepts of property, and year after year, during the nineteenth century, thousands of the dispossessed fled the country, bearing with them "an unrequited hatred of landlordism" and of England.

But a number of these emigrants—at least seeking requital—had been coming back during the late 1870's, protected, they thought, by their status as American citizens. This status, they felt, would afford them immunity against the edicts of the English Parliament; they could agitate as much as they pleased, unmolested. The mother country offered concessions in 1881, acknowledging finally a principle of dual ownership: The peasant could no longer be arbitrarily evicted; he was accorded the right to remain on the land, subject only to his payment of the fair rent. Also he could dispose of his legally acknowledged interest in the holding.[3]

Yet this concession did not in any sense bring peace. It was merely a first triumph, and the people's leaders were ambitious. They turned next to the clamor for Home Rule, as a panacea for all evils, and a handful of astute young men worked that clamor to the limit. The peasants, however, continued to ask for something more tangible than protests; they continued to want the land. When their representatives, therefore, gained new concessions, they were supported; "but when they lagged, the people had recourse to a 'Land League,' a 'Plan of Campaign,' or a 'United Irish League.' There was a magic in the formula, 'the land for the people.'"[4]

The aims of one of these protest groups, the 'Land League,' were clearly defined. It wanted rents gradually reduced; ultimately it wanted a peasant proprietary. Throughout Lowell's last year in Spain its leader, Parnell, had been advising the peasants to do two things: to keep a firm grip on their homesteads, and to commit no illegal act. On at least one occasion his method became the now traditional one of picketing. He led a procession of eight thousand men to the scene of an eviction. There were troops present to see that the law was not interfered with, and they managed to keep order. No bloodshed occurred. But the landlord, confronted by the organized sentiment of the community, dared not permit his tenant to be thrown out.[5]

Parnell went even further. A few months after Lowell arrived in London, this Irish leader defined a program which was to prove highly inconvenient to the landlords. "Now what are you to do," he asked at a meeting, "to a tenant who bids for a farm from which another has been evicted? (*Shoot him!*) I think I heard somebody say 'Shoot him!' I wish to point out to you a very much better way—a more Christian and charitable way, which will give the lost man an opportunity of repenting. When a man takes a farm from which another has been unjustly evicted, you must shun him on the roadside when you meet him; you must shun him in the streets of the town; you must shun him in the shop; you must shun him in the fair-green and in the market place; and even in the place of worship, by leaving him alone; by putting him into a moral coventry; by isolating him from the rest of his country, as if he were the leper of old—you must show him your destestation of the crime he has committed."[6]

A method was even found of applying this system to the landlords. In November, 1880, a certain agent of Lord Erne, Captain Boycott (the significance of his name is proverbial!), refused to accept the rents which the tenants offered. He demanded payment in full, threatening eviction. Learning of this, "his servants deserted him, shop-keepers refused to sell to him, and he was soon completely isolated. He was unable to secure men to harvest his crop." Orangemen, protected by troops, came to his rescue; but as one author phrased it, "every pound of potatoes and every turnip cost the government a shilling."[7] It was a policy of "aggressive moral force," financed largely by the American Irish. Toward the close of 1880 the Land League's income exceeded £1,000 a week, "nine-tenths of which came from the United States."[8]

This sort of thing was proving entirely too much for Gladstone's government in London. It simmered down to the question of whether Parnell's law should be the law of the land. The Chief Secretary for Ireland, W. E. Forster, decided that the outrages against property would diminish only if the leaders of the Land League were imprisoned. Fourteen were finally indicted, including Parnell, and the date of their trial set at December 28. It was a blundering act. A large defense fund was raised in America. Wavering Irish politicians dedicated themselves to the support of the native cause. Landlords became afraid to evict; yet violence spread, despite the appearance of military reënforcements in the country.

Forster concluded that only one solution to the difficulty was left: the Habeas Corpus Act would have to be suspended. Under the name of "the Coercion Bill," a measure was introduced into Parliament in January, 1881. "Its provisions were simple. It empowered the lord lieutenant to issue a warrant for the arrest of any person whom he might reasonably suspect of treasonable practices or agrarian offenses and to detail such persons as unconvicted prisoners for a period not to exceed any time after September 30, 1882." [9] On March 2, despite elaborate protests from Irish representatives in the House, the Bill became law.

Lowell's troubles with his Irish-Americans began almost at once. He had already written Secretary Evarts an analysis of the general issue, declaring that the condition of Ireland "and the question of what remedy should be sought for it have deeply divided and embittered public opinion. Not only has the Law been rendered powerless and order disturbed (both of them, things almost superstitiously sacred in England), but the sensitive nerve of property has been rudely touched." [10] He admitted that the Irish had many legitimate grievances, but added that their leaders must surely see the folly of expecting England ever to consent to the country's independence. "The landlords," he went on, "are represented as the minions of a foreign and hated domination, and the use of the epithet *foreign* has at least this justification, that there is certainly an imperfect sympathy between the English and Irish characters, which prevents each from comprehending either the better qualities of the other or, what is worse, the manner of their manifestation." Then Lowell submitted his own deliberate judgment on the problem, in one of the most revealing statements of his life. No reform measure would ever be effectual, he declared, that did not "gradually nullify through many generations the pitiable travesty of feudal relations between landlord and tenant, making that relation personal instead of mercantile, and thus insensibly debauching both."

One week after the Coercion Bill became effective, Lowell was faced with the case of Michael P. Boyton. Mr. Boyton lay in grievous straits in Kilmainham Jail, Dublin, charged, he wrote, with being "reasonably suspected of inciting divers persons to murder divers other persons." He added that his incarceration was under circumstances that precluded any possibility of reply or defense on his part. He wished to protest formally and violently against this outrage upon his freedom. It represented to him an effort "to destroy my reputation and cast an infamous stigma upon my whole life." "I am an American citizen," he went on indignantly, "and in the name of Justice, I ask of you, Sir, to demand from the British government, either that it try me for the crime imputed, on the foul and unfounded suspicion of I know not whom, or else release me at once from what I am competently advised is an imprisonment contrary to International Law and a gross outrage to the person and liberty of an American citizen." [11]

Lowell's reply to this petition defined in large measure his subsequent treatment of many others like it. His first insistence was that the victim prove his citizenship, and in Boyton's case this became no easy task. He had made conflicting statements to the American consul at Dublin, statements which, moreover, were at variance with those he had subscribed to on his fifteen-year-old passport. The prisoner admitted these discrepancies, pleading in excuse that one had been set out from memory, the other after mature deliberation. Moreover, he could easily establish the fact that his father was a naturalized citizen; quite normally, he assumed, the privilege would pass to the son. Lowell replied that this assumption did not follow; the son would himself have to apply formally for citizenship. Then Boyton laid down his trump. He was an American, he contended, because during the war he had served for the Union in one of the national vessels, a service which made him *"ipso facto* a citizen of the United States." He named the vessel on which he had sailed.

The Minister, in answer, proceeded to quote the law from which his petitioner was arguing. "Any alien of the age of twenty-one years and upward," it read, "who.has enlisted or may enlist in the Armies of the United States, either the regular or volunteer forces, and has been or may be hereafter honorably discharged shall be admitted to become a citizen of the United States upon his petition." Mr. Boyton would observe, Lowell said, in closing: "First: that this law applies only to the *Armies* of the United States. It has been decided in Bailey's case . . . that the expression "Armies" does not even include Marines. Second: That the service does not by itself constitute a man a citizen. It is still necessary for him to prove one year's residence."[12]

Boyton was indignant, but he had exhausted his arguments. Without abandoning any of his previous claims, he asserted, "I now ask you, Sir, to inform me definitely whether you decline to accept the Passport issued to me by Mr. W. H. Seward, Secretary of State, in November, 1866, as evidence of my American citizenship." Lowell replied by return post: "For reasons which sufficiently appear in the correspondence which I have already had with you on the subject, I beg to inform you that I decline to accept the passport issued by Mr. Seward in November, 1866, as evidence of your American citizenship."[13]

His routine in cases of doubtful citizenship was thus comparatively simple: he had merely to demand proof before consenting to act. When citizenship could be clearly established, his problems were more complex and considerably more interesting. There was, for instance, the Daniel Sweeney affair, which first came to his attention through the following letter:

Dundalk Gaol, June 7th, 1881.

To the American Minister to England.

Sir,

I am an American citizen having resided twenty-five years in the United States, twenty of which I spent in San Francisco, California. During that time I never was either charged, accused, or even suspected of any crime nor in fact never was accused of any crime in my life until on the 2nd of the present month my house was surrounded by an armed force and I was forcibly dragged from the bosom of my family and lodged in jail. The charge against me now is inciting persons to unlawfully assemble and commit riot and assault. Now there was no unlawful assembly, no riot or assault committed in the district from which I was arrested, neither was there any incitement to commit such. The Government kindly furnished me with a short-hand reporter who carefully took down every word I said in the English or Irish languages, and I challenge him, or the Government, or all the Landlords in Ireland to prove that I uttered one word which could by any possibility be construed to mean incitement to crime. On the contrary, from every platform I advised the people to commit no crime, to violate no law, but to carefully work within the lines of the constitution. Now Sir, I want a fair trial; if I am innocent, I want as an American to be released. I want to know if my naturalization papers are worth preserving; Whether, when an American leaves home his mouth must be sealed, though slavery in its worst form should exist in every country through which he may travel.

Yours respectfully,
Daniel Sweeney.[14]

Here was a man who meant business. Lowell wrote immediately to the American vice consul at Belfast, William Simms, declaring his belief that Mr. Sweeney was a citizen; that Simms should examine closely into the grounds of the arrest; and that, should it appear that Sweeney was innocent of the charge made against him, his trial or speedy release should be requested. "You will of course do this in respectful terms and without any suggestion of threats."[15]

A month passed without action, and Mr. Sweeney became impatient. The information Consul Simms desired could be obtained in an hour from his keepers; yet "here I am in jail for over six weeks." He desired to know Mr. Lowell's exact address.

By the time he got that address, apparently, another tedious delay had occurred. "I am now fifteen weeks locked up in a British dungeon and my health is a complete wreck. I deny and defy the British government to show that I am guilty of any crime. I sincerely hope that your Excellency will demand my immediate release and urge my claim for damages for false imprisonment." [16]

Lowell's reply set forth a principle which animated his dealing with every prisoner who could prove his citizenship, adding that he had "communicated his views" to the American Secretary of State. "The Coercion Act," he wrote, "however exceptional and arbitrary, and contrary to the spirit of both English and American jurisprudence, is still the law of the land and controls all parties domiciled in the proclaimed districts of Ireland, whether they are British subjects or not. It would be manifestly futile to claim that naturalized citizens of the United States should be excepted from its operations. The only case, in my opinion, in which I ought to intervene, could be where an American citizen who is in Ireland attending exclusively to his private business, and taking no part whatever in public meetings or political discussions, should be arrested. Under such circumstances it would be proper to appeal to the Courtesy of the government here on the ground of mistake or misapprehension and ask for the release of the prisoner." [17]

It was a safe but unaggressive attitude, and it made Mr. Sweeney hopping mad—so mad, indeed, that before their lengthy correspondence ended Lowell had been forced to read more pages of personal abuse than in his previous experience he had ever, likely, deemed imaginable. Lowell was termed servile, he was denounced as a virtual coward; he was said to have no real interest in the misfortunes of his countrymen when they found themselves trapped by the tyrannous laws of England. And hard upon the Sweeney charges came similar ones from other prisoners. They pleaded for trials, protested their innocence, but the Minister's course did not vary: As long as the operation of the law failed to lead to obvious discrimination against Americans, they must submit to it, he advised them. Once, more tartly, he asked that all such persons as were under arrest be made to understand clearly "that they cannot be Irishmen and Americans at the same time, as they seem to suppose, and that they are subject to the operation of the laws of the country in which they choose to live." [18]

Matters came to a head in March, 1882, when news reached

him of the passage by the House of Representatives of a resolution demanding a copy of the Coercion Bill and a full report upon every case involving American citizens. His reply to the Secretary of State was the longest of the thousand and one dispatches that comprise the story of his English diplomatic career. It is an able and lucid summary, set down case by case. To it he appended fifty-one inclosures, the entire series of documents relating to the problem. As far as the record discloses, this report was entirely satisfactory in Washington; certainly he was not censured by his superior for his stand. Tension between the two countries was eased soon afterwards when the British resorted to the device of releasing most of the foreigners quietly and encouraging them to leave the country. In April, 1882, Lowell was able to report to the Secretary of State that only three remained in prison.[19]

It had been a delicate situation, by far the most delicate of his official career. He had handled it with an abiding tact, though, as is evident, with little enthusiasm for the abstract rights of his countrymen. Those rights, he felt, were temporarily suspended in Ireland, and the eloquence or scorn of people with names like *Sweeney* was in no sense going to provoke a change in his point of view!

Yet his course of action left him with lasting enemies in America. He was derided in cartoons and denounced in public meetings as traitor to a holy trust. Perhaps the attitude of his detractors was nowhere more sharply or more pitifully condensed than in a sentence of the communication which a half-literate prisoner wrote to the American consul from his narrow cell in Queenstown. Michael Hart was the prisoner's name—a man who had petitioned in vain for Lowell's aid. "In my estimation," he said, "the U. S. Minister do think we are after committing some great breach of the law, and I really think if the truth of his mind was known he have very little sympathy for me or any one like me." [20] In a single penetrating line he had drawn His Excellency to the life!

XXII

"But the throng was such as only London could pour forth
—eight miles of it—and the growing and sinking
surge of sound as sacred majesty passed was
something I was glad to have heard."

Lowell to Henry James, May 17, 1887.
New Letters, 307

LOWELL'S other diplomatic problems while in England were numerous but relatively minor; in few respects can they be said to rival in significance his treatment of the Irish question. The disease of cholera among American hogs caused him a good deal of worry, however, and his manner of dealing with it is worth noting. Rumors of its spread reached him for the first time in March, 1881. The British vice-consul in Philadelphia, a Mr. Crump, had recently issued an alarming statement. During the previous year, this gentleman declared, 700,000 hogs had died of the malady in Illinois alone. He added that several cases of trichinosis had also occurred in the United States—"giving the idea," Lowell afterwards complained, "that the two diseases are correlated, and he further announced the possibility of communicating *trichina* to the human body by adulteration of butter and cheese with fatty products supposed to be taken from places where hogs die of disease." [1] It was imperative that such a statement not be allowed to go unchallenged, for it threatened the entire export trade in pork to England, a trade which approximated 350,000 tons each year.

Lowell wrote at once to Secretary Evarts, stating his opinion that speculators, aiming at a sudden fall in prices, had imposed upon Mr. Crump's credulity, and asking "whether any system of inspection of pork exists in the United States and whether it is so applied as to be efficacious." [2] Evarts, meanwhile, had been succeeded by James G. Blaine, who explained to his minister in detail about the difference between the two maladies. Hog cholera was a contagious catarrhal pneumonia; trichinosis was due to the development, in the muscular tissue, of minute parasites. But he added his fears to those of Lowell that "in the popular mind this distinction is far from evident."[3] Despite the elaborate length of Blaine's communication, no reference was made to Lowell's inquiry about a system of meat inspection. Meanwhile J. Warrack, British vice consul in Chicago, had sent in to the Foreign Office a survey of the mortality rate of swine in Illinois which confirmed Mr. Crump's charges.[4]

Lowell was convinced by Warrack's evidence, which was based, the consul declared, on published reports. He communicated his opinion to Blaine immediately, and in unmistakable terms. "Unless something be done, and promptly done," he said, "to render the exportation of diseased cattle from America impossible, there is an imminent probability that the importation of live stock [to Great Britain] will be absolutely prohibited. It will not have escaped your notice also that should the foot-and-mouth disease,[5] which is so easily contagious, once fairly establish itself on our vast grazing tracts, there would be no hope of our exterminating it. Supervision of a thoroughly scientific character would seem to be an absolute necessity both at the points where the cattle are herded, where they are gathered for carriage by rail, and at the ports whence they are shipped for Europe."[6] Perhaps the most significant fact about Lowell's blunt statement is that it antedates by a full quarter of a century the passage of our Pure Food and Drug Law during the second administration of Theodore Roosevelt.[7]

Of course there were scores of other problems to engage his attention. Should the government buy a collection of Benjamin Franklin's papers for the Library of Congress? Lowell regarded the amount requested for them as exorbitant (it was £5,000), but acknowledged their intangible value to be beyond estimate. "I should consider Congress entirely justified in paying what the Italians call a "price of affection" for them.[8] And there was correspondence about a copyright law; fisheries claim to be settled;

better protection for American missionaries in Persia to be requested; the skull of "the American Privateer Paul Jones" to be sought for, vainly, after the story that it was owned and exhibited by the British Museum had reached the State Department. Bodies had to be shipped to America—notably the body of John Howard Payne, the friend of Irving, from distant Tunis. And, recurrently, there were gold watches to be awarded—upon the due signing of receipts—to captains and other officers who had distinguished themselves for valor at sea.[9]

And yet Lowell's life in England would seem to have been rich, and more than eventful, even if none of these formal duties had come his way. It was not without cause that he earned the tribute of finding the English strangers and leaving them cousins. He met a number of the leading men of letters of the country, and he read the new books of many others and passed on his opinion about them. There was the aged Cardinal Newman, for example, whom he visited by appointment in Birmingham. "He was benignly courteous, and we excellencied and eminenced each other by turns. A more gracious senescence I never saw. There was no 'monumental pomp,' but a serene decay, like that of some ruined abbey in a woodland dell, consolingly forlorn."[10] He read Mrs. Carlyle's published *Correspondence*—"a very painful book in more ways than one. There are disclosures there that never should have been made, as if they had been caught up from the babblings of discharged housemaids. One blushes in reading and feels like a person caught listening at the keyhole."[11] And there were the celebrated Carlyle-Emerson letters. He examined them with pathetic interest. "It pleased, but not surprised me in what an ampler ether and diviner air the mind and thought of Emerson dwelt, than those that were habitual to his contemporary." He did not reverse, in other words, his thirty-five-year-old judgment of the two men as set forth in the *Fable for Critics*. Emerson's failure as a writer was in poetry, he added. He was "absolutely insensitive" to its harmonies. "I never shall forget the good humored puzzled smile with which he once confessed to me his inability to apprehend the value of accent in verse." [12]

But unanalyzable moods would settle upon him at times, moods which made the present appear wholly unreal and even his own personality an illusion. In the spring of 1884 he was seized with one of these strange experiences, after the receipt of two old letters from Norton. They had apparently been written soon after Maria's death, and they brought back, unsoftened by time, that dreary interval he had dragged through, thirty years ago it was, in his study at Elmwood. He remembered the unaccountable consolation he derived from repeating the service of the dead, which he had learned by heart. He saw in his mind's eye the old scribblings on the wall, which he had traced there after the fashion of prisoners. "I remember the ugly fancy I had sometimes that I was another person, and used to hesitate at the door when I came back from my late night walks, lest I should find the real owner of the room sitting in my chair before the fire." [13]

And then the queer obsessions that would seize him, obsessions with no apparent basis in his own history. One could understand his dislike of the Irish; they were taking over his native Cambridge as they had already taken over Boston. Besides, he had just wound up a two years' fight with them. But why his remarkable obsession about the Jewish race? An anonymous writer for the *Atlantic,* six years after Lowell's death,[14] recalled hearing him on his topic at a dinner in Paris. He had come over from London for a vacation during the autumn of 1883. The table talk had drifted around to a discussion of the France of the twelfth and thirteenth centuries, and Lowell was describing the students of a celebrated philosopher of the times, seated on their bundles of straw. Suddenly he stated his conviction that the teacher was a Jew.

"He instantly began to talk of the Jews, a subject which turned out to be almost a monomania with him. He detected a Jew in every hiding-place and under every disguise, even when the fugitive had no suspicion of himself. To begin with nomenclature: all persons named for countries or towns are Jews; all with fantastic, compound names, such as Lilienthal, Morgenroth; all with names derived from colors, trades, animals, vegetables, minerals; all with Biblical names, except Puritan first names; all patronymics ending *son,—sohn, sen,* or any other version; all Russells, originally so called from red-haired Israelites; all Walters by long descended derivation from wolves and foxes in some ancient tongue; the Caecilii, therefore Cecilia Metella, no doubt St. Cecilia too, consequently the Cecils, including Lord Burleigh and Lord Salisbury; he cited some old chronicle in which he had cornered one Robert de Caecilia and exposed him as an English Jew. He gave examples and instances of these various classes with amazing readiness and precision, but I will not pretend that I have set down even these few correctly. Of course there was Jewish blood in many royal houses and in most noble ones, notably in Spain. In short, it appeared that this insidious race had penetrated and permeated the human family more universally than any other influence except original sin. He spoke of their talent and versatility, and of the numbers who had been illustrious in literature, the learned professions, art, science, and even war, until by degrees, from being shut out of society and every honorable and desirable pursuit, they had gained the prominent positions everywhere.

"Then he began his classifications again: all bankers were Jews, likewise brokers, most of the great financiers—and that was to be expected; the majority of barons, also baronets; they had got possession of the press, they were getting into politics, they had forced their entrance into the army and navy; they had made their way into the cabinets of Europe and become prime ministers; they had slipped into diplomacy and become ambassadors. But a short time ago they were packed into the Ghetto: now they inhabited palaces, the most aristocratic quarters, and were members of the most exclusive clubs. A few years ago they could not own land; they were acquiring it by purchase and mortgage in every part of Europe, and buying so many old estates in England that they owned the larger part of several counties.

"Mr. Lowell said more, much more, to illustrate the ubiquity, the universal ability of the Hebrew, and gave examples and statistics for every statement, however astonishing, drawn from his inexhaustible information. He was conscious of the sort of infatuation which possessed him, and his dissertation alternated between earnestness and drollery: but whenever a burst of laughter greeted some new development of this theme, although he joined in it, he immediately returned to the charge with abundant proof of his paradoxes. Finally he came to a stop, but not a conclusion, and as no one else spoke, I said, 'And when the Jews have got absolute control of finance, the army and navy, the press, diplomacy, society, titles, the government, and the earth's surface, what do you suppose they will do with them and with us?' 'That,' he answered, turning towards me, and in a whisper audible to the whole table, 'that is the question which will eventually drive me mad.'"

The description of this writer agrees with that of Leslie Stephen. "To say the truth," the latter wrote of his friend's fascination with this topic, "this was the only subject upon which I could conceive of Lowell's approaching within measurable distance of boring." [15]

Lowell, as has been suggested, was more than frequent visitor and diner-out, while in England; preserved among his papers at Harvard are literally hundreds of invitations. Vacations on the island itself often took him to Whitby, in Yorkshire; the Du Mauriers and the G. W. Smalleys were there. Or he would go to St. Ives, in Cornwall, to be with Mr. and Mrs. Stephen. Then there was Lady Lyttelton, who was devoted to him; Mrs. W. K. Clifford, who could discuss literature with remarkable penetration and wit; and always his old friend Thomas Hughes. He appears to have been uniformly entertaining at such times, yet, according to at least two accounts, prone to make few apologies for America. One Englishman who was often his host put it in this way. "I like Mr. Lowell. I like to have him here. I keep him as long as I can, and I am always in terror lest somebody shall say something about America that would provoke an explosion." This statement accords with that of Max Müller, who found him on occasion capable of very sharp replies. "Everybody knows," Mr. Müller wrote, "that the salaries paid by America to her diplomatic staff are insufficient, and no one knew it better than he himself. But when the remark was made in his presence that the United States treated their diplomatic representatives stingily, he fired up, and discoursed most eloquently on the advantages of high thoughts and humble living." [16]

Lowell felt no real desire to remain permanently in England, no matter how gracious might be the people he knew there. When his time for retirement drew near, he was certain of it. In fact, there was no inclination even to move to any other part of America; he was content with Cambridge. John W. Field tried to tempt him with the excitements of Washington, but he refused to be impressed. Perhaps the capital was all very well for those who, as the saying went, had "struck ile." But Mr. Lowell had certainly not struck anything like ile! "Besides," he added, "I have but one home in America, and that is the house where I was born and where, if it shall please God, I hope to die." [17]

Yet his love for Cambridge did not militate against his urbanity; indeed, at least one important American found him rather too urbane. Moses Coit Tyler, the literary historian, visited him during this period and recorded the occasion in a statement not wholly flattering. In June, 1882, he called at the legation. "After some delay," he wrote in his Journal, "I was ushered into Lowell's rooms. My first impression was of the gracefulness and graciousness of the man; his elegance in dress and form; his manly beauty. As he told me, he is sixty-three years old; his dark auburn hair still abundant and rich, just touched with silver and parted in the middle. His whiskers are more whitened. His eyes bright; his whole face mobile, artistocratic, refined. The perfect courtier and man of the world, dashed by scholarship, wit, genius, consciousness of reputation, and success. His voice was very pleasant and sweet; his tones indescribably pleasant, a pronunciation not copied from the English, and as pure and melodious as theirs at the best. His fluency in words perfect, his diction neat, pointed, with merry implications and fine turns. He is an immense success in England, in society and public meetings; petted and flattered like a prince; admired by men and worshipped by women. He has the pick and run of the best society in the kingdom. His manners have the ease, poise, facility, and polish of one who has got used to courts and palaces. I must say I never saw a more perfect gentleman. Indeed, he is too perfect; it would have pleased me better to have found the poet, satirist, and man of letters less worldly, more simple in style. I revere the sturdy dignity and homely simplicity of men like Emerson and Whittier."

One medium of expression in which Lowell appeared to be uniformly successful while in England was public speaking. He always seemed able, as Tyler implied, to say the right thing effectively, and without the tedium of length. Actually, he derived little pleasure from this sort of work, complaining frequently of the sacrifice in nervous strength it demanded. But he managed to conceal his discomfort; to his auditors he seemed always supremely at ease. His theory regarding the requirements of an after-dinner speech—most of his at that time belong in this category—he once set forth in the course of certain remarks to members of the Provincial Newspaper Society. "I think it should be in the first place short; I think it should be both extemporaneous and contemporaneous. I think it should have the meaning of the moment in it, and nothing more." The great majority of his public comments were patterned after this formula, certainly an agreeable one for the speaker whose major aim is to be entertaining.

But there were occasions considerably more official in tone, and at them he was expected to say something memorable. He was the American Minister, it should not be forgotten, speaking seriously and in character. Seven of these addresses were deemed worthy of survival in his collected works. They treat four men of letters— Fielding, Coleridge, Wordsworth, and Cervantes ("Don Quixote"); two public figures—Dean Stanley and President Garfield; and finally, the ambitious subject of "Democracy."

The literary addresses are uneven, but revealing. Lowell, for instance, could not condone Fielding's immorality, ignoring the moral intention behind practically everything this author wrote.

He found his early plays "shamefully gross," and his personal nature "coarse and animal," even "sensual." Yet, in Fielding's defense, he declared, it should be remembered that he belonged to an incredible age, to "a generation whose sense of smell was undisturbed by odors that would now evoke a sanitary commission." Moreover, "he had so hearty an English contempt for sentimentality that he did not always distinguish true sentiment from false, and setting perhaps an overvalue on manliness looked upon refinement as the ornament and protection of womanly weakness rather than as what it quite as truly is—the crown and compliment of manly strength." Lowell was asserting here a profound and abiding aesthetic conviction, was saying that any treatment of the less "ethereal" attributes of human nature represented a falling-short of true virility.[18]

The Coleridge, Don Quixote, and Wordsworth addresses were less ambitious. The occasion of the first one, he said, "was not to consider what Coleridge owed to himself, to his family, or to the world, but what we owe to him. Let us at least not volunteer to draw his frailties from their dread abode." Such a statement is hardly very promising critically, but it is entirely explainable: Lowell's remarks were phrased for a special occasion, the unveiling of a bust of the poet in Westminster Abbey.[19] They were incidental and perfunctory, as a matter of course.

The Wordsworth speech, an outgrowth of his position as president of the Wordsworth Society, left him handicapped, for a reason he was quick to name: he had already, twenty years before, in fact, set forth in an essay his considered opinion of the poet.[20] He found it wearisome to repeat himself and profitless to repeat others. Yet there was one subject that still needed comment—the subject of Wordsworth's change from liberalism to conservatism. Let the student read Wordsworth's poetry in chronological order, he implied, and the argument of Browning's "The Lost Leader" will be seen to be manifestly unfair. Lowell made his point rather heavily, but it remains one which later criticism has not challenged. "Whatever modifications Wordsworth's ideas concerning certain social and political questions may have undergone, these modifications . . .

were the natural and unconscious outcome of enlarged experience, and of more profound reflection upon it. I see no reason to think that he ever swerved from his early faith in the beneficence of freedom, but rather that he learned the necessity of defining more exactly in what freedom consisted." [21]

"Don Quixote"—delivered at the Workingman's College in London—he termed a few illustrative comments on its author's one immortal book. But they were founded upon repeated readings of the volume. He labeled Cervantes the father of the modern novel, and he praised his unexcelled humor. This Spaniard was an artist who took his reader out of himself and away from his ordinary neighbors. Don Quixote belonged with Hector and Achilles, with Antigone and Clytemnestra, Macbeth and King Lear. Lowell analyzed the work with remarkable penetration, and regarding its author he wrote at least one brilliant sentence. It was good for us to remember, he said "that this man whose life was outwardly a failure restored to Spain the universal empire she had lost." One could demand no more of an occasional speech, or hope for more in many soberly prepared critical essays.[22]

The comments on Dean Stanley were the briefest among those he chose to publish. He rejoiced in the meeting which called forth his own and other tributes, he said. It was an augury of the day, admittedly distant, "when the character and services of every eminent man of the British race in every land, under whatever distant skies he may have been born, shall be the common possession and the common pride of every branch which is sprung from our ancestral stem." [23] It was, of course, an ambitious statement, and only the liberties of the moment could fully excuse it. The polite thing to say of it is that Lowell was being occasional and polite himself, was submitting to the exigencies his position demanded.

The "Garfield" speech was one of a number that were delivered in Exeter Hall, London, at a memorial meeting held shortly after the President's death. What can one say at such times, after all, without violating amenities more valuable than any critical analysis can be? Lowell's tribute appears wholly sincere. He described the death scene in detail, and the good humor of the bullet's victim, who acknowledged as the prime defect of his character the fact that he could not hate anybody. "I find the word coming back to my lips in spite of me, 'He was so human.' An example of it was his kissing his venerable mother on the day of his inauguration."

Lowell was making no very discriminating statement, surely. One may wonder why such an ordinary tribute to one's mother, at any time, merits particular recognition. Yet Lowell regarded the opportunities of the occasion as fruitful, and he made the most of them. He buried his old resentments of the English, his shrewd analyses of their condescending temperament and opportunism, laying these things aside, forever, it would appear, in an effort to draw the two countries inseparably together. It was an amicable, if purely verbal, gesture. Garfield's assassination had been shocking, past doubt, and when news of it reached London, two great nations "looked at each other kindly through their tears." He added, in the Introductory Note to the entire published proceedings at Exeter Hall, another remarkable sentiment: "Never before," he said, "have Americans speaking in England felt so clearly that they were in a land, not only of their fathers but of their brethren." [24] It would be wholly unfair to call Lowell either a sentimentalist or a renegade on the basis of such a comment as this. He was speaking by his formula, was expressing the "meaning of the moment." And he was also the United States Minister to the Court of St. James's.

"Democracy" was the most important address he delivered in England, as it is likewise his best-known. And yet that reader curious enough to seek in it for Lowell's mature opinions of his subject is faced with remarkable difficulties. There is simply no telling what his opinions were; he glides from a defense of the idea of universal suffrage to an indorsement of a ballot only for the wise, or the propertied classes, with the baffling skill of a necromancer. To begin with, there is his definition: Democracy is "nothing more than an experiment in government, more likely to succeed in a new soil, but likely to be tried in all soils, which must stand or fall on its own merits as others have done before it." This does not lead us very far; we are told simply that it is an experiment in government. But the definition is immediately elaborated with a quotation from Theodore Parker. "Democracy," that gentleman had said, "meant not 'I'm as good as you are,' but 'You're as good as I am.'" Such was its import ethically, and Christ was labeled the first true democrat. A good deal farther on Lowell declared that democracy was "that form of society, no matter what its political classification, in which every man had a chance and knew he had it."

More important is the question of how far the privilege of the ballot might, in Lowell's view, be safely extended. He recalled the old fears of the conservative on this score, the voice of Proverbial Wisdom. "The beggar is in the saddle at last," this voice shouted, "Why, in the name of all experience, doesn't he ride to the devil?" Lowell's reply was comforting. "Because in the very act of mounting he ceased to be a beggar and became part owner of the piece of property he bestrides. The last thing we need be anxious about is property. It always has friends or the means of making them." No one could doubt him on this latter point, yet one might be privileged to wonder how the beggar becomes a property owner through the simple expedient of being allowed to vote.

But what did he think of the propertied classes in general, of the authority they should be allowed to exercise in the State? He returned to the question with these words: "The right of individual property is no doubt the very corner stone of civilization as hitherto undertsood, but I am a little impatient of being told that property is entitled to exceptional consideration because it bears all the burdens of the State. It bears those, indeed, which can most easily be borne, but poverty pays with its person the chief expenses of war, pestilence, and famine." Yet he did not wish to be misunderstood! He knew the value of wealth, saw it as clearly as any man. "Old gold has a civilizing value." Lowell was everybody's friend. He picked up the question another time, but again he did nothing but toy with it. No longer was the query, "Is it wise to give every man the ballot?" an academic one. Practical considerations asked with equal emphasis, "Is it prudent to deprive whole classes of it any longer." Perhaps men will not value any privilege indiscriminately bestowed, but if this one is denied them, will they not conceive some illegitimate method of making up for the want of it? This much, at least, was certain, he declared, remembering Carlyle: "Those who have the divine right to govern will be found to govern in the end . . . and the highest privilege to which the majority of mankind can aspire is that of being governed by those wiser than they." Yet why should this be, his audience might have wondered, if any validity could be attached to a later sentence in the same paragraph: "An appeal to the reason of the people has never been known to fail in the long run." Are not the people the "majority of mankind," and would any honest man wish to be governed by an influence stronger than the reason?

These comments may read like quibbles, but they are not. They are, rather, efforts to suggest the incoherence of which Lowell was capable when he tried to speak pleasantly on all phases of a problem at once. "Democracy in its best sense is merely the letting in of light and air." . . . "Socialism means the practical application of Christianity to life." The first statement is meaningless; the second, pious but entirely vague.

He began his final paragraph with a disavowal of violent changes in a nation's political economy. Later on, he praised the sensitiveness of men of wealth to many of society's evils. They build hospitals, he explained, establish missions, and endow schools. "It is one of the advantages of accumulated wealth, and of the leisure it renders possible, that people have time to think of the wants and sorrows of their fellows." Did this remark represent, then, a final indorsement of the capitalistic system? It did not. "All these remedies," he declared immediately afterwards, "are partial and palliative merely. It is as if we should apply plasters to a single pustule of the small-pox with a view of driving out the disease.

The true way is to discover and to extirpate the germs." What are the germs then, the real causes? The reader is never told. He is admonished, instead, to "be of good cheer," and is comforted with the advice that "in the scales of the destinies brawn will never weigh so much as brain."

Everybody should have been happy and consoled, even—if they were present—those Englishmen who had joined the new Fabian Society organized in the country the year before. For Mr. Lowell seemed at least to believe in the "inevitability of gradualism" as thoroughly as did its most ardent members. Indeed, he seemed to believe in everything. In most felicitous language he had stated the position of every important group in the country—capitalist, socialist, even laborite, in passages it seems unnecessary to cite. He had rebuked each gently, but he had afterwards praised each, separately and elaborately. For a diplomat it was, perhaps, the perfect speech. For the semanticist or the student of Lowell's ideas, it will likely remain a lasting series of vagaries and contradictions.[25]

Yet against the bright and glittering generalizations of these addresses the shadow of his domestic misfortune remained undispelled. On the first of his two extended vacations on the continent, Mrs. Lowell had been unable to accompany him, though still capable, apparently, of appreciating the frank and even lively letters he sent back to her. Two years later, in the autumn of 1883, she actually did make a visit with him to Paris. She was feeling at this date "hopeful enough about her health to enjoy her life." But she was not to enjoy it very long. February 19, 1885, she died in London of an "organic and incurable lesion of the brain."

She was buried four days later in the Kensal Green cemetery, where lay, among many others, the bodies of Thackeray, Leigh Hunt, Trollope, Thomas Hood, Robert Owen, and Sydney Smith. It was a private funeral, attended only by Lowell's closest friends— Smalley, Leslie Stephen, Henry James, the Hon. Waldgrove Leslie, and Lady Lyttelton.[26] Writing his daughter of his loss, he expressed a conviction that was to suffer no change: "I have never," he said, "known a nature more noble all round than hers." [27]

What could he do now, what controlling metaphor was available to make coherent the shreds of his shattered world? His friends were gravely doubtful about him—even Norton. "Overcome as Lowell may be by the calamity of her death," he wrote Leslie Stephen, "he must be glad that her life was not prolonged like her sister's with a shattered mind. But I could wish that he too might die. With all his vigor and force of individuality, he was unusually dependent on his wife; his temperament made her essential to him. I have always hoped he might die before her. . . . I see no future comfort, or even occupation for him. The best thing, perhaps, would be for him to be left in his present position, and thus compelled to some distraction of mind. I do not see how he can come home to his solitary house, unless for the sake of dying. Before he went away, Elmwood was already too full of ghosts for him." [28]

But Norton's theory of "the best thing for him" did not square with the designs of President Cleveland's new Democratic administration. In the spring, Lowell was succeeded as minister by Edward J. Phelps. He sailed for America in early June. But the zest he had known on former returnings, the glad expectations at the end of them, were tenuous, now, and forceless. He had left behind his last compelling tie with the world, in a land which he had at length learned almost without reservation to love.

XXIII

*"Come early and come often, as they say to the voters in
New York."*
Lowell to Thomas Hughes, June 11, 1870.
Works, XV, 256

BACK in America, Lowell went to Southborough, Massachusetts, to "Deerfoot Farm," with his daughter, Mabel. Elmwood was leased, and besides he lacked the heart for it. The
village lay some two hours by rail from Boston, a quiet place,
unviolated by factories, all hill and dale. The family, which included five grandchildren, lived in a large rambling house of three
stories and with spacious grounds.

Once here, he began what was probably the most industrious
correspondence of his life. Occasionally the routine of it overwhelmed him. "How should one write letters worth reading who
has so many to write as I?" He addressed this question to Mrs. Leslie
Stephen, and the fact that he did is significant. For a trait that
had been evident from the beginning of his career came to the
fore now with renewed emphasis. He grew to be increasingly
dependent upon women—seemed, like Washington Irving and
the later Poe, invariably happiest when they were present, or, when
they were absent, delighted in communicating with them. And,
on their part, the wistful whimsicalities of his nature apparently
proved always satisfying.

He knew the wisest of the many secrets about them—that it was
unnecessary to say anything important in order to win their interest
and affection. It was all in one's manner, and, as everybody knew,
Mr. Lowell was a poet! His usual theme was Time's Violations,
set out in phrases suggestive of no tragic sense (for Lowell mainly
lacked this) but in tones of fragile, feminine sadness. "Goethe,
you know," he wrote Mrs. Stephen, "talks of the roaring loom of

LOWELL IN HIS LIBRARY AT ELMWOOD

Time, and I suppose he weaves us all in somehow or other, whether we like it or no. Of you, no doubt, he will make a lovely white rose. I shan't cut much of a figure, I am afraid, but shall be content to be the dull ground on which you are woven." [1]

There were many others. Let not the sister of one scold him for his delayed replies to her notes: "I take my letters in order, and yours came before hers; and oh, if I am tardy, remember how many I have to write and that my life is eventless." He could be waggish at will: "It is very droll to be seventy. Don't scold me for it—I'll never do it again; but I don't feel any older, I think, and am sure I don't feel any wiser than I did before." And again, the simple line that would bring tears, and that was possibly so designed: "Goodbye till next spring, if next spring shall come to me."

The charm of these later letters rests largely in the fact that they followed the pattern he had defined for his speeches—they contained "the meaning of the moment" in them, little more. Whatever vagary crossed his mind he would set down, always in graceful diction. A bluebird might come to rest gingerly outside his study, or some robin, in September, pretending it was the very fresh of the year. Or again he would recall a certain rook he had watched, in Whitby. Every morning it busied itself among the chimneypots opposite his window. "For a good while I used to hear his chuckle but thought he was only flying over. But one day I got out of bed and looked out. There he was on the top of a chimney opposite, perambulating gravely, and now and then cocking his head and looking down a flue. Then he would chuckle and go to another. Then to the next chimney and *de capo*. He found out what they were going to have for breakfast in every house." Or Lowell would describe the weather, or raise his eyes and detail a scene—the blossoming of an apple tree, the greenness of a lawn, a glad brook he had walked beside, or, more somberly— though with no less pleasure—the long rows of headstones (as at Whitby) which stared at him unspeakingly from the churchyard on a hill. [2]

He recalled in another letter to his daughter a dream of his dead wife, Fanny, with a fullness that must have impressed this busy mother of five children as somewhat gratuitous. He had visited the Stephens at St. Ives, a delightful place, though fraught with indescribably sad memories. "I had a singular vision of her the first night," he said. "I dreamed that I had come in from a walk and found your aunt Rebecca waiting to tell me that Fanny had wandered away in a fit of delirium and could nowhere be found. As I was rushing out I met her coming back and fell upon my knees before her shouting 'Thank God! Thank God!' The sound of my voice awakened me, and I could not help hoping for a moment that I should see her. But I never can, though I have prayed for it many times. It was a gruesome thing, but it made me feel somehow as if she were near. I couldn't help longing to go again to Land's End whither I went with her. We drove over and back in a pouring rain, but I was glad I went, for in those solitudes I seemed to feel the traces of her blessed feet as I never can here in the multitudinous trample of London." [3]

It was the sort of acknowledgment that explained in part the charm of his conversation. He told everything that was proper. It was an infallible formula for one who sought for and stood in constant need of sympathy. But it must at the same time have augmented his internal restlessness and emptiness. Certainly it involved a sacrifice of his pride.

When the fall of 1885 came, he found himself rather impatient with Southborough; indeed, he never fully adjusted himself to the place. "I walk to the post office or over the hills," he later confessed, "and though I have every evidence that earth is solid under my feet, yet it crumbles away at every step and leaves me in dreamland." The result was that he agreed to take a class in Dante and one in Cervantes for the first term at Harvard. It would be over in January, and his income from the work would enable him to spend the following summer in England.

His classes finished, he made a visit to Washington, at the urgent request of the Copyright League. It was beginning to seem that the oversweated members of the writing profession would at last be given some safeguards against their exploiters. But, as he walked into the meeting room of the Committee on Patents, he heard some highly remarkable words. Mr. Gardiner G. Hubbard, well known as the most active promoter of the Bell telephone interests, was speaking. An author's right in his literary property, he was contending, differed from that in any other kind of property. While he has the manuscript of his thoughts in his own possession, the manuscript belongs to him alone, but when, through publication, he gives it to the world, it becomes the possession of the world. Moreover, Mr. Hubbard insisted, an international copyright would prove injurious to the public, by tending to raise the price of books.[4]

Lowell was called upon as soon as this gentleman had had his say, and he disposed of him with a devastating neatness. Mr. Hubbard's contention was that there was no such thing as property in books, or, as it was generally phrased, there could be no such thing as property in an idea. This was perfectly true. What was equally true, he went on, was that there *was* a property in the fashioning an idea is given, in the work a man has put into it. This the Constitution had plainly recognized in authorizing the granting of patents. "Patents are nothing but ideas fashioned in a certain way. For instance, the Bell telephone is precisely a parallel case to that of books, and I think there are a great many people in this country who are interested in the Bell telephone and believe it to be property."

He went on to offer convincing arguments against the theory that a copyright law would make books more expensive. This would depend upon the market, he said; if the market demanded cheap books, the producers would manage to supply them. But his real contention came later, and it was characteristic: "I myself take the moral view of the question. I believe that this is a simple question of morality and justice; that many of the arguments which Mr. Hubbard used are arguments which might be used for picking a man's pocket. One could live a great deal cheaper, undoubtedly, if he could supply himself from other people without any labor or cost. But at the same time—well it was not called honest when I was young, and that is all I can say. I cannot help thinking that a Book which was, I believe, more read when I was young than it is now, is quite right when its says that "righteousness exalteth a nation." I believe this is a question of righteousness. I do not wish to urge that too far, because it is considered a little too ideal, I believe. But that is my view of it, and if I were asked what book is better than a cheap book, I should answer that there is one book better than a cheap book, and that is a book honestly come by." Mr. Lowell sat down.

It was an obviously effective statement, and in the questionings which followed he added a great deal which the committee found useful to hear. None of it seems to have been entirely lost; he deserves every credit for his advice in framing the law that finally became effective in 1891. One might still be curious to know, however, why it apparently never occurred to Lowell to emphasize the obvious fact that copyright protection was desirable because it would tend to enable authors as a class to support themselves and their families. Could it have been that such an argument automatically disqualified itself in his mind for the simple reason that it was economic, and not moral, in its emphasis? Of course no one can be sure. But the economic phase of an issue, as we have seen, he had always found himself reluctant to face—it seemed, somehow, wanting in dignity. At all events, God's shadowy purposes could not very conveniently be marshaled in its support.

By May he was back in London, steeling himself for the round of dinners and receptions already being planned for him, and excited anew over the Irish question. Lowell, as a citizen, entertained a very decided opinion on this latter score, and he displayed little reticence about letting it be known. It was a "clot of blood in England's veins, always discomforting, and liable always to lodge in the brain." [5] The only permanent solution, he finally concluded the following summer, was "Home Rule," which, he seemed convinced, would carry "one of these days." His friends in England always considered him a radical in his view, but they failed to change it, nor has history proved his position unsound.

It was a pleasant summer, but it had to end. He left, planning to return the following year. Casting up his accounts when winter came, he found his income sufficient for his needs, if not bountiful. He could still preserve his way of life without, as he phrased it, "defrauding his grandchildren" by selling off more of his land. There was £400 a year assured him from his copyrights. Another "three or four hundred pounds" was likewise certain, in 1887, as payment for six lectures at the Lowell Institute.[6] And, of course, there were checks from time to time for poems and for occasional introductions to books. His total resources, it is safe to say, were approximately $5,000 a year. He needed the entire sum for his regular pilgrimages to England.

During each of the three successive years after his return to America in 1885, Lowell found himself plagued with the necessity of delivering at least one speech that caused him no end of worry. He groaned over his problem like a woman in labor. If only he could be left alone! All sorts of people were after him, foraging on his equanimity and laying waste his time. If he could only conquer his shyness so far as to be able to stand up and let himself go, it would be different; he wouldn't mind. How he had dared speak with such freedom years ago—as he had—was a source of constant amazement to him.[7]

Yet he did not mince words in his remarks to the friends of Harvard in 1886. The occasion was auspicious. It was the two-hundred-and-fiftieth anniversary of the college, and the event was celebrated for four days, during early November. Some 2,200 alumni and 300 guests, including President and Mrs. Cleveland, were in attendance. Holmes read one of his last occasional poems, greetings were extended from leading universities in America and abroad, Phillips Brooks preached a noble sermon, Mr. Justice Holmes addressed the Law School alumni, and President Eliot urged the motto "Press On" to listeners apparently coöperative, even eager. There was also Lowell, whose remarks deserve considerably more attention than Harvard's scholarly historian was able to allow them.[8]

He began by praising the early Puritans for founding an institution that symbolized "our intellectual independence of the old world." They were narrow, but "only as the sword of Righteousness is narrow." They wished to teach the Humanities, to train a learned and godly clergy, and to educate the Indians. In the first two of these objects they succeeded, but the third proved a soon-admitted failure. A lone savage was finally graduated, only to disappear into the wilderness from whence he had come. Lowell found himself unable even to pronounce the Indian's name!

He turned to the present status of the college. Its professors were overworked, he declared, were underpaid and fretted with trivial and routine duties. Moreover, with the influence which German scholarship was effecting at Harvard he confessed himself out of sympathy. Young men were being trained in the languages as if they were all to be editors, not lovers of polite literature, and humanistic values were suffering in consequence. What was his conception of a university, then? He answered his question by quoting the statement he had made years before, to President Walker: "A University is a place where nothing useful [*i.e.* utilitarian] is taught; but a University is possible only where a man may get his livelihood by digging Sanskrit roots." He hoped to see the day when a competent professor might lecture at Harvard for three years on the first three vowels of the Romance alphabet, and find fit audience, though few. But he hoped even more strongly that the time would never come when the Humanities no longer dominated the teaching which the University made available for the majority of its students.

He addressed himself next to the elective system, President Eliot's innovation, whereby a young man was permitted, within limits, to choose for himself the subjects he would study. Lowell was largely skeptical of this tendency; it seemed to be making headway too fast. For one thing, he argued, Harvard was still partly a college, and therefore only in part a university. It still spoke "with that ambiguous voice, half bass, half treble, or mixed of both, which is proper to a certain stage of adolescence." Again, he was worried about the students upon whom the problem of selection devolved: were they old enough to understand the import of the decision that was being left to them? Or were their parents capable of any pertinent guidance? Then he came to his real objection: "You may," he felt, was not nearly so wholesome a lesson for youth as "you must." He framed his confession as a statement, but he was defining his own attitude in unmistakable terms. He suggested, vaguely, less mechanical methods of instruction as a means of solving the problem—at least for the present. He wanted to see a university so well equipped that it would no longer be necessary for young men to go abroad for their final training. He wanted a system of post-graduate fellowships established, and numerous scholars brought in, men who would enjoy with their professors a social as well as an academic relationship. Culture, he said finally, should be the aim of the university, and insofar as it failed to train cultured men it registered itself as derelict to its trust.[9]

His next speech, on "Tariff Reform," was delivered before a league of that name which met in Boston, December 29, 1887. Lowell served as chairman for the occasion. His remarks fail to indicate his precise stand on the question itself, except to show that he felt existent tariffs to be exorbitant. Yet what he said is wholly plain insofar as it involves an analysis of the country's political condition. Its condition was rotten, he was convinced, had been rotten for a long time, and Mr. Cleveland—though a Democrat—seemed the only representative of the "higher type of Americanism since Lincoln was snatched from us." For the President was a man who understood the word politics "to mean business, not chicanery." He had had the courage to tell the truth to the nation "without regard to personal or party consequences." Indeed, Lowell went on, "our politics call loudly for a broom. . . . Mr. Cleveland has found a broom and begun to apply it. He has shown us that there was such a thing as being protected too much, and that we had protected our shipping interests so effectively that they had ceased to need protection by ceasing to exist." The significant fact about the address is that Lowell, in making it, was aligning himself unmistakably with the liberal or independent Republicans. They were a group that had already, in 1884, won for themselves the jarring epithet of "Mugwumps."

This last was merely one of the less obvious of any number of damning phrases which conservatives in the party had heaped upon them. George W. Curtis, Theodore Roosevelt, Henry Cabot Lodge, Henry Ward Beecher, and Carl Schurz were but a few among many who had found the rule of the old-line Republicans of the past two decades too sordid to tolerate with equanimity. For their rebellion they had been termed, variously, saints, gentle hermits, doctrinaires, aristocrats from the Back Bay and Beacon Hill, Anglomaniacs, visionaries, and dudes. Nor was this enough. They were likewise labeled Pharisees who raved and frothed at the mouth. "They were soreheads, blackguards, apostates, holy willies, Democrats at heart but Republicans in name, hypocrites, mutineers, conspirators, snakes, hired assassins, and so on." [10]

"Mugwumps" was the name that stuck. Meanwhile, many wondered, what did it signify? Colonel T. W. Higginson, a victim and an old friend of Lowell's, took comfort amid the fusillade. He, at least, was not ashamed of being called a Mugwump, he confessed, for "in the Indian language the word means a chief with a large following." The Colonel ignored a somewhat earlier usage which identified the noun with "a man who thinks himself of consequence." [11] Lowell's sympathies were with this group from the beginning. He would have aided them in their support of Cleveland in 1884, he admitted (though still a servant of the opposing administration), had he not been in England and consequently outside the picture.

But four years later the story was different. He was then in the United States, an uncommitted citizen, and decidedly eager to see a basic reform in American politics. Men like Walt Whitman had for years been crying out against the sickening record that followed 1865. What had happened proved a strange but unmistakable revelation, and no one now was able to deny its meaning. The revelation disclosed that, once the Vartu of the North had won for itself undisputed authority in the nation, the most corrupt elements in American political history immediately established themselves in power.

But Lowell, for his part, had not meant it that way at all; he had not for one moment intended to support the army of reckless spoliation in government. There had been scandals, scores of them, dating from a long time back, but they had occurred without his conscious connivance or approval. They stretched, these scandals, row after row behind him, almost too numerous and too sickening to remember. One recalled them with definite humiliation. There had been, to name a few, the Credit Mobilier frauds, the Salary Grab, the Sanborn Contracts, and the Whiskey Ring, which had involved even the President, General Grant. And, of course, back in 1869 there had been Black Friday, a day thousands still poignantly remembered; the none-too-precocious hero of Appomattox had stupidly got himself mixed up in that calamity, too. Walt Whitman had undertaken to define his country's condition at about this time (the same Whitman, it should be remembered, whose poetry Lowell had resolved to keep out of the way of Harvard students). He described it in the following terms: "The depravity of the business classes of our country, is not less than has been supposed, but infinitely greater. The official services of America, national, state, and municipal, in all their branches and departments except the judiciary, is tainted. The great cities reek of bribery, falsehood, mal-administration; and the judiciary are saturated in corruption, with respectable as much as non-respectable robbery and scoundrelism." [12]

No one could, thus, fairly claim for Lowell any peculiar virtue or insight in recording his indignant analysis of the American political scene. He was doing what almost any honest and discerning man would have done, granted the personal freedom to make a choice or a public statement. He made such a statement

April 18, 1888, in his address, "The Place of the Independent in Politics."

He began it with the defensive argument that scholars are as capable as men of the world in comprehending the business of government. He admitted his status as a bookman, alluded to his English address on Democracy, and then settled down to his purpose. That purpose, he declared, was to point out the weakness and perils in a system (the democratic) which had never before been undertaken on so broad a scale as in the United States. What was politics, anyhow, he then inquired, except an art that concerned itself with the national housekeeping?

He turned to the "Bosses" who had that housekeeping in charge. If only we could have a traveling exhibition of them, circus fashion, and say to the American people, "Behold the shapers of your own destiny." He mentioned a major scandal of the age: "It is publicly asserted that admission to the Senate of the United States is a marketable thing." Moreover, our political conventions are systematically packed; we allow ourselves to be bilked of our rights by rascals and charlatans. What is the remedy? The remedy is that if parties will not look after their own drainage and ventilation, there must somewhere be people who will do it for them. And this duty, he went on, can only be performed by men dissociated from the interests of party. "The Independents have undertaken it, and with God's help will carry it through. A moral purpose multiplies us by ten, as it multiplied the early abolitionists. They emancipated the negro; and we mean to emancipate the respectable white man."

He looked about him at the strident tendencies which were making over the nation of his early love. The continuance of unrestricted emigration evoked the gravest doubts in his mind. Thinking of the abuses of which the Irish-Americans had been guilty in recent years, he seriously wondered whether the privilege of citizenship should any longer be indiscriminately bestowed. Might it not become harmful, even dangerous, "when interpreted and applied politically by millions of newcomers alien to our traditions, unsteadied by lifelong training and qualifying associations? We have great and thus far well-warranted faith in the digestive and assimilative powers of our system; but may not these be overtaxed?" He stressed this argument more than once. The ballot was a blessing only when intelligently exercised, he urged; and again, thinking more directly in terms of his own experience, he recalled an incident heavy with meaning: "As I was walking not long ago in the Boston Public Garden, I saw two Irishmen looking at Ball's equestrian statue of Washington, and wondering who was the person thus commemorated." Meanwhile, what of their hearts? They were otherwhere, and their basic loyalties were otherwhere, beside an old hearthstone dedicated to an old cause, three thousand miles away, in Ireland. "I laid the lesson to heart," Lowell said. "I would in my own way be as faithful as they to what I believed to be the best interests of my country."

Yet what if those interests proved unrealizable under the present party system? This was the very condition in which the Independent found his excuse for being. For, contended Lowell, it was to the advantage of the best men in both parties "that there should be a neutral body, not large enough to form a party by itself, nay, which would lose its power for good if it attempted to form such a party, and yet large enough to moderate between both, and to make both more cautious in their choice of candidates and in their connivance with evil practices. . . . It has been proved, I think, that the old parties are not to be reformed from within. It is from without that the attempt must be made, and it is the Independents who must make it. If the attempt should fail, the failure of the experiment of democracy would inevitably follow." [13]

But he was not to go out as an orator or a prose writer: his first venture into print had been poetry, and a group of poems likewise proved the last of the volumes he lived to see through the press. He entitled it *Heartsease and Rue,* and in it he collected the best of the verses he had written during the past two decades. It appeared during the winter of 1888. Compared with it, the six lectures on the "Old English Dramatists" he had delivered at the Lowell Institute were unimportant; so unimportant, in fact, that he had given no thought to publishing them. After all, he had had little to say about Marlowe, Webster, Chapman, Beaumont and Fletcher, or Massinger and Ford. He had contented himself mainly with readings from their works, had chided the late Elizabethans for their decadence and the early ones for their indifference to plot.[14] His rôle had remained throughout the series that of an interpreter of the works of other and greater men. Yet he had not lost his status as America's most genteel and now most venerable poet. Longfellow and Emerson were dead, Whittier was burnt out, Holmes had read his last occasional verses—the twilight of the gods was everywhere acknowledged and deplored. But Lowell, being somewhat younger, had not yet surrendered utterly to the finalities of implacable time.

Heartsease and Rue was a solid and impressive volume, certainly more impressive than anyone then living in America, except Whitman, could have submitted to a publisher. Its importance in Lowell's career is chiefly spiritual; he records in it his confessions and his doubts in the midst of a changing world. Those doubts at times engaged him seriously, but they were never triumphant. He stated them, over and over, often in phrases unforgettably smooth and reminiscent of less trammeled hours. But he never allowed himself to waver from the traditional faith for very long:

> Our dear and admirable Huxley
> Cannot explain to me why ducks lay,
> Or, rather, how into their eggs
> Blunder potential wings and legs
> With will to move them and decide
> Whether in air or lymph to glide.[15]

His dominant theme in the book is optimism; the good will always prove ultimately triumphant. Indeed, he draws his little morals all too often with the persistence of men like Bryant and Longfellow at their worst. A large number of incidental pieces stand as evidence that this vein was never wholly relaxed in him. He never, for all his awareness of the tendency, quite mastered in himself the chasmic difference between "singing and preaching."

Yet this limitation was not one for him to fret over. He had rhymed himself out, that was the secret, though his waning passions, his doubts, and his desires had achieved for themselves a final serious and public statement. Other disclosures were likewise unmistakable. They made plain the fact that his inspiration had irretrievably disintegrated since the lusty days of the *Biglow Papers*. These last poems, in truth, were no more than distressing reminders of a once stalwart tree, fallen, at length, into the sere and yellow leaf. There was not a single distinguished piece among them. As is true with most writers, he had already, in his prime, created the work by which posterity would remember him.

XXIV

*"Death is a private tutor. We have no fellow-scholars, and
must lay our lessons to heart alone."*
Lowell to S. H. Gay, March 17, 1850.
Works, XIV, 238

LOWELL left England for the last time in late October, 1889,
and returned to Cambridge to die. The symptoms were unmistakable. There was his gout, that throbbing familiar, shattering his feet "with lightning," able now to keep him in bed for
as long as five weeks at a stretch. Added to this were severe pains in
his back. He would be insensible for forty-eight hours consecu-
tively. His doctor, an old friend, more than once watched beside
him for three nights without stopping. His letters grew shorter
and shorter; composing more than a few paragraphs left him light-
headed, he said. He was taking opium almost steadily, unable
to sleep without it.

Mabel had moved back to Elmwood to keep house for him. He
would mark the seasons come and go, the flowers that came with
them, and the days, steadily fewer, during which he found himself
relatively free of pain. How delightful and rare an experience it
was to awaken and discover that one's body no longer suffered, that
it was merely weaker!

During such intervals he read, as always. He went through Bos-
well's *Johnson* for the fourth time, also through Walter Scott's
Diary, pronouncing it—familiar adjective—a "manly" book. He
even began to look into novels, "a new habit with me." Meanwhile, the gayety of his mind did not falter. Suppose he were a
centipede, with the gout assailing each of his hundred squirming
feet! He had come to reasonable terms with his malady. He
called it, he declared, "the unearned increment from my good
grandfather's Madeira, and think how excellent it must have been,

and sip it cool from the bin of fancy, and wish he had left me the cause instead of the effect. I dare say he would, had he known I was coming and was to be so unreasonable." [1]

He even attempted some consecutive writing. There was an introduction to Milton's "Areopagitica," and a short essay on Parkman for the *Century*. But what excited him most, and with justice, was the printing in 1890 of a collected edition of his works—the Riverside Edition. The ten crisp volumes were evidence in plenty that the indolence of which he complained so often had been mainly fictitious. And there were several supplements to be made to this number after his death.

There were also, of course, many inquiries about his well-being from friends in England. To one of them, Mrs. W. K. Clifford, he proved fairly explicit, in the spring of 1890. "I have been really ill," he confessed—"six weeks in bed whither I refused to go till I could sit up no longer. I couldn't conceive of anything but Death strong enough to throw me, and he *did* look in at the door once, they tell me, when I was worst, but changed his mind and took his ugly mug away." At least once, however, Lowell said, he had managed to crawl about for almost a hundred yards—"one of the triumphs of pedestrianism." But venturing across the water again seemed out of the question. His most recent warning had been too sharp to ignore.[2]

Still, measured intervals of good health would evoke from him an old playfulness. There was Mrs. J. T. Fields, for instance, with whom he was always as gay as his condition permitted. A year before his death, she wrote him requesting a note she might show to other admirers. His previous ones she treasured too greatly to share. He replied in rhyme:

> This note I write at your command, with all my might
> Endeavoring not to be *too* bright,
>
> Because my usual scrawls, you say,
> Have always too much *je ne sais*
> *Quoi* to be lightly given away.

I write this (frugal man) to you
And to the other lady too,
Just as Poe did his *billets—doux.*

No personal matter it contains
No spoil for Lit'rary remains,
And, by express desire, no brains.

"A fool the author might divine,"
I hear you mock, "by that last line;
"Merci! Your name you needn't sign.

"You've done my bidding to a *t,*
"The autograph is Q.E.D.,
"And proves its own identity.

"You think all others may not so well
"Know you by intuition? O, well,
"Write underneath, then, J. R. Lowell." [3]

But when the summer of 1891 came, it was clear that the span
of his life was measurable in terms of weeks, perhaps of days. Meanwhile, what did truly ail him? Was it gout alone? It was not,
by any means. Cancer of the kidney and liver, the doctor pronounced it, but he was able to do so only after the racked body it
finally conquered had become tenantless forever.

Yet Lowell declined by degrees, his faculties undimmed; the
senility of his dead friend Emerson was spared him. There was,
instead, the all-engrossing lassitude from the opium that now proved
wholly indispensable. But the courtesy which almost everybody
had marked in him remained unabated to the end. He was able,
on the last day of his life, August 12, to comfort his nurse with the
agonized whisper that the pain she caused in shifting him in his
bed had been, he knew, unavoidable. But the old rapture, the old
fire, the old bitterness; and, beyond these, the old savage resentments against a people he could never, for all his "nationalism," understand; the eloquent blindness of his starry-eyed days—where
were they in this dense hour, in what memories did they still rankle?
The answer is that they were nowhere, except in already long-
neglected records, or in the neatly lettered set of books that bound
him so obviously to the past. They had faded with a faded age,

had merged with a victory now twenty-six years established. The world we know had overtaken, and inundated with an ultimate arrogance, his early incredible Cambridge, his early illusions, and most of his work. They had all been swept with an identical gesture into the unpredictable retirements of history. He fell asleep and his spirit dissolved within the waveless summer afternoon.

NOTES
CHAPTER I

1. This is substantially Lowell's account. See "Cambridge Thirty Years Ago," *Works,* I, 15–16. References throughout are to the Elmwood Edition, 16 vols. (Boston, 1904).
2. S. E. Morison, *Three Centuries of Harvard* (Cambridge, 1936), 216, 219–20.
3. *Ibid.,* 224–30, *passim.*
4. Lowell, "Cambridge Thirty Years Ago," *Works,* I, 18–19.
5. Alice Longfellow (Ed.), *Letters of John Holmes to J. R. Lowell and Others* (Cambridge, 1917), xx.
6. See, on the fair and the native characters, *Works,* I, 21–26, *passim.*
7. Quoted in V. L. Parrington, *Main Currents in American Thought,* II, 281.
8. S. E. Morison, *op. cit.,* 208.
9. Quoted in H. E. Scudder, *James Russell Lowell* (2 vols.; Boston, 1901), I, 5.

CHAPTER II

1. The Lowell family is discussed in detail in Scudder, *op cit.,* I, 6–15. Scudder also prints a genealogy, both maternal and paternal, in II (Appendix A), 409–18.
2. Quoted in *ibid.,* I, 20.
3. See "The Cathedral," *Works,* XIII, 43–46, *passim.*
4. See "An Indian Summer Reverie," *Works,* IX, 197–98.
5. See *Works,* XIV, 8–9 (1/25/27).
6. Quoted in Scudder, *op. cit.,* I, 19.
7. See *ibid.,* I, 23.
8. See *Works,* XIV, 9–10.
9. On his reading see Scudder, *op. cit.,* 24–25.

CHAPTER III

1. For Lowell's account of Quincy see "A Great Public Character," *Works,* II, 24. See also Morison, *op. cit.,* p. 252.
2. *Ibid.,* pp. 252-53.
3. See Scudder, *op. cit.,* I, 29. Lowell apparently studied Chemistry as a sophomore. See *Works,* XIV, 14.
4. *Works,* XIV, 12 (7/21/35).
5. *Ibid.,* XIV, 15 (Lowell to G. B. Loring 2/1/36).
6. Shackford to Lowell 8/26/37. *Lowell Mss.* (Harvard).
7. See *Harvardiana,* IV (1837–38), *passim.*
8. The *Journal,* in 8 volumes of varying sizes, may be found among the *Lowell Mss.* (Harvard). It was haphazardly kept. The earliest date is 1837–39; the latest entry lists his silver plate "as of 1882."
9. See Loring to Lowell, 4/11/38. *Lowell Mss.* (Harvard).
10. The most reliable account of this incident is in T. W. Higginson, *Old Cambridge* (N. Y., 1899), p. 157.
11. Loring to Lowell, 6/29/38. *Lowell Mss.* (Harvard).
12. Eben Wright to Lowell, 7/3/38. *Ibid.*
13. *Works,* XIV, 34.
14. E. E. Hale, *J. R. Lowell and His Friends* (Boston, 1901). p. 50.
15. On this theory see *ibid.,* p. 45.
16. See Lowell, *Class Poem* (1838).

CHAPTER IV

1. See Scudder, *op. cit.,* I, 58–59 (Lowell to Emerson, 9/1/38).
2. See R. L. Rusk, *Letters of Ralph Waldo Emerson* (N. Y., 1939), *passim.*
3. *Works,* XIV, 38–39 (Lowell to Loring, 9/22/38).
4. Loring replied the same night he heard from Lowell—11/2/38. See *Lowell Mss.* (Harvard).

5. See *Works*, XIV, 44 (2/27/39).
6. Lowell to Loring. *Lowell Mss.* (Harvard).
7. *Lowell* (Boston, 1905), p. 28.
8. *James Russell Lowell*, I, 71.
9. Lowell to Loring. Dec. (?), 1840. *Lowell Mss.* (Harvard).
10. *Works*, XIV, 61–62 (12/2/39).
11. See Hope J. Vernon, *Maria Lowell, Poems and Letters* (Providence, 1936), pp. 7 ff.
12. Scudder, *op. cit.*, I, 87.
13. The book was actually out in December, 1840. See Greenslet, *op. cit.*, p. 49.
14. E. E. Hale, *J. R. Lowell and his Friends* (Boston, 1901), p. 71.
15. See *ibid.*, pp. 71–76, *passim*.
16. L. L. Thaxter to T. W. Higginson, 1/19/42. See Scudder, *op. cit.*, I, 89–90.
17. Lowell to Loring, 7/6/42. *Letters*, I, 89–90.
18. Loring to Lowell, 4/28. *Lowell Mss.* (Harvard).
19. Lowell to Loring, 9/22/38. *Ibid.*
20. Lowell to Emerson, 11/18/41. See M. A. DeWolfe Howe, *New Letters of James Russell Lowell* (N. Y., 1932), pp. 5–6.
21. Lowell to Loring, 11/30/42. *Lowell Mss.* (Harvard).
22. Later editor of Appleton's *New American Encyclopaedia.*
23. For an excellent brief discussion see F. L. Mott, *History of American Magazines*, 1740–1850. pp. 435–38.
24. See J. A. Harrison, *Life and Letters of E. A. Poe* (N. Y., 1903), II, 120–21.
25. *Ibid.*, II, 126. See also G. E. Woodberry, *Poe* (A.M.L.S.), p. 178.
26. These figures include reviews. Scudder, *op. cit.*, II, 485, is more accurate on the point than is G. W. Cooke, *A Bibliography of J. R. Lowell* (Boston, 1906), pp. 77–78.
27. F. L. Mott, *op. cit.*, p. 737.
28. See Scudder, *op. cit.*, I, 113–14.
29. See G. E. Woodberry, "Lowell's Letters to Poe," *Scribner's* (Aug., 1894).
30. Lowell to Poe, 3/24/43. *Works*, XIV, 104.
31. J. T. Adams, *New England in the Republic*, pp. 411–12.
32. *Ibid.*, p. 405.
33. *Ibid.*, pp. 406–7.
34. Lowell to Loring, 11/15/38. *Works*, XIV, 43.
35. See *Lowell Mss.* (Harvard).
36. See Ralph Strauss, *Dickens* (London, 1928), p. 166.
37. Lowell to J. F. Heath, 1/30/42. *Works*, XIV, 80–81.
38. *Ibid.*, 12/15/42. XIV, 102–3.
39. Lowell to C. F. Briggs, 8/9/43. *Works*, XIV, 110–11.
40. 1844 is the date which appears on the title page.
41. E. Barrett to Lowell, July, 1844. *Lowell Mss.* (Harvard).
42. Lowell to C. F. Briggs, 3/6/44. *Works*, XIV, 116.

CHAPTER V

1. See G. E. Woodberry, *op. cit.*, pp. 186-87.
2. Lowell to Briggs, 8/30/44. *Works*, XIV, 118.
3. See Scudder, *op. cit.*, I, 130–31.
4. See G. W. Cooke, *op. cit.*, p. 84.
5. For ample excerpts from this essay, with comment, see Scudder, *op. cit.*, I, 133–45.
6. *Works*, XIV, 126.
7. See *ibid.*, XIV, 123–24, and Scudder, *op. cit.*, I, 154.
8. See L. P. Mott, *op. cit.*, pp. 458–59.
9. Hope J. Vernon, *op. cit.*, pp. 80 ff.
10. *Works*, XIV, 131–33.
11. Scudder, *op. cit.*, I, 159–60.
12. *Works*, XIV, 133–37.
13. *Ibid.*, XIV, 142-45.
14. *Ibid.*, XIV, 146–47; 147–50.
15. For full excerpts from the more than 50 articles belonging to this period see *The Anti-Slavery Papers of James Russell Lowell* (2 vols. Boston, 1902).
16. *Ibid.*, I, 15.
17. *Ibid.*, I, 40.

18. It is worth noting that this term was used by Lowell almost four years before Whittier applied it to Webster.
19. *Ibid.*, I, 54–55.
20. *Ibid.*, I, 62–63.
21. *Ibid.*, I, 148–50.
22. See Lowell's paper of 3/7/50, which bears this title. *Ibid.*, II, 173–74.
23. *Ibid.*, II, 173–74.
24. *Ibid.*, II, 175–76.
25. See Lowell to Briggs, 9/18/44. *Works*, XIV, 121–22.
26. A. Y. Lloyd, *The Slavery Controversy* (Chapel Hill, 1939), p. 52.
27. The New England Non-Resistance Society endorsed this view in 1838.
28. See Lloyd, *op. cit.*, p. 65.
29. See *Ibid.*, p. 76.
30. *Ibid.*, p. 80.
31. *Ibid.*, p. 83.
32. This is only a slight paraphrase from the Rev. Bourne. See *ibid.*, p. 91.
33. *Ibid.*, p. 96.
34. J. A. Harrison, *Works of E. A. Poe* (N. Y., 1902), I, 202.

CHAPTER VI.

1. *Works*, XIV, 152 (Lowell to E. M. Davis, 2/23/46).
2. See Scudder, *op. cit.*, pp. 186–88.
3. See G. W. Cooke, *op. cit.*, *passim.*
4. See "Introduction" to *Biglow Papers* (Second Series), *Works*, XI, 6–7.
5. Lowell writes here entirely in the dialect of the New England rustic. I have simplified and of course in part vitiated it for the simple reason that I should like to have the present book read. We no longer know this dialect in other sections—if indeed it is generally known at Harvard or Yale.
6. The letter appeared in the Boston *Courier* of Aug. 18, 1847.
7. See *Works*, XI, 73–83.
8. Compare *op. cit.*, p. 85.
9. *Ibid.*, p. 85.
10. See *Works*, X, 98–112 (It appeared in the *Courier* of 12/28/47).
11. See *Works*, X, 113–21.
12. *Ibid.*, X, 128–31.
13. *Ibid.*, X, 162.
14. *Ibid.*, X, 164–82.
15. See "Lowell's Biglow Papers," *Proceedings of the Massachusetts Historical Society*, XLC (1911–12), 602–11.
16. One interested in the question might examine A. T. Beveridge, *Abraham Lincoln*, II, 112–16; Justin Smith, *The War with Mexico*, I, 58–72; Benjamin Lundy, *The War in Texas;* E. D. Adams, *British Interests and Activities in Texas*, p. 228; and N. W. Stephenson, *Texas and the Mexican War*, p. 257.

CHAPTER VII

1. Actually out by Christmas, 1847, but dated 1848 by the publisher.
2. See *Works*, IX, 301–04.
3. *Works*, I, 185 ff.
4. *Works*, XII, 7.
5. W. P. Trent, *American Literature 1607–1865* (N. Y., 1908), p. 251.
6. See her *Papers on Literature and Art*, p. 308.
7. *Works*, XIV, 176–77 (3/26/48).
8. Of course, as is generally known, she was drowned off Fire Island on her return from Italy, in 1850. The finest and fairest statement of her character is perhaps that which appears in Emerson's *Journals.*
9. The entire poem may be found in *Works*, XII, 5–87.
10. Lowell's statement to Briggs that the satire remained "just as it was. About six hundred lines I think are written" would appear to disprove the legend that the entire work was dashed off within forty-eight hours. See *Works*, XIV, 166 (11/13/47).

CHAPTER VIII

1. Longfellow's phrase for it. See Samuel Longfellow, *H. W. Longfellow*, II, 40.
2. J. T. Morse, Jr., *O. W. Holmes*, II, 107–09.
3. *Ibid.*, II, 109–10.
4. See Samuel Longfellow, *op. cit.*, II, 106, 123, 136.
5. H. W. Parker to Lowell, *Lowell Mss.* (Harvard), 4/10/50.
6. Ben Cassidy to Lowell, *Lowell Mss.* (Harvard), 8/20/48.
7. See *Letters*, I, 224. This letter is dated September 23, 1849. Obviously *Oct.* 23 is meant.
8. Griswold to Lowell, 10/31/49, and Nov. (undated, 49). *Lowell Mss.* (Harvard).
9. See *Works of E. A. Poe* (1857 ed.), I, xlvii.
10. *Lowell Mss.* (Harvard), *loc. cit.*
11. See Poe's *Works* (1857 ed.), I, 12.
12. George Woodberry, *Edgar Allan Poe* (Boston, 1909), II, 137.
13. *Ibid.*, II, 138.
14. *Ibid.*, II, 138.
15. Phillips to Lowell, 5/24/49, *Lowell Mss.* (Harvard).
16. *Works*, XIV, 173-75 (3/6/48).
17. Lowell to S. H. Gay, *Works*, XIV, 206 (2/26/49).
18. *Ibid.*, I, 212–13, May 21, 1849.
19. *Ibid.*, April 17, 1850, I, 242–43.
20. Lowell to Gay, Nov., Election Day, 1850, *ibid.*, I, 252.
21. *Works*, X, 66.
22. *Works* XIV, 229–34 (1/23/50).
23. *The Homes of the New World* (2 vols., N. Y., 1853), I, 130–31.
24. Lowell to Gay, 3/17/50. *Works*, XIV, 236–37.
25. *Ibid.*, I, 255 (4/20/51).
26. Hope J. Vernon, *op. cit.*, p. 35.

CHAPTER IX

1. "Leaves from My Journal in Italy." See *Works*, I, 136.
2. *Ibid.*, I, 133-34.
3. The fact that these elaborations were deliberate is seen clearly in Lowell's reference to Hawthorne's stay in Italy in 1859, five years after the "Leaves" first appeared in *Graham's*. The Journal was reprinted in *Fireside Travels* (1864). See *Works*, I, 151.
4. *Ibid.*, I, 201.
5. *Ibid.*, I, 229.
6. *Ibid.*, I, 246–47.
7. *Works*, XIV, 319 (10/12/55).
8. M. A. DeWolfe Howe, *New Letters of J. R. Lowell*, pp. 115–16 (To W. L. Gage, 12/7/63).
9. Scudder, *op. cit.*, I, 316–17.
10. Hope J. Vernon, *op. cit.*, p. 154 (9/11/52).
11. Scudder, *op. cit.*, I, 324.
12. Hope J. Vernon, *op. cit.*, pp. 143–44.
13. Scudder is inaccurate on the date of his death—6/5/52—implying that the loss occurred before the family left Rome, in April. See *op. cit.*, I, 338.
14. *Ibid.*, I, 337.
15. Hope J. Vernon, *op. cit.*, p. 149.

CHAPTER X

1. Longfellow records several of these occasions in his *Journal*. See Samuel Longfellow, *Life of H. W. Longfellow*, II, 244; 245; 246.
2. See *Poems and Prose Remains of A. H. Clough*, I, 188. Quoted in Scudder, *op. cit.*, I, 347.
3. Hope Vernon, *op. cit.*, p. 157.
4. See on contents of *Journal*, *Works*, I, 71–115. It was first published in *Putnam's Monthly*, II (1853), 457 ff.
5. *Works*, XIV, 271.

6. See Scudder, *op. cit.*, I, 357–58. This "visionary faculty" of Lowell's amounted almost to a sixth sense, Scudder declares.
7. The substance of this piece has already been indicated. See Chapter I.
8. *Works*, XIV, 281 (To Miss Loring, 5/29/54).
9. See Scudder, *op. cit.*, I, 366 (paraphrased from a letter to Norton 8/14/54).
10. M. A. DeWolfe, Howe, *op. cit.*, p. 55 (8/22/54).
11. *Works*, XIV, 287 (12/6/54).
12. Samuel Longfellow, *op. cit.*, II, 90.
13. *Ibid.*, II, 281.
14. L. H. Sigourney to Lowell, 3/13/55. *Lowell Mss.* (Harvard). For an excellent life of her see Gordon Haight, *Mrs. Sigourney, The Sweet Singer of Hartford* (New Haven, 1932).
15. Samuel Longfellow, *op. cit.*, II, 281.
16. *Works*, XIV, 297 (to Miss Norton, 4/9/55).
17. M. A. DeWolfe Howe, *op. cit.*, p. 57.
18. Mrs. Howe was formerly Lois White, Maria's sister.
19. *Works*, XIV, 310–11 (to C. E. Norton, 8/11/55).
20. Howe. *op. cit.*, pp. 61-62.
21. *Works*, XIV, 319 (to Miss Loring, from Dresden, 10/3/55).
22. *Ibid.*, XIV, 320 (to Norton, 10/12/55).
23. Howe, *op. cit.*, 70–71 (11/4/55).
24. *Ibid.*, p. 87 (3/2/56).
25. *Ibid.*, I, 343 (6/9/56).
26. See V. L. Parrington, *Main Currents in American Thought*, II, 465.

CHAPTER XI

1. This is counting Lowell. E. E. Hale, *op. cit.*, p. 170.
2. See S. E. Morison, *op. cit.*, p. 300.
3. The fact, already mentioned, that he would be expected to give only two courses of lectures a year did not mean exemption from routine classwork.
4. See "The Study of Modern Languages," *Works*, VII, 303–36.
5. *Ibid.*, VII, 335.
6. E. E. Hale, *op. cit.*, p. 144–45.
7. Barrett Wendell, "Mr. Lowell as a Teacher," *Stelligeri* (N. Y., 1893), p. 207. This essay was first published in *Scribner's* (Nov., 1891).
8. *Ibid.*, pp. 207-8.
9. *Ibid.*, p. 212.
10. *Ibid.*, p. 211.
11. Howe, *op. cit.*, pp. 92–94 (8/13/57).
12. Quoted in Scudder, *op. cit.*, I, 402 (8/31/57).
13. E. E. Hale, *op. cit.*, p. 161.
14. *Ibid.*, p. 156. Hale terms this the first of the famous Saturday Club dinners.
15. M. A. DeWolfe Howe, *op. cit.*, p. 98 (11/22/59).
16. *Ibid.*, p. 99 (to J. T. Fields, May ?, 1860).
17. *Works*, XIV, 29 (12/9/58).
18. Scudder, *op. cit.*, I, 415.
19. *Ibid.*, I, 442–43.
20. Scudder, *op. cit.*, I, 438.
21. *Lowell Mss.* (Harvard). Thoreau to Lowell, 6/22/58. This letter is quoted in H. S. Canby, *Thoreau* (Boston, 1939), pp. 375–76.
22. Lowell to Fields, 3/1/61. *Huntington Library Mss.*
23. See *Atlantic Monthly Index* (1857–76), *passim*.
24. *Lowell Mss.* (Harvard) (Hayne to Lowell, 12/28/59).
25. Lowell to Fields, 5/23/61. *Huntington Library Mss.* This note is quoted in *Works*, XV, 58.

CHAPTER XII

1. See *Works*, VI, 1–20 (published first in the *Atlantic*, II, 246 ff., July, 1858).
2. See "The Pocket Celebration of the Fourth," *Atlantic*, II, 374 ff. Lowell did not republish this essay.

3. Essay not later republished. See "A Sample of Consistency," *Atlantic*, II (1858, 750 ff.).
4. See *D. A. B.*, IV, 626–27.
5. A party made up of the former "Know Nothings" and Whig groups.
6. See on this Summary, "The Election in November," *Works*, VI, 21–54, *passim*.
7. W. M. West, *A History of the American Nation* (N. Y., 1929), p. 593. Lincoln's electoral vote was 180 against 123 for his opponents.
8. Published first in *Atlantic* (Feb., 1861). See *Works*, VI, 55–90, *passim*.
9. It is true that his humanistic period is said by Professor H. H. Clark to have come after the war. See his "Lowell—Humanitarian, Nationalist, Humanist," *Studies in Philology*, XXVII (July, 1930), 411–41. I find myself unconvinced that the three periods of his life were quite so sharply defined as this scholarly and useful article implies. Lowell appears, for instance, to have been a humanitarian (cf. his sentimental view on slavery as the central issue of the war) throughout his second, or Nationalist period. There are traces of this attitude, recurrent, indeed, until his death.
10. See *Biglow Papers* (First Series), *Works*, X, 66.
11. See *Works*, VI, 91–112.
12. Scudder, *op. cit.*, II, 45.
13. *Ibid.*, II, 48.
14. Thus titled when it first appeared in the *North American Review* (Dec., 1863). Lowell revised its conclusion slightly, after Lincoln's death, and published it as "Abraham Lincoln" in his *Political Essays*. See *Works*, VI, 217–56.
15. See *Works*, VI, 113–64, *passim*. Lowell's essay was based upon the General's *Letter of the Secretary of War, Transmitting Report on the Organization of the Army of the Potomac, and of the Campaigns in Virginia and Maryland Under the Command of Major General Geo. B. McClellan, from July 26, 1861, to November 7, 1862*. (Washington: Gov't Printing Office, 1864). The essay first appeared in the *North American Review* (April, 1864).
16. See *Works*, VI, 145–86, *passim* (first printed, July, 1864).
17. Emerson's "Evil is privative," and the self-evident Transcendentalism (here in its Platonic phrase) of this passage are worth remembering in view of Lowell's indictment of the whole movement in his Thoreau essay, two years later.
18. Present author's italics.
19. *Ibid.*, present author's italics.
20. *Works*, VI, 187–216.
21. Donald Davidson, *The Attack on Leviathan* (Chapel Hill, 1938), p. 114.

CHAPTER XIII

1. *Works*, XV, 68.
2. Numbers VIII and IX do not seem to have been printed individually. See G. W. Cooke, *op. cit.*
3. *Works*, XI, 87–113, *passim*.
4. *Ibid.*, XI, 113–46, *passim*.
5. *Ibid.*, XI, 146–47, *passim*.
6. *Ibid.*, XI, 174–89, *passim*.
7. *Ibid.*, XI, 189–206.
8. *Ibid.*, XI, 207–19, *passim*.
9. *Ibid.*, XI, 220–33.
10. *Ibid.*, XI, 233–40.
11. *Ibid.*, XI, 253–59.
12. According to the Federal census of 1860 the "Paddies" comprised eight and one-half percent of the population of New England. The Negroes at the same date represented thirty-five percent of the total population of the South.
13. See *Works*, XI, 260–80.
14. See "Reconstruction," *Works*, VI, 257–92, *passim*.
15. See "Scotch the Snake, or Kill It?" *Works*, VI, 293–322, *passim*.

CHAPTER XIV

1. The three letters which bear on this period are dated from Vienna, May 3, 1862; Aug. 28, 1864; and Feb. 11, 1865. All are extremely long. See *Lowell Mss.* (Harvard).
2. See *Works*, XV, 88–92 (Lowell to Motley, 7/28/64).

3. *Ibid.*, XV, 98–100 (Lowell to C. E. Norton, January, 1865).
4. See V. L. Parrington, *op. cit.*, II, 465.
5. Lowell is not referring to the present house. The one he criticizes was torn down in 1912.
6. See M. A. DeW. Howe, *op. cit.*, 107–11 (Lowell to Hoar, 11/18/62).
7. See *Lowell Mss.* (Harvard).
8. *Works*, XV, 92–93 (Lowell to Howells, 7/28/64).
9. *Ibid.*, XV, 78–79 (Lowell to Mrs. F. G. Shaw, 8/28/63).
10. Motley to Lowell (2/11/65). *Lowell Mss.* (Harvard).
11. "Ode Recited at the Harvard Commemoration" is his exact title.
12. See his letters to William James, the psychologist. Quoted in Scudder, *op. cit.*, II, 67–68.
13. See, for the entire poem, *Works*, XIII, 18–32. The sixth stanza, on Lincoln, was not read at the services but was added immediately afterwards.

CHAPTER XV

1. *Works*, VI, 349–98.
2. See on the convention, G. F. Milton's detailed statement in *The Age of Hate*, pp. 344–55 (New York, 1930).
3. Present author's italics.
4. G. F. Milton, *op. cit.*, p. 353.
5. See *Works*, VI, 377.
6. *Ibid.*, VI, 377.
7. *Life and Letters of E. L. Godkin* (Rollo Ogden, ed., N. Y., 1907), II, 48. Godkin refers specifically to Lowell's essay on "Reconstruction."
8. See *North American Review*, CVIII (1869), 255–73. Lowell's view here is referred to as one of *timidity* because it was not consistently held. In his uncollected essay, "The Political Campaign of 1872," *N.A.R.*, CXV (1872), 401–22, he argues (1) that if Horace Greeley is elected, reconstruction will be retarded and the forces of rebellion again let loose in the South (2) that seven years of its discipline is insufficient to restore the southern whites "to their right minds" (3) that, granting the chaos of Reconstruction, the ballot *had* to be given the freedman despite his ignorance, and (4) that it would constitute a violation of the rights of the states had the government interfered in the former Confederacy to modify the villainies of carpet-bag rule. The present Chicago *Tribune* would be considerably pressed to match his sophistry regarding the rights of the States. See also Basil Gildersleeve, "The Creed of the Old South," *Atlantic Monthly*, LXIX (1892), 75–85, on his meeting with Lowell in Baltimore in February, 1877. In the course of one of their conversations the name of Robert E. Lee was mentioned. Lowell immediately denounced the General "for turning against the government to which he had sworn allegiance." Gildersleeve adds: "it instantly became evident that this was a theme that could not be profitably pursued, and we walked on in silence the rest of the way." Again the States Rights theme had obtruded, and once more, forgetting his "Under the Old Elm" recantation, Lowell had defined his true position.
9. *Ibid.*, 267.
10. *New England Quarterly*, VII (1934), 115–41.
11. See "The Independent in Politics," *Works*, VII, 265 and *passim*.

CHAPTER XVI

1. Leslie Stephen, *Letters*, I, 408. Quoted in Scudder, *op. cit.*, II, 115–16.
2. See *Lowell Mss.* (Harvard). Mrs. Clemm to Lowell, 3/9/50. There was at least one other similar request from Mrs. Clemm. See *Ibid.*, 2/20/57.
3. *Lowell Mss.* (Harvard), Mrs. Hawthorne to Lowell, 9/7/66.
4. *Op. cit.*, II, 102.
5. See his editorial of the *American Notebooks*, Introduction, XIII. Stewart's view is based upon an explicit statement of C. E. Norton to Lowell. It appears in his *Letters*, I, 292–93 Boston, 1913).
6. *Lowell Mss.* (Harvard). Stedman to Lowell. See also on the point *Works*, XV, 127, 272.
7. *Lowell Mss.* (Harvard), Lowell to W. C. Church, 10/17/66.

8. The ms. of Lowell's chapter of his novel, to which he never gave a title, may be found among his papers at Harvard.
9. See Scudder, *op. cit.*, II, 123–24.
10. *Ibid.*, II, 133. A comparative study of Lowell's and Coleridge's comments on Words-worth—the former in his essay on the subject; the latter in his *Biographia Literaria*—arouses strong doubt that Lowell respected his own precept in this instance.
11. *Works*, XV, 209 (Lowell to Godkin, 5/2/69).
12. For the entire document see *Works*, XV, 219–23. I have slightly altered its form.
13. See *Atlantic Monthly* (July, 1869). Reprinted in *Fireside Travels*. See *Works*, I, 291–332.
14. *Works*, XV, 205 (Lowell to Godkin, 5/2/69).
15. *Works*, I, 312.
16. *Ibid.*, I, 319–20.
17. The opportunity for alliteration seems to have proved too much for Lowell here. See on the dominant motive behind colonization in America—which were economic—J. T. Adams, *The Founding of New England*, and T. J. Wertenbaker, *The Planters of Colonial Virginia*.
18. *Works*, I, 328.
19. *Ibid.*, XV, 231–36 (Lowell to Hughes, 9/18/71).
20. *Ibid.*, XV, 159 (Lowell to Norton, 9/25/67).
21. *Ibid.*, XV, 242 (Lowell to Miss Norton, 9/28/69).
22. *Ibid.*, XV, 245 (Lowell to Godkin, 12/3/69).
23. See M. A. DeWolfe Howe, *New Letters of J. R. Lowell*, pp. 117–19 (Lowell to Eliot, 12/26/66).
24. *Ibid.*, p. 127–28.
25. The need for this action was obviously apparent as early as 1869. See *Works*, XV, 250 (Lowell to Norton, 12/10/69).
26. *Ibid.*, XV, 273–74 (Lowell to Stephen, 7/31/71).
27. *Ibid.*, XV, 282 (Lowell to Miss Norton, 2/17/72).

CHAPTER XVII

1. This introduction is reprinted in G. W. Cooke, *op. cit.*, pp. 114–15.
2. See especially the title poem. *Works*, XII, 152–65.
3. See "The Dead House," *Works*, II, 25.
4. Compare, for example, Tennyson's "Battle of Brunanburh" with Lowell's meters in the greater part of his "Voyage to Vinland," *Works*, XII, 224–34.
5. See "The Fountain of Youth," for an example. *Works*, XII, 238–46.
6. *Works*, III, 215–320.
7. *Ibid.*, 243.
8. *Works*, III, 3–112.
9. *Ibid.*, IV, 173–217 (published first in *N.A.R.*, July, 1867).
10. *Ibid.*, IV, 91–169 (published first in *N.A.R.*, April, 1867).
11. *Ibid.*, III, 115–211 (published first in *N.A.R.*, Jan., 1868).
12. This quotation is from Lowell's "New England Two Centuries Ago," *Works*, IV, 14.
13. See J. T. Adams, *The Founding of New England*, Perry Miller and T. H. Johnson, *The Puritans*, and Perry Miller, *The Puritan Mind*, *passim*.
14. *Works*, IV, 5 (the Essay was first published in the *N.A.R.*, Jan., 1865). It is strangely contradictory to find Lowell making this statement, with evident approval, and yet recommending the same year that the freed slaves of the South be given the ballot, immediately.
15. Preface to *My Study Windows*. Quoted in G. W. Cooke, *op. cit.*, 6. 118.
16. See the essay in *Works*, I, 333–75.
17. See *Works*, I, 257–90.
18. See the essay in *Works*, VI, 217–56.
19. See S. E. Morison, *op. cit.*, p. 260.
20. The essay may be found in *Works*, II, 3–49.
21. See the essay in *ibid.*, II, 181–270.
22. Yet see Norman Foerster, *American Criticism*, p. 120. Foerster implies here, it seems, that judging a writer in terms of his age—*i.e.*, historically—was a settled principle of criticism with Lowell.
23. See the essay in *Works*, II, 405–72.

24. *Ibid.*, II, 51–100.
25. *Ibid.*, II, 155–80.
26. See *ibid*, II, 129–54.
27. See Salt to Lowell, *Lowell Mss.* (Harvard).
28. The essay is reprinted in *Works*, II, 103–27.
29. *American Criticism*, pp. 146–47.
30. *Ibid.*, p. 149.
31. Regarding the thesis of J. J. Reilly's careful volume, *Lowell as a Critic* (New York, 1915), in which the contention is made that Lowell was an "impressionist," I believe the truth is as follows: He was an impressionist in method. But certain convictions which are in line with those Mr. Foerster catalogues do emerge occasionally, though after no entirely predictable pattern.

CHAPTER XVIII

1. *Works*, XV, 287 (Lowell to Jane Norton, 8/19/72).
2. *New Letters*, p. 159 (Lowell to his daughter, Mrs. Burnett, 8/4/72).
3. *Ibid.*, p. 163 (Lowell to his daughter, Mrs. Burnett, 8/4/72).
4. See *Works*, XV, 288 (Lowell to C. E. Norton, 12/4/72).
5. *Ibid.*, XV, 290.
6. *New Letters*, p. 168 (Lowell to his daughter, 12/20/72).
7. See Scudder, *op. cit.*, II, 160–61 (Lowell to Norton, 11/1/72).
8. Quoted in *ibid.*, II, 187.
9. *Works*, XV, 295–96 (Lowell to Jane Norton, 3/14/73).
10. *Ibid*, XV, 306–07 (Lowell to T. B. Aldrich, 5/28/73).
11. The public orator for the occasion was Viscount James Bryce, who, using the new Latin pronunciation, introduced Lowell with the phrase: "In celeberrimâ illa atque nobis dilectissimâ academia Harvardiensi olim professorem."
12. *New Letters*, p. 194 (Lowell to Lilla Cabot, 6/6/73).
13. *Works*, XV, 338 (Lowell to George Putnam, 5/19/74).
14. *Ibid.*, XV, 337.
15. Quoted in Scudder, *op. cit.*, II, 173.
16. For an excellent analysis of this poem see Cleanth Brooks and R. P. Warren, *Understanding Poetry*, p. 319–23.
17. *Works*, XV, 362 (Lowell to Mrs. S. B. Herrick, 8/5/75).
18. *Ibid.*, XV, 364-65.
19. *Ibid.*, XV, 388-89 (Lowell to Stephen, 5/15/76). His statement here should indicate the inaccuracy of such stark classifications as "Transcendentalist" and "Brahmin." The ideas of Lowell, the "authentic Brahmin," are thick with Transcendental tendencies.
20. Printed in *The Nation*, XXI (1875), 82. Reprinted in Scudder, *op. cit.*, II, 192.
21. *Works*, XIII, 252.
22. See *Works*, XV, 376–77 (Lowell to Benton, 1/19/76).
23. *Works*, XVI, 7–8 (Lowell to J. B. Thayer, 1/14/77).
24. The three odes may be found in *Works*, XIII, 73–108. Lowell published them separately in December, 1876, under the title *Three Memorial Poems*.
25. *Ibid.*, XIII, 97.
26. *Works*, XV, 357 (Lowell to Mrs. S. B. Herrick, 7/6/75).
27. *The Road to Reunion* (Boston, 1937), p. 308.

CHAPTER XIX

1. M. A. DeWolfe Howe, *op. cit.*, pp. 209–10 (Lowell to his daughter Mabel, 11/25/74).
2. See *Works*, XV, 379.
3. *Ibid.*, XV, 380 (Lowell to Stephen, 4/10/76).
4. *Ibid.*, XV, 392–93 (Lowell to Mrs. S. B. Herrick, 7/4/76).
5. J. S. Bassett, *Short History of the United States, 1492–1929*, p. 653.
6. *Ibid.*, p. 697. This, it should be remembered, dates from Lowell's so called "Nationalist" period, which means, I take it, a period in which he was interested, with relative impartiality, in the condition of the country as a whole. This entire address, under the title, "Draft of Speech at Caucus, Cambridge, in the Presidential Campaign of 1876," may be found in the *Lowell Mss.* (Harvard).
7. The speech is amply quoted from in Scudder, *op. cit.*, II, 206–11.

8. A clear recital of the facts in this election may be found in J. S. Bassett, *op. cit.*, pp. 664–67.
9. See W. D. Howells, *Literary Friends and Acquaintances*, pp. 237–38.
10. *Works*, XVI, 14–15 (Lowell to Miss Grace Norton, 7/1/77).
11. See *ibid.*, for his own statement on this point.
12. The publisher's date is 1876. Actually the volume appeared in December, 1875.
13. They may be found in *Works*, V, with the exception of the Spenser essay which appears in *Works*, IV, 219–321.
14. The Brownell essay in his *American Prose Masters*, along with that of Robert M. Lovett in *American Writers on American Literature* (John Macy, ed.), are among the most illuminating studies of Lowell that exist, in my opinion.
15. *Works*, IV, 259.
16. *Works*, V, 248.
17. See Coleridge's *Biographia Literaria*, Chapter 22, for a detailed comparison.

CHAPTER XX

1. See *Walden* (Chapter II).
2. See *Diplomatic Correspondence: Spain.* Vols. 95–99. Department of State, Archives Bldg., Washington.'
3. See *Letters*, XVI, 17–18 (Lowell to Grace Norton, 7/29/77).
4. *Ibid.*, XVI, 19 (Lowell to George Putnam, 8/16/77).
5. *Ibid.*, XVI, 21–22 (Lowell to Mrs. Burnett, 8/24/77).
6. *Ibid.*, XVI, 52–53 (8/11/78).
7. *Ibid.*, XVI, 62 (Lowell to Thomas Hughes, 11/17/78).
8. *Diplomatic Correspondence: Spain*, Vol. 96, No. 109 (Lowell to Evarts, 8/20/78).
9. *Ibid.*, Vol. 95, No. 10 (Lowell to his Excellency Mr. Silvela, 8/31/77).
10. See the "Death of Queen Mercedes," *Works*, XIII, 197–98.
11. See *Diplomatic Correspondence: Spain*, Vol. 97, No. 109 (Lowell to Evarts, 8/26/78), *passim*.
12. Quoted in M. A. DeWolfe Howe, *op. cit.*, pp. 233–34.
13. *Works*, XVI, 55 (9/1/79).
14. *Ibid.*, XVI, 73 (9/12/79).
15. *Ibid.*, XVI, 30 (3/16/78).
16. F. A. Shannon's *Economic History of the People of the United States* (N. Y., 1934), 475 ff., contains an excellent discussion of this movement.
17. *Letters*, III, 28–29 (3/7/78).
18. Quoted in H. E. Scudder, *op. cit.*, II, 250–51.
19. Quoted in Howe, *op. cit.*, p. 245.
20. H. E. Scudder, *op. cit.*, II, 252.
21. *Letters*, III, 75 (Lowell to Mrs. Burnett, 1/22/80).
22. Howe, *op. cit.*, p. 250, April 4, 1880.

CHAPTER XXI

1. G. M. Smalley, in the New York *Tribune*, 8/16/91.
2. John E. Pomfret, *The Struggle for Land in Ireland* (Princeton, 1930), Preface, ix–x.
3. *Ibid.*, Preface, x. This "fair rent" was based upon an old government valuation of the land, the Griffith valuation of 1852. See p. 146.
4. See *ibid.*, Preface, x–xi.
5. See *ibid.*, p. 142–43.
6. Quoted in M. O'Hara, *Chief and Tribune*, p. 144. See Pomfret, *op. cit.*, p. 144.
7. See *idem*.
8. *Ibid.*, p. 146.
9. *Ibid.*, p. 155.
10. *Diplomatic Correspondence: Great Britain* (Vols. 139–51, cover Lowell's period as Minister). This citation is from Dispatch No. 115 (1/8/81).
11. *Ibid.*, Dispatch No. 144 (Boyton to Lowell, 3/11/81).
12. *Ibid.*, Lowell to Boyton, 3/25/81. Dispatch No. 154.
13. *Ibid.*, Lowell to Boyton, 4/2/81. Dispatch No. 154.
14. *Ibid.*
15. *Ibid.* (Lowell to William Simms, 6/10/81).

16. *Ibid.* (Sweeney to Lowell, 9/17/81).
17. *Ibid.* (Lowell to Sweeney, 9/22/81).
18. *Ibid.* (Lowell to Consul General E. A. Merrett, 2/10/82).
19. *Ibid.* (Lowell to Frelinghuysen, 4/12/82).
20. *Ibid.* The letter itself is undated, but is enclosed in a report of Consul G. B. Dawson to Lowell of 2/18/82.

CHAPTER XXII

1. *Diplomatic Correspondence: Great Britain* (Lowell to Lord Granville, 4/1/81).
2. *Ibid.,* 3/9/81. Dispatch No. 139.
3. *Ibid.,* 3/17/81.
4. *Ibid.* See Enclosure in Granville to Lowell, 4/8/81.
5. A cipher telegram Lowell had sent Blaine, 3/28/81, reads in part: "371 cattle landed here March 23 by *City of Liverpool* from New York, all with foot and mouth disease. Unless rigorous inspection is made at shipping ports there is much danger that the importation of American cattle will be strictly prohibited. Highly important this intelligence should not become public." *Ibid.,* Vol. 141.
6. *Ibid.,* 4/9/81. Dispatch No. 161.
7. See J. S. Bassett, *Short History of the United States* (N. Y., 1932), p. 833.
8. *Diplomatic Correspondence: Great Britain* (Lowell to Frelinghuysen, 2/6/82).
9. See *ibid., passim.* (Jones's body was finally found near Paris and returned to the United States in 1901.)
10. *Works,* XVI, 114 (Lowell to C. E. Norton, 10/17/84).
11. *Ibid.,* XVI, 104 (Lowell to C. E. Norton, 4/22/83).
12. *Ibid.,* XVI, 107 (Lowell to Norton, 12/24/83).
13. *Ibid.,* XVI, 111–12 (4/13/84).
14. See "Conversations with Mr. Lowell," *Atlantic* (Jan., 1897). The Stephen comment may be found in *Works,* XVI, 336.
15. *Works,* XVI, 336. E. E. Hale, *op. cit.,* p. 276, terms this interest one of Lowell's "fads" and treats it with indulgence. But Hale's work impresses me as, naturally, almost entirely uncritical. Moreover, it was written in his seventy-ninth year.
16. *Auld Lang Syne,* quoted in Scudder, *op. cit.,* II, 263.
17. *Works,* XVI, 122 (12/11/84).
18. For the entire speech see *Works,* VII, 57-58.
19. See *Works,* XII, 79–92.
20. His essay appeared first as an "Introduction to Wordsworth's Poetical Works," in 1854, and was reprinted in *Among My Books,* Second Series, 1876.
21. See *Works,* XII, 119–38 for the entire address.
22. *Ibid.,* XII, 139–64.
23. *Ibid.*
24. For the speech and introduction see *ibid.,* XII, 41–50.
25. The address may be found in *ibid.,* XII, 1–37.
26. See H. S. Burrage, "James Russell Lowell's Two Visits to Portland," *Partlow Daily Press* (April 9, 1921).
27. See M. A. DeWolfe Howe, *op. cit.,* p. 281 (Lowell to Mabel, 2/20/85).
28. *Letters of Charles Eliot Norton,* II, 171 (3/6/85).

CHAPTER XXIII

1. *Works,* XVI, 192 (8/16/87). See also, Lowell's letters to Mrs. Owen I. Wister, 12/25/86. *New Letters,* p. 301.
2. These allusions may all be run down in *ibid.,* XVI, *passim.*
3. Howe, *op. cit.,* p. 317 (9/19/87).
4. This entire incident is well summarized in Scudder, *op. cit.,* II, 326–33.
5. *Works,* XVI, 147 (Lowell to the Misses Lawrence, 1/4/86).
6. *Ibid.,* 178–79 (Lowell to Thomas Hughes, 1/10/87).
7. See *ibid.,* 169–70 (Lowell to C. E. Norton, 12/24/86).
8. See S. E. Morison, *op. cit.,* pp. 362–64. The statement "James Russell Lowell delivered a learned and witty oration, as full of quotations from ancient and modern writers as a treatise by Cotton Mather," is scarcely instructive, or accurate.
9. The entire speech may be found in *Works,* VII, 217–30.

10. E. P. Oberholzer, *History of the United States,* IV (1878–88), 195–96.
11. Quoted in New York *World* (10/31/84). See *ibid.,* IV, 196.
12. See *Democratic Vistas* (1871), *passim.* Parts of Whitman's volume had appeared in 1867–68 in the *Galaxy*—twenty years before Lowell's speech on "The Independent in Politics."
13. For the entire speech see *Works,* VII, 231–68.
14. The lectures may be found in *Works,* VIII, 165–316.
15. See "Credidimus Jovem Regnare," *Works,* XIII, 249.

CHAPTER XXIV

1. See *Works,* XVI, 319 (Lowell to E. R. Hoar, 6/1/91).
2. Lowell to Mrs. Clifford, 4/9/90, *Huntington Library Mss.*
3. Lowell to Mrs. Fields, 5/18/90, *ibid.*

BIBLIOGRAPHICAL NOTE

THE definitive edition of Lowell's works is *The Complete Writings of James Russell Lowell* (Elmwood Edition; Boston, 1904; 16 vols.), an edition which includes the three volumes of the author's letters which were edited by his literary executor, Charles Eliot Norton. It is referred to in this biography as *Works*. To these should be added the valuable *New Letters of James Russell Lowell* (New York, 1932), edited by M. A. DeWolfe Howe; *The Anti-Slavery Papers of James Russell Lowell* (Boston, 1902; 2 vols.); and *The Function of the Poet, and Other Essays* (Boston, 1920), edited by Albert Mordell. Some half-dozen of Lowell's essays remain uncollected.

George Willis Cooke's *Bibliography of James Russell Lowell* (Boston, 1906) is invaluable for items about Lowell that had appeared to that year, as well as for initial publication dates and for sources and arrangement given both essays and poems in their first editions. The forthcoming American Writers selections, by H. H. Clark and Norman Foerster, will contain the usual excellent bibliography which has characterized previous offerings in this series. I have been privileged to read the Introduction in manuscript, and I have great respect for it.

The most complete and useful biography is that by Horace Elisha Scudder: *James Russell Lowell: A Biography* (Boston, 1901; 2 vols.). Ferris Greenslet's *James Russell Lowell* (Riverside Popular Biographies; Boston, 1905) is brief but reliable. As for the others, such as Francis H. Underwood's *The Poet and the Man: Recollections and Appreciations of James Russell Lowell* (Boston, 1893) and Edward Everett Hales's *James Russell Lowell and his Friends* (Boston, 1901), I found them only incidentally worth noting. Much more important is the large collection of Lowell manuscripts in the Widener Library at Harvard (which none of the scholars just mentioned seems to have used as profitably as he might have), the sixty letters in the Huntington Library, and Lowell's Diplomatic correspondence in the Archives Building in Washington. The twelve hundred-odd despatches which Lowell addressed to our Secretaries of State from Madrid and London have hitherto been almost completely unnoticed.

Of course there are also the various scholarly and popular articles and reviews—and occasional books like J. J. Reilly's *Lowell as a Critic* (New York, 1915)—which have been appearing now for almost half a century. I believe I have examined them all. But I have not referred to them all, by any means. For I cannot subscribe to the notion that every rediscovered phase of the career of a figure deserving biographical treatment is important, or that the life of any man of letters, in this age, is worth something like the two or three thousand pages which would be demanded were notice taken of every item of patient research that—in Lowell's case, for instance —has been devoted to his activities. The world is too much with us. And when we venture *in great detail* into our subject's largely inconsequential interests, and the motives behind them, we are guilty of a needless encroachment upon the field of the social historian, or the prosodist, or the semanticist, or the editor—even though through so doing we may earn for ourselves the impressive compliment of having produced a "monumental" work. Just what material one finally does select and stress will always remain a matter of taste, a commentary upon the nature of the critic's mind. It is an exposure, a violation of privacy, which every maker of books must endure. The only prescription I have ever found for this is toughness, or indifference.

Index

Aldrich, T. B., 229
Ames, Fisher, 7
Among My Books (First Series), 211-17
Among My Books (Second Series), 243-45

Barrett, Eliz. (Browning), 48
Bell, John, 155
Benton, Joel, 235
Biglow Papers (First Series), 75-90, 99
Biglow Papers (Second Series), 166-76
Bourne, Rev. George, 72
Bowen, Francis, 29
Boyton, M. P., 260-61
Breckenridge, J. C., 155
Bremer, Fredericka, 110-112
Briggs, C. F., 57, 61, 62-4, 107, 110, 124, 127, 128, 129, 194
Brownell, W. C., 244
Browning, Rob't., 132
Bryant, W. C., 97
Buchanan, Jas., 156
Buffum, Arnold, 50
Burns, Anthony, 129

Cabot, Arthur, 7
Cabot, J. E., 143
Calhoun, J. C., 69, 82
Cambridge, 1, 2
"Cambridge Thirty Years Ago," 128-29
Carlyle, Thos., 229, 267
Carter, Robt., 46, 49
Cassady, Ben, 102
Channing, E. T., 3, 21
Charles River, 1
Child, Lydia Maria, 50
Chivers, T. H., 106
Choate, Rufus, 152-53
Clark, J. F., 239
Clay, Henry, 69
Clemm, Mrs. Wm., 104, 106, 196
Cleveland, Grover, 285, 287

Clough, A. H., 123, 124
Conversations on Some of the Old Poets, 58-60
Cooper, Jas. F., 99
Courier (Boston), 62, 75
Craigie House, 2
Curtis, G. T., 15
Cushing, Caleb, 78, 79, 80, 153, 154

Daily News (London), 75
Dana, R. H., Jr., 97
Davis, Jefferson, 159
"Democracy," address by Lowell, 275-78
Dickens, Chas., 52, 75
Douglas, Stephen A., 155
Dunlap, Miss Frances (the second Mrs. Lowell), 132, 133, 141-42, 254-55, 278-79
Duyckinck, E. A., 95, 130
Dwight, J. S., 48

Emerson, R. W., 24, 25, 29, 31, 49, 95-6, 100, 101, 124, 143, 144, 145, 199, 267-68
Everett, Edw., 3

Fable for Critics, 53, 74, 91, 94-100, 111
Fields, J. T., 147, 148
Fields, Mrs. J. T., 295
Filmore, Millard, 132
Foerster, Norman, 225-26
Follen, Karl, 50
Forster, W. E., 259
Frost, Rev. Barzillai, 29, 30, 32-3
Fuller, Margaret, 97-8, 99-100, 101, 111

Garrison, W. L., 50, 72, 107, 108
Gay, Sidney H., 75, 107, 108, 112
Gerry, Elbridge, 7
Godkin, E. L., 191-92, 201, 203
Grant, U. S., 193, 250
Greenslet, F., 39-79
Griswold, R. P., 95, 104, 105

Gurney, E. W., 200

Hale, Nathan, 24, 44
Halleck, Fitz Greene, 97
Harvard, 2, 3, 4, 9, 10, 15, 17, 18, 183-84
Harvardiana, 24-6, 44
Hart, Michael, 264
Hasty Pudding Club, 22
Hawthorne, Nathaniel, 48, 197
Hawthorne, Sophia, 197-98
Hayes, Rutherford B., 239-40, 243
Hayne, P. H., 103, 148
Higginson, T. W., 144, 288
Hoar, Judge E. R., 183-84
Holmes, John, 4, 229, 248
Holmes, O. W., 100, 101-02, 143, 144, 145, 147, 199, 205, 285
Howells, W. D., 184, 242-43
Hughes, Thos., 205, 270

Irving, Washington, 99, 112

Jenkins, Warren, 194-95
Johnson, Andrew, 177, 188-90

King, John G., 44
King, Rufus, 24
Kingsley, Chas., 227

Lanier, Sidney, 103
Latimer, Geo., 52
Leaves from My Journal in Italy, 115-21
Leland, Chas. G., 184
Leland and Whiting, publishers, 46, 49
Liberator, 62
Lincoln, Abraham, 155, 159, 160, 161
Lippitt, G. W., 24
Longfellow, H. W., 98-99, 100, 102, 124, 143, 199, 206
Loring, C. G., 45
Loring, G. B., 20, 27-8, 30, 31, 46, 51
Lowell, Blanche, daughter of J. R. L., 65, 66, 112, 131
Lowell, Rev. Chas., father of J. R. L., 8, 10, 11, 12, 22-3, 61, 72, 111, 112, 121, 125
Lowell, Chas. R., brother of J. R. L., 12, 112
Lowell, Chas. R., nephew of J. R. L., 185
Lowell, Chas., cousin of J. R. L., 126
Lowell, Ebenezer, 9

Lowell, Francis C., 10
Lowell, Harriet Brackett Spence, mother of J. R. L., 11, 16, 45, 61, 112
Lowell, James Russell: birth, 7; childhood, 12; early letter, 14-16; qualifies for Harvard, 16; Views on the Railroad, 20; his undergraduate reading, 21, 26-7; absence from recitations and prayers, 22; editor of and contributor to *Harvardiana,* 24-26; his Journal, 27; elected Class Poet, 28; rusticated to Concord, 29; contents of Class Poem, 33-5; is graduated, 36; seeks a profession, 37-9; receives LL.B., 39; meets Maria White, 40; betrothal, 42; publishes *A Year's Life,* 43; founds the *Pioneer,* 46; failure of *Pioneer,* 49-50; his growing radicalism, 50-53; publishes *Poems,* 53-56; publishes *Conversations on Some of the Old Poets,* 58-60; marriage to Maria, 60; winter in Philadelphia, 60-1, first daughter, Blanche, born, 65; begins *Biglow Papers,* 75; their contents summarized and criticized, 76-90; his *Annus Mirabilis* (1848), 91; reception of 1848 publications, 101-103; relations with *Anti-Slavery Standard,* 106-9; sails with family for Italy, 112-13; observations in *Leaves from My Journal in Italy,* 115-21; friendship with Thackeray and Clough, 123-4; makes trip recorded in *Moosehead Journal,* 126-7; death of Maria, 127; lectures at Lowell Institute, Boston, 130; named Smith Professor of Modern Languages at Harvard, 131; studies in Europe, 132-35; begins teaching at Harvard, 136; his teaching manner, 137-41; Editor of *Atlantic,* 144-49; his essays in the *Atlantic,* 150-65; contents of *Biglow Papers* (2nd series), 166-76; writes Reconstruction essays for *N. A. R.,* 176-83; delivers the Harvard "Commemoration Ode," 186-87; contents of other Reconstruction essays, 188-91; asked to do Hawthorne's life, 197-98; troubles as editor of *N. A. R.,* 199-200; views on Economic Reform (1869), 201-02; dissatisfaction with teaching, 207; publishes *Under the Willows,* 209-11; publishes *Among My Books,* 211-217; publishes *My Study Windows,* 217-26; goes abroad with second Mrs. Lowell

(1872), 227-29; receives D.C.L. from Oxford, 229-30; returns to Elmwood (1874), 231; resumes teaching at Harvard, 232-33; explains his religious views, 233, 253; criticizes Republican Party, 234-35; contents of three Memorial Odes, 236-37; asked to serve as Minister to Russia, 238; named delegate to Republican Convention (1874), 238-40; named Minister to Spain, 243; publishes *Among My Books* (2nd series), 243-45; residence and duties in Spain, 247-55; his wife's illness, 254-55; Minister to Great Britain, his problems and duties, 256-69; his opinion of the Jews, 268-70; his speeches in England, 272-78; death of Mrs. Lowell, 278-79; return to America, 280; views on Copyright law, 282-84; visits England, 284-85; views on Harvard in 1886, 285-87; on Tariff Reform (1887), 287-88; as "Mugwump," 288-91; publishes *Heartsease and Rue* and *Old English Dramatists*, 291-93; illness, 294-96; Riverside Edition of Works published (1890), 295; death (August 12, 1891), 297.

Lowell, John, 9, 10

Lowell, Mabel, daughter of J. R. L., 112, 113, 123, 124, 126, 136, 201, 280

Lowell, Mary Traill, sister of J. R. L., 12, 112

Lowell, Percival, 9

Lowell, Rebecca R., sister of J. R. L., 12, 61, 112, 128

Lowell, Robert Traill, 12, 14, 15, 112

Lowell, Rose, daughter of J. R. L., 112

Lowell, Walter, son of J. R. L., 112, 113, 123

Lowell, Wm. Keith, 12

Madison, James, 1

May, S. J., 50

Methodist Church, South, 73-4

Monroe, James, 1

Moosehead Journal, 126-27, 185

Morison, S. E., 18

Motley, J. L., 143, 179-82, 185

McClellan, Genl., 160, 161, 162, 163, 182

My Study Windows, 217-25

National Anti-Slavery Standard, 66, 75, 83, 106-09

Neal, John, 97

Norton, Andrews, 3

Norton, Chas. E., 120, 129, 207

Norton, Grace, 253

"Ode Recited at the Harvard Commemoration," 186-87

Oliver, Thos., 7

"On a Certain Condescension in Foreigners," 203-06

Parker, Theodore, 96

Parker, W. H., 102

Parnell, Irish patriot, 258

Phillips and Sampson, printers, 142-44, 148

Phillips, Wendell, 50, 103, 107

Pioneer, 46-7

Poe, E. A., 47, 61, 64-5, 74, 98, 100, 103-06, 197-98

Poems, 53-6

Poems (2nd series), 90, 93-4

Poems (collected, 2 vols.), 110

Putnams Monthly, 124, 128

Quincy, Edmund, 72, 107, 129

Quincy, Josiah, 17-20, 29

Ruskin, John, 229

Salt, H. S., 223

Scott, Walter, 16

Scudder, H. E., 39, 44

Shackford, W. H., 20, 21, 23

Shannon, F. A., 154-55

Shaw, Mrs. Francis G., 184

Sigourney, Lydia H., 131

Stephen, Leslie, 197, 205, 233, 238, 270, 280, 282

Stewart, Randall, 198

Story, W. W., 44, 126

Stowe, H. B. (Mrs.), 144

Sumner, Chas., 135

Sweeney, Daniel, 261-63

Taylor, Bayard, 118

Taylor, Zachary, 69

Tennyson, Alfred, 132

Thackeray, W. M., 123, 124, 133
Thoreau, H. D., 29, 31-2, 96, 100, 126, 144,
   146-47, 199, 222-23, 247
Ticknor, Geo., 3, 131
Tilden, Samuel J., 240, 241
Tuckerman, A. T., 47
"Twain, Mark" (S. L. Clemens), 103, 118
Tyler, Moses C., 271-72

Under the Willows, 209-11
Underwood, Francis H., 142, 143

Very, Jones, 48
Vision of Sir Launfal, 54, 55, 91-2, 101

Walker, Jas., 136
Ware, Rev. Henry, 28
Washington, Geo., 2, 10

Washington, Martha, 2
Webster, Daniel, 67, 68, 70-1
Wells, Wm., 15, 16
Wendell, Barrett, 138-40
White, Andrew D., 208
White, Maria (the first Mrs. Lowell), 40-3,
   44, 57-8, 60, 63, 112-13, 122-23, 124,
   126-7, 130, 268
White, W. W., 44
Willis, N. P., 40, 60, 96
Winthrop, John, 1
Whitman, Walt, 103, 120, 133-34
Woodberry, Geo., 106
Wright, Eben, 30
Wright, I. B., 48

Years Life, 43